The
Rock 'n' Roll
Classroom

*Rich Allen dedicates this book to all those individuals
who have helped to make music such a magical part of his professional
and personal life, including* **James McCray, Lance Tomlinson,
Doug Tidaback, Greg Johnson,** *and so very many more . . .*

W. W. Wood dedicates this book to his mother,
Judy Douglas, *whose model of grace under pressure taught him
how to persevere through life's challenges; to* **Earl Lomax,** *whose encouragement
and mentorship set him on the path toward a literate life; and to his wife,* **Debbie Wood,**
without whose constant love and support this book would never have been written.

The Rock 'n' Roll Classroom

Using Music to Manage Mood, Energy, and Learning

Rich Allen
W. W. Wood

www.rockandrollclassroom.com

CORWIN
A SAGE Company

CORWIN
A SAGE Company

FOR INFORMATION:

Corwin
A SAGE Company
2455 Teller Road
Thousand Oaks, California 91320
(800) 233-9936
www.corwin.com

SAGE Publications Ltd.
1 Oliver's Yard
55 City Road
London EC1Y 1SP
United Kingdom

SAGE Publications India Pvt. Ltd.
B 1/I 1 Mohan Cooperative Industrial Area
Mathura Road, New Delhi 110 044
India

SAGE Publications Asia-Pacific Pte. Ltd.
3 Church Street
#10-04 Samsung Hub
Singapore 049483

Acquisitions Editor: Jessica Allan
Associate Editor: Allison Scott
Editorial Assistant: Lisa Whitney
Permissions Editor: Jason Kelley
Project Editor: Veronica Stapleton
Copy Editor: Diane DiMura
Typesetter: C&M Digitals (P) Ltd.
Proofreader: Scott Oney
Indexer: Karen Wiley
Cover Designer: Karine Hovsepian

Printed in the United States of America

Library of Congress Cataloging-in-Publication Data

Allen, Richard, 1957 Sept. 28-

The rock 'n' roll classroom : using music to manage mood, energy, and learning/Rich Allen, W. W. Wood.

p. cm.
Includes bibliographical references and index.

ISBN 978-1-4129-9976-2 (pbk.)

1. Music in education. 2. Music—Psychological aspects. I. Wood, W. W. (Willy Wray), 1957- II. Title.

MT1.A48 2013
371.33—dc23   2012020444

This book is printed on acid-free paper.

SUSTAINABLE FORESTRY INITIATIVE
Certified Chain of Custody
Promoting Sustainable Forestry
www.sfiprogram.org
SFI-01268

SFI label applies to text stock

12 13 14 15 16 10 9 8 7 6 5 4 3 2 1

Contents

Additional materials and resources related to *The Rock 'n' Roll Classroom* can be found at www.rockandrollclassroom.com

Foreword

Why Education Needs a Soundtrack

For over a century, researchers have explored the power of music, with the last decade in particular yielding considerable scientific evidence about its extraordinary neurological effects. For example, in

May 2010, researchers from Boston University School of Medicine found that patients with Alzheimer's disease—with virtually nonexistent short-term memories—achieve close to normal memory of new verbal information when it is provided in the context of music.

As the evidence has piled up, many sectors, from health, to manufacturing, to advertising, have deliberately harnessed music, not just to heal, but to control, influence, and modify human behavior. Indeed, we are now at the point where the music that plays in every store, restaurant, and sporting venue is scientifically selected to create a specific effect on patrons.

Yet, education has not followed suit. Despite a widespread knowledge and acceptance of these concepts, teacher education still fails to include the use of music as a deliberate teaching strategy or classroom management tool. As a result, educators lack the understanding, skills, and resources to use one of the most powerful teaching tools at their disposal—a tool that offers at least five scientifically proven benefits in the classroom.

1. **Music acts directly on the body,** specifically on metabolism and heartbeat. Listening to certain types of music can trigger the release of endorphins, producing a tranquil state that leads to faster learning.

2. **Music relaxes the mind and lowers stress levels that inhibit learning,** and when used effectively, music increases alpha levels in the brain, boosting memory and recall and allowing the brain to access reserve capacities.

3. **Music stimulates and awakens,** reviving bored or sleepy learners and increasing blood and oxygen flow to the brain.

4. **Music is a state-changer** and can be used effectively to get students into an effective learning state or support transitional activities.

5. **Music aids memory,** both acting as a powerful anchor that moors learning in memory and also inspiring emotion to create a clear passage to long-term memory.

Please note this book is not about the "Mozart effect," the controversial theory that listening to Mozart increases intelligence in children. This theory is not based on solid research, but a single study, whose authors claim their findings were misrepresented; whereas, the five effects noted above have been demonstrated by multiple studies—opening the door to new teaching and classroom management strategies.

So Why Don't We Use More Music in Our Classrooms?

As with so many decisions in education, the real reason our sector has lagged so far behind others in using music comes down to resources. Until very recently, the equipment required to use music effectively in the classroom was prohibitively expensive. But today, music players and speakers are relatively cheap and extremely easy to use. The major hurdle to education harnessing the power of music has been removed.

However, two smaller but significant hurdles remain. First, using music effectively in the classroom is a practical skill. Different types of music used in different ways produce different effects. Teachers must understand what these different types of music are, why they work, what effects they create, and how to use them. Second, not all music is appropriate for use in the classroom—and not just because it includes inappropriate lyrics. Only certain types of music, with certain beats, or instrumental complexity, work in certain situations. Education playlists must be properly researched—and this can be extremely time-consuming.

This book removes these final two barriers. It clearly explains the different research-supported uses of music in the classroom—*what* the possible uses are, *why* they work, and *how* to apply this knowledge in the classroom. And it also provides appropriate playlists for each application, along with guides to help teachers create their own lists.

We hope it will be the catalyst for education to act on the evidence that other sectors are currently using—to great effect. Research suggests that, if every classroom had an appropriate sound track, we could boost academic results, improve student behavior, and reduce teacher burnout.

This final benefit is the hidden but vitally important reason that we are passionate about getting our schools wired for sound. Music takes much of the stress out of teaching. In many ways, it offers you a "remote" for your class. Touch a button and your students shift from bored to engaged. Touch another and they calm down. Change the volume and get every single student's attention—without ever having to raise your voice. These are just a few of the seemingly magical results possible through the effective use of music. We hope this book helps you to make them happen in your classroom.

W. W. Wood and Rich Allen

Acknowledgments

T he authors wish to thank the following people for their invaluable contributions to the development of this manuscript:

♪ **Karen Pryor,** editor. Your ideas for structure, sequencing, connectivity, and flow have pushed the level of readability to amazing heights. We hope this book is immediately useful to *any* reader—if that truly happens, much of our success will actually be *your* success. Thank you!

♪ **Wayne Logue,** illustrator. Your images in this book *rock*! They are humorous, witty, and most important—thought provoking. You have managed to do something quite challenging—taken *auditory* concepts and made them come alive *visually*. That, really, is nothing less than the magic of genius. Thank you!

♪ **Lauren Virshup,** thematic music expert extraordinaire! Your suggestions for songs in Chapter 7 were simply *stunning*. The breadth and depth of your knowledge in this arena of music is utterly astonishing—truly, you stand alone as the complete and total authority in the field, and we appreciate you giving so freely of your time, energy, and insights. Thank you!

Publisher's Acknowledgments

Corwin Press gratefully acknowledges the contributions of the following reviewers:

Emmalee Callaway
2/3 Gifted and Talented Program Teacher
Acres Green Elementary School
Littleton, CO

Melanie S. Hedges
Art Teacher, NBCT
West Gate Elementary School
West Palm Beach, FL

Steve Knobl
Principal
Gulf High School
New Port Richey, FL

Jeff Loftus
Teacher, 7th-Grade Humanities
Stoller Middle School
Beaverton, OR

Beth Madison
Principal
George Middle School
Portland, OR

Kathryn McCormick
7th-Grade Teacher
Gahanna Middle School East
Gahanna, OH

Lauren Mittermann
7th- and 8th-Grade Social Studies Teacher
Gibraltar Secondary School
Fish Creek, WI

Pamela L. Opel
Science Curriculum Specialist
Gulfport School District
Biloxi, MS

Debra A. Scarpelli
7th-Grade Math Teacher and Adjunct Professor for RIC
RIMLE President and Slater Jr. High School
North Smithfield, RI

About the Authors

 **Rich Allen**, PhD, is a highly regarded educator with more than twenty-five years' experience coaching teachers. Founder and president of Green Light Education, he is the author of numerous popular educational books, including most recently *Humane Teaching* (2012); *Sparking Student Synapses 9–12: Think Critically and Accelerate Learning* (2012); *High-Five Teaching K–5: Using Green Light Strategies to Create Dynamic, Student-Focused Classrooms* (2011); *High-Impact Teaching Strategies for the 'XYZ' Era of Education* (2010); and *Green Light Classrooms: Teaching Techniques That Accelerate Learning* (2008).

He has shared his dynamic instructional strategies not only in the United States and Canada, but also in such diverse countries as the United Kingdom, Australia, New Zealand, Hong Kong, Singapore, Thailand, Brunei, Russia, Jordan, and Brazil. Dr. Allen is also a popular keynote speaker at international education conferences and works with schools and school districts to embed effective teaching methods into mainstream curriculum.

Dr. Allen first took to the stage as an off-Broadway actor, before starting his educational career as a high school math and drama teacher. In 1985 he became a lead facilitator for SuperCamp—an accelerated learning program for teens—and has since worked with more than 25,000 students worldwide. Dr. Allen completed his doctorate in educational psychology at Arizona State University, where he studied how the human brain receives, processes, and recalls information—knowledge that informs all aspects of his teaching strategies. The author divides his time between his home in the U.S. Virgin Islands, on the sun-kissed paradise of St. Croix, and his wife's home in Sydney, Australia, where he is learning to be a step-dad. He can be reached at his e-mail address: rich@drrichallen.com.

W. W. Wood, MA, is a highly sought-after speaker on how the human brain learns and effective teaching practices. He speaks regularly in school districts across the United States and at national and international brain and education conferences, with a focus on sharing and modeling practical classroom approaches extrapolated from current cognitive psychology and neuroscience.

Mr. Wood began his educational career as an English teacher, teaching high school and university level literature and writing classes for fourteen years. He then served as the Communication Arts Consultant for the Missouri Department of Elementary and Secondary Education for five years. During his time at DESE, Mr. Wood wrote the state's Curriculum Frameworks for Communication Arts, led the development of the state's communication arts assessment, and started the state's first intensive K–3 professional development model for improving reading instruction (the Missouri Reading Initiative). During his time as a teacher and state educational consultant, Mr. Wood became fascinated with exploring the biological underpinnings of effective teaching and learning. He left DESE in 2000 to become a full-time educational consultant and presenter so he could share his passion for brain-compatible teaching practices with educators around the world. He now serves as president of Open Mind Technologies, Inc., an educational consulting firm. The author lives in Missouri with his wife, Debbie, and has three sons. He can be reached at his e-mail address: wordmanw@yahoo.com.

1

Music

A Powerful Teaching Tool

Writing about music is like dancing about architecture—it's a really stupid thing to want to do.

—Elvis Costello

Music and Mankind—Arguments and Theories

Music has a powerful influence on our lives. It can calm us down when we are stressed or energize us when we are tired. It can move us to laughter or tears. It can raise goose bumps on our arms or raise us to the heights of religious feeling. For years, philosophers, psychologists, and musicologists have been asking *why* and *how* does something as simple as the structured arrangement of sound waves achieve all of this? While we are still far from having any kind of detailed, definitive explanation for all of music's effects, each year research unravels a bit more of the mystery. This book reveals the practical implications of this research on the use of music in educational settings.

Before we begin our more specific discussion of how teachers can harness the power of music in their classrooms, let's take a few minutes to glance at the bigger picture. To understand the wonderful possibilities we see for an expanded role for music in the classroom, we first need to grasp the current arguments and theories about music's origins and uses, its effects on the human psyche and physiology, and how fields other than education have begun to use it in various ways.

Cultural or Universal?

One of the biggest of the big picture questions, which has been hotly debated for years, is whether our response to music is cultural or universal. This is one of those "nonargument arguments" similar to the old nature versus nurture debate—neither side is *right* (to put it another way, *both* sides are right to some extent). The argument really comes down to one about percentages: How much of our response to and appreciation of music is universal and how much is culturally determined?

In his classic 1956 book, *Emotion and Meaning in Music*, musicologist Leonard Meyer argues that the musical experience of any listener involves expectations, and these expectations are based on the listener's cultural experiences with music. When the music conforms to our expectations, Meyer explains, we relax and enjoy the ride. However, when our expectations are not met, we experience tension. Artful composers play with these expectations, establishing a musical theme or structure, then violating it in any number of ways, before (usually) resolving those violations and bringing the tune back "home" to satisfy our expectations. Most people tend to prefer music that teases our expectations like this—if it's too predictable, it's boring—but only if our expectations are ultimately satisfied. If the music wanders too far from our expectations, it simply sounds wrong. This is why most people tend to enjoy the music of their own culture more than music from other cultures.

On the other hand, while different cultures certainly have different expectations of their music, there is plenty of evidence to support the case for universality. For example, all human cultures make music and have done so for a very, very long time. Archaeological evidence—such as bone flutes and drums—proves that mankind has been making music for at least 30,000 years.

Also, while we may prefer music from our own cultures, some elements of music produce consistent effects across cultures. Research by Laura-Lee Balkwill and William Forde Thompson (1999) found that when Western listeners were asked to identify what emotion (joy, sadness, anger, or peace) was being conveyed by twelve Hindustani ragas, they performed at a better than chance level, despite the fact that they were completely unfamiliar with the tonal system and the raga-rasa system of conveying moods. Similarly, Fritz and colleagues (2009) at the Max Planck Institute for Human Cognitive and Brain Sciences asked members of a native African population (Mafa) what basic emotion Western music was intended to convey. Once again, subjects were able to identify the correct emotion (happy, sad, or scared/fearful) at a better than chance level, though less reliably than native Westerners.

Weighing in heavily on the side of innate versus learned, recent studies have shown that infants can detect a number of musical features even before they can talk! In carefully constructed experiments by patient researchers such as Sandra Trehub (2003), infants sit on their mothers' laps between two speakers, while a researcher plays

with a toy in front of them to focus attention. Music plays from one or both of the speakers while the researchers subtly change something about the music (its key, tempo, or pitch). These experiments have determined that, when sound features change, infants will turn toward the speaker. In most cases, infants can detect these fundamental musical features as well as adults.

Why does any of this matter for teachers? We think that there are two broad "take away points": (1) wherever in the world you teach, and no matter what culture your students come from, they *will* respond positively to music in your classroom—that's pretty much universal; and (2) if you can find and use a number of musical selections in your classroom that come from your students' culture(s), they will be even *more* likely to enjoy them, as they will have a certain familiarity and comfort level with that music.

Why Does Music Affect Us? Some Theories

Research has yet to establish a definitive answer to the question of *why* we get such pleasure from the artful arrangement of sound. However, several interesting theories have been proposed.

One is that music has some yet-to-be-understood adaptive evolutionary value. Some evolutionary psychologists have theorized that the arts (storytelling, humor, wit, music—indeed creativity itself) evolved as forms of courtship behavior. If music doesn't have a clearly "practical" use, maybe it's the sonic equivalent of the peacock's tail.

Other theorists who believe in music's adaptive value point to the fact that human beings prefer note combinations that mimic natural sounds. Since as far back as Pythagoras, we have known that two notes played simultaneously sound harmonious if their acoustic frequencies are related in simple ratios. For example, notes an octave apart have frequencies in the ratio of 1:2, and the so-called "perfect fifth," such as a C and the G above it, have a ratio of 2:3. Researchers note that these preferred combinations of notes with simple frequency ratios are also generated in the natural world, whereas combinations of sounds with complex frequency ratios tend to sound jarring. Some scientists have theorized that an auditory system that seamlessly blends more natural sound frequencies into a single perceived note (as our human auditory system does) would be selected for by evolution, since it would provide a more accurate representation of the sonic world around us. And since we clearly prefer to hear such consonant sounds, music makes use of them the vast majority of the time—and therein may lie much of its appeal.

Others believe music acts as social glue, pointing to its use in important events. Within any culture, whenever people get together to celebrate (a birthday, wedding, or graduation), mourn (funerals), or worship, music is almost always a key component. For that matter, whenever people gather with no other object than to simply have a good time, music is almost always present. Why does music help create social cohesiveness? Robin Dunbar (1997) of the University of Liverpool suggests that music originally helped to bond social groups that had grown too large for grooming. Other researchers have suggested that the social benefits of music grow out of our tendency to want to move to a beat. Studies have shown that when people listen to music, motor regions of the brain activate to process the rhythm. These regions include the cerebellum, which helps us to smoothly coordinate physical movements—movements as simple as tapping a foot or as complex as dancing—to match a rhythm. Thus, when a group of people synchronize their movements to the same rhythm, you have a party—or at least a line dance!

One final theory challenges both the evolutionary adaptation theory and the social-glue theory. Noted psychologist Steven Pinker believes that music is no more than a happy evolutionary accident, a by-product of the development of other parts of the brain that evolved for more "useful" functions, such as language. In fact, in his book, *How the Mind Works,* Pinker (1997) famously called music "auditory cheesecake," suggesting that it is no more than a pleasant evolutionary add-on to the main course (p. 534).

Who's right? Who knows? And more important, for our purposes, why should teachers care? Certainly, it doesn't much matter to us whether music served some unknown evolutionary purpose, or whether, as Pinker believes, it is just some fortuitous accident. What really matters is not so much music's origins as its obvious importance in everyday life. Clearly, music plays an important role in the emotional lives of most people, and especially in the lives of our students outside of school. If music permeates all other aspects of life, surely there are potential benefits to using it in the classroom. To us, it's really not a matter of *whether* we should use music in the classroom, but *how* we can use it effectively—and that's what this book is all about.

How We Use Music in Everyday Life

> Music is rapidly becoming the common tongue of the modern world. People today spend more money, time, and energy on music than on books, movies, and sports. The most popular cultural icons of our era are not statesmen or saints, but singers.
>
> —Don Campbell

Today, more than at any other time in history, music pervades our lives. Most people—especially young people—listen to music several times a day. Thanks to technological advances and recent changes in the music industry, never before has so much music been so easily and inexpensively available, and never before have individuals had so much control over what music they listen to and under what conditions. And even when the listener is not in control of the music selection, or even actively listening to it, music permeates the environment all around us—we play it while we do housework, when we ride in the car, and while we eat, exercise, and socialize.[1]

Why is music so ubiquitous? For the simple reason that it improves the quality of our lives. Numerous research studies have cataloged the many benefits that music confers upon listeners. But for now, let's just focus on the top three most common uses for music, which are universally practiced all over the world: (1) to regulate mood (to make us feel better); (2) to manipulate energy levels (to help us either energize or relax); and (3) to sharpen and maintain focus (to filter out distractions).

Mood

Mood management is one of the most basic of all human activities. We constantly make decisions, large and small, with the goal of improving our moods. Whether it's as simple as going for a walk or getting a snack out of the refrigerator, or as complex as planning a family vacation, our goal in a broad sense is always the same—to make ourselves feel good.

Research conducted through questionnaires, surveys, and psychotherapist interviews indicates only a handful of effective ways for reliably turning a bad mood into a good one. The top four approaches, as rated in the research,[2] are

1. Physical—getting some exercise

2. Musical—listening to our favorite music

3. Social—calling, talking to, or being with a friend or loved one

4. Intrapersonal—giving ourselves a pep talk or trying to figure out why we are in a bad mood in the first place

In one study, nearly 1,000 subjects, aged 12–29, were surveyed about their listening habits and their uses of music in their daily lives. Of the group,

♪ 20% were high-involved listeners—people to whom music was a central part of their lives;
♪ 74% were medium-involved listeners—people whose use of music was more casual and recreational; and
♪ 6% were low-involved listeners—people who chose to listen to music infrequently.

Those percentages in themselves show just how pervasive music is. But perhaps the most interesting finding of this research was that people from *all three* categories used music regularly to manage their moods and fend off boredom—even the low-involved group (Ter Bogt, Mulder, Raaijmakers, & Gabhainn, 2011).

Energy

While research shows that the number one use of music is as a mood enhancer, using music to adjust one's energy level runs a close second. According to one study, listening to music ranked equally with caffeine as the fifth best method of raising our energy levels when we are feeling tired. The top four are

♪ taking a nap,
♪ taking a shower or bath,
♪ going outside for some fresh air, and
♪ doing something to keep busy.

In fact, 41% of people report regularly using music to raise their energy levels (Thayer, Newman, & McClain, 1994). And music's power to influence energy levels works in the other direction, as well. When we are stressed out or anxious, we often use music to calm and relax us.

Focus

Many people realize intuitively that a "pad" of sound in the immediate environment can be used to filter out distractions, allowing them to focus on the task at hand. Some people like to work with the television or radio on in the background to provide this sonic pad. But human voices can be highly distracting in themselves, so having the television or radio on doesn't always work. Instead, many people use instrumental background music as their "distraction filter."

The important point for teachers is that people don't just listen to music for pleasure. Yes, this experience can be wonderful in itself. But music is also incredibly useful. We deliberately use it to lift us up when we're feeling down, give us a shot of energy, calm us when we are frazzled or anxious, and help us focus and work. Our students already intuitively use music for all these purposes outside of school. Perhaps we could put music to similar use in our classrooms.

How Other Fields Use Music

How Business Uses Music to Manipulate Us

Researchers have been investigating the effects of music in a variety of business contexts for nearly a century, but the pace of this research has picked up greatly in the last thirty years. Today, the three main areas of research in this field look at the power of music to increase the

1. Productivity of workers

2. Purchasing behavior of consumers in retail settings

3. Effectiveness of advertising

Using music to boost productivity

One of the earliest examples of using music in manufacturing settings was the BBC radio program *Music While You Work*, which was launched in 1940 and ran for twenty-seven years. This half-hour program, which aired twice daily and featured popular, up-tempo dance music of the time, was meant especially for factory workers to listen to as they worked. *Music While You Work* was credited with reducing the occurrence of accidents due to the increased alertness and improved mood of the workers. The British Minister of Labor even wrote that the program "made the hours pass more quickly and resulted in increased production (Le Roux, 2005)." And he was right. Research into the use of music in the workplace shows the following:

- ♪ The vast majority of workers find music to be pleasant and a positive mood enhancer.
- ♪ Workers rate themselves as feeling less tired in the presence of music than when no music is playing (Middleton, Fay, Kerr, and Amft, 1944).[3]
- ♪ Music reduces boredom and leads to increased productivity.
- ♪ There is some evidence that music leads to a decrease in errors in manufacturing.
- ♪ Using more arousing music during repetitive work leads to greater efficiency and economic benefits for the business.[4]

These findings are not lost on a business world desperate to increase productivity. Today, millions of people do their work to a carefully selected "soundtrack," specifically designed to boost energy levels, improve focus, and increase accuracy.

Using music to increase retail sales

The retail and restaurant businesses are highly adept at using music to influence shoppers and patrons. Next time you enter an establishment with its own sound track, pay attention—there is nothing random about the music you're hearing. Your friendly local barista did not just bring his favorite CD from home to pop in the stereo system. Considerable thought and even research has gone into the music you hear in your favorite mall, restaurant, bar, or coffee-house. Retail researchers have examined the effects of different aspects of background music, such as tempo, volume, familiarity, and liking, on a number of business metrics—with eye-opening results.

- ♪ **Tempo**—Research shows that slow tempo music makes shoppers[5] and diners[6] spend more time and money in the store or restaurant. On the other hand, faster tempo music makes bar patrons drink faster (and spend more money).[7] Thus, retailers choose music to encourage the behavior that boosts profitability: 5-star restaurants use slower tempo music to encourage their patrons to stay longer and spend more, while fast-food chains play fast tempo music to "turn over" as many customers as possible.

♪ **Volume**—People spend more money in a restaurant when the background music is played more softly (Lammers, 2003). On the other hand, bar patrons consume more drinks and drink them faster when the music is louder, possibly because you can't talk to someone and drink at the same time (Gueguen, Jacob, Le Guellec, Morineau, and Lourel, 2008). Interestingly, the results of research on music volume in a supermarket setting are mixed, with louder music leading to shorter stays in the store, but no significant difference in sales (Smith & Curnow, 1966).

♪ **Liking** (pleasantness) and **arousal**—When music is both pleasant and mildly arousing, customers tend to approach business personnel more readily and interact in a more friendly manner (Dube, Chebat, & Morin, 1995). Customers also rate the entire buying experience—service quality and merchandise quality—more highly in the presence of background music that they find pleasurable (Sweeney & Wyber, 2002).

♪ **Fit**—Music has a more powerful retail effect when it matches customers' perceptions of the business. For example, several studies have shown that, for some businesses, playing classical music in the background increases profits. One such experiment, conducted in a wine store, found that while customers didn't buy *more* wine when classical music was playing, they did buy more *expensive* wine. The hypothesis is that patrons viewed the store as being "classier" because of the classical music playing in the background, and that since classier people (supposedly) visit classier stores and buy more expensive products, the store's patrons followed suit (Areni & Kim, 1993). If you have trouble believing in the manipulative power of classical music, this same finding has been replicated in other settings— customers in a British restaurant were shown to consistently spend more with classical music playing in the background, as were college students in a student cafeteria.[8] Of course, in other retail settings, the best musical fit might be pop music, or country music, or . . . whatever fits the customer profile best.[9] Rest assured, business owners worldwide make conscious decisions about what music to play in their stores because they know that the right music works to increase sales.

Retailers—along with medical clinics and sporting venues—also use music to lift the mood of their patrons. Studies show that people will wait longer when listening to music than in silence, and that they don't mind the wait so much and have better feelings toward the business if they enjoy the music being played (even when it makes the wait seem longer).[10] This is why there is almost always music playing while you wait for your car to be fixed, in the doctor's office, or in line to have a prescription filled. This is why every sporting venue has energizing music playing (either over the loudspeakers or performed by a live band) at every opportunity—as you enter the venue, at half-time, during time outs—to lift the mood and make the experience more enjoyable, so patrons return.

Using music to make advertising more effective

Research shows that a good, catchy jingle embeds a business slogan in our heads very effectively for branding purposes (though you can only embed so much information in a jingle).[11] Similarly, the background music used in commercials creates positive associations with a brand, increasing sales. Not surprisingly, this effect increases the more attention-getting the music, the more the listener likes the music, and the better the music fits the product.[12] But music in advertising can be tricky, as well. Research has found that when consumers have to think hard about product features to make a purchasing decision, attention-getting music can be distracting (Park & Young, 1986). Likewise, appealing, up-tempo background music, when played behind educational television programming, tends to distract viewers' attention from the content of the program and impair recall (Wakshlag, Reitz, & Zillman, 1982).

Music in the Health Care Field

> Each illness has a musical solution. The shorter and more complete the solution, the greater the musical talent of the physician.
>
> —Novalis

In his book *Awakenings*, physician and neurologist Oliver Sacks (1973) writes that "the power of music to integrate and cure . . . is quite fundamental (p. 60). [It is the] profoundest nonchemical medication." In the United States, music therapy began as far back as the 1800s, first in the Perkins School for the Blind in South Boston, and later in hospitals treating physical and mental disabilities and emotional disturbances, especially depression and mania. Today, across the world, licensed music therapists are frequently included as key members of teams of medical professionals, most commonly using music to reduce stress in patients (Heller, 1987).

Considerable research supports the anxiolytic (stress reducing) benefits of certain kinds of music. For example, in one study by Knight and Rickard (2001), college undergraduates were given a stress-inducing task (a short time to prepare an oral presentation on a challenging topic). Subjects' heart rate, blood pressure, and levels of cortisol (a stress hormone) were taken prior to being told of the task. The experimental group then listened to calming music (Pachelbel's Canon in D Major) as they worked, while the control group worked in silence. After the preparation period, physiological measures were taken again (the subjects didn't actually have to give the presentations—even researchers have a heart!). The control (no music) group reported increased subjective stress levels, and physiological measures showed increased heart rate and blood pressure due to the stressful task. The group listening to the music, however, showed *no stress-induced effects* of the task! Relaxing music has also been found to work well when used in combination with other stress-reduction techniques such as biofeedback and muscle-relaxation training.[13]

Music is also highly effective in reducing stress prior to, during, and after surgery. A number of studies have shown that with both children and adult patients, using music, either by itself or in combination with other stress-reduction methods, can reduce anxiety about upcoming surgical procedures.[14] In addition, patients who listened to music during surgery where a nongeneral anesthetic was used reported that the music eased their anxiety, acted as an effective distracter, and increased their threshold for pain (Stevens, 1990). And for surgical patients undergoing general anesthesia, those given postoperative music therapy reported less anxiety and pain and required less pain medication (Nilsson, Unosson, & Rawal, 2005).

Research also supports the effectiveness of using music in obstetrics. Women report much more satisfaction with their deliveries when music is used as part of a predelivery routine during the third trimester of pregnancy and then subsequently used during delivery to cue breathing, assist in relaxation between contractions, and focus attention away from discomfort. Women who followed the music therapy program prior to and during their deliveries also reported significantly less pain than those delivering without music.[15]

In addition to its use for stress reduction, in surgery, and during childbirth, music's other research-supported health applications include the following:

- ♪ **Exercise**—Listening to music while exercising has been shown to significantly increase the amount of time spent working out.[16]
- ♪ **Physical therapy**—Matching muscle movements to a rhythm has been shown to lead to a more efficient recruitment of motor units and smoother movements (Thaut, Schleiffers, & Davis, 1991).
- ♪ **Addiction**—Patients recovering from chemical or alcohol dependency reported a decrease in chronic stress following a series of treatment sessions combining music with guided imagery (Hammer, 1996).
- ♪ **Sleep**—A program of music, progressive muscle relaxation, and guided imagery was found to significantly decrease the amplitude of circadian rhythms, allowing a group of nurses to more quickly adjust their sleep patterns when switching from daytime work shifts to night shifts, and vice versa (Rider, Floyd, & Kirkpatrick, 1985). Likewise, listening to soft music just prior to bedtime was shown to provide a variety of sleep benefits for elderly people, including better sleep quality, longer sleep duration, and less sleep disturbance, and the benefits of listening were shown to increase over time (Lai & Good, 2005).
- ♪ **ICU support**—Nearly 60% of intensive care patients, when exposed to music therapy, demonstrated lowered blood pressure, heart rate, and respiration, indicating less stress.[17]

The bottom line is that *business people and clinicians pay attention to the research.* If some use of music (or any other atmospheric variable) can help business owners to influence customers to purchase more of their products, they are going to use it. They understand the power music has to affect us, and they aren't shy about using it to manipulate our feelings and direct our decision making. Similarly, while physicians are focused on more altruistic outcomes, they nevertheless also pay attention to research and aren't afraid to try new techniques when warranted. After all, in the final analysis, both business and health care are driven by a "results orientation"—what works (for profit in business, for quality of life in health care) is what counts, and pretty much all that counts. Perhaps it's time for educators to follow suit.

Our Turn Now—Using Music as a Powerful Teaching Tool

Despite the pervasive nature of music in our modern society, and its extensive use in the fields of business and health care, music has yet to be fully harnessed in education. It almost seems as if there is some unwritten rule prohibiting music on school property, especially with older students. This is a sad situation, because there are so many ways music can be used effectively in the classroom.

Please realize this is not the fault of teachers. There are any number of reasons why schools are not filled with music, starting with the inertia of tradition. Using music in the classroom has never become a mainstream, accepted educational practice, and we know how hard it is to be the first teacher in a school to break with tradition. In addition, music is often excluded from the teacher education curriculum. While teaching methods courses for elementary level teachers often include at least some techniques for using music in the classroom (to teach some content and for management purposes, mainly), secondary methods courses rarely even mention the topic. And we can't ignore the role of administration. A teacher may wish to use more music in his or her classroom, but if the school administrators are not supportive, the teacher is not likely to give it a try.

Despite these challenges, we believe the potential benefits of using music will make overcoming these difficulties worthwhile. Teachers who learn to use music well find it a powerful force for

- ♪ **Mood Management**—As teachers, we also know how challenging it is to teach a room full of students when they are in a bad mood. Chapter 2 shows you how and when to use music to lift the mood of your students and get them into a better frame of mind for learning.
- ♪ **Energy Management**—You know how hard it can be to teach when your students are bouncing off the walls with excess energy, or conversely, when they are all dragging around the room with no energy at all. In either situation, music is a wonderful tool for manipulating student energy. Chapter 3 explains how to use calming music to bring your students' energy level down so they can focus on their work. Chapter 4 shows you how to use energizing, "pump-up" music to raise student energy when needed.
- ♪ **Establishing and Maintaining Focus**—One of the bigger challenges all teachers face is getting and keeping students "on

task." Once again, music is an amazing tool for achieving this goal. Chapter 5 explains how to use background music effectively when students are doing individual seatwork and Chapter 6 shows you how to use music behind small group activities to help students focus on their work.

♪ **Increasing Learning**—One of the most powerful uses of music is as a mnemonic (memory) aid. When curricular content is embedded in song lyrics, students learn it more quickly and retain it better. Chapter 7 demonstrates a variety of ways you can use music with embedded content to supercharge learning in your classroom.

♪ **Classroom Management**—Music can be used as a cue for students to do certain tasks, to manipulate the speed of transitions, and as a tool for modulating classroom noise. You can also use it to add an element of fun and engagement to simple classroom chores, such as passing out papers and cleaning up after activities. Chapter 8 describes a number of ways you can use music to make your classroom run smoothly throughout the day.

If this all sounds a bit daunting, don't worry. You can start with a single use of music and take it nice and slow. Once you are comfortable with that use, you can add another. There's no timetable, and no particular order in which you need to read the chapters. Feel free to dip into the book at any point; each chapter can be read as a stand-alone piece. In addition, Chapter 9 offers you a number of tips about equipment and policies you might find helpful for getting started. No matter how you approach the task, this book offers you guidance and resources to make the trip easier and more enjoyable.

Notes

1. Juslin and Laukka (2004) used a questionnaire approach to assess how 141 music listeners between the ages of seventeen and seventy-four years used music in their everyday lives. The researchers found that 64% of the subjects listened to music "several times a day" and that over 80% listened to music at least once a day. The data also showed that nearly 50% of the time, subjects were engaged with other activities, with music comprising one component of the environment (217–238).

2. Thayer, Newman, and McClain (1994) conducted four studies to evaluate the success of different behaviors used by people

to regulate their moods, energy levels, and stress. They found that exercise was the most effective strategy for elevating mood, followed closely by listening to music, which ranked higher than strategies such as talking to or being with others or taking a nap (910–925).

3. Middleton, Fay, Kerr, and Amft (1944) conducted one of the earliest studies on the use of music in a manufacturing setting. They found that both male and female workers reported being less tired and in a better mood with music in the environment than with no music. They also found that workers were more energized by popular vocal music than by waltz music (299–318).

4. Fox and Embrey (1972) report that, in repetitive work situations, research has found that background music raises efficiency even when the music has to compete with machine noise. The results support the contention that economic benefits can accrue to business from using music in this fashion (202–205).

5. Milliman (1982) found that the tempo of background music significantly influenced buying behavior. The supermarket in which this study was conducted had an average increase of 38.2% in sales volume when slow tempo music was played (86–91). This general conclusion may not hold up in all cases, however, as research by Eroglu, Machleit, and Chebat (2005) has found that the right tempo of background music depends upon how crowded the store is. When a store was crowded, shoppers were found to enjoy the shopping experience more if slower tempo music was playing in the background; alternatively, in less crowded conditions, they enjoyed the shopping experience more with faster tempo background music (577–589).

6. Milliman (1986) found that restaurant patrons stayed longer with slower tempo background music playing, and while they ate about the same amount of food, they consumed more alcoholic beverages (286–289). Caldwell and Hibbert (1999) also found that diners spent more time dining with slower tempo music, and that they spent more money on both food and drink (58–62).

7. McElrea and Standing (1992) tested how much bar patrons drank with different tempos of background music playing.

When faster tempo music was playing (132 beats per minute), patrons drank significantly faster (and more) than with slower tempo music playing (54 beats per minute) (362).

8. North, Shilcock, and Hargreaves (2003) found that restaurant patrons spent more money on starters, coffee, and food with classical background music as opposed to pop music or no music (712–718). North and Hargreaves (1998) also conducted a study in a college cafeteria where they played either classical, easy listening, pop music, or no music in the background while students dined. Subsequent interviews showed that diners felt prepared to spend more money with classical music playing than in the other conditions. Both classical music and pop music led to higher spending than easy listening or no music (2254–2273).

9. Yalch and Spangenberg (1990) examined the effect of different types of music on the shopping behaviors of clothing store patrons. They concluded that trying to satisfy customers' preferences may not always be the optimal approach. Instead, they suggest that music should be varied across different areas of the store that appeal to different-aged customers (55–63).

10. North and Hargreaves (1999a) examined subjects' willingness to wait while listening to music at one of three different levels of complexity, or in silence. They found that the complexity of the music didn't matter to wait time, but that subjects were more willing to wait with music (of any level of complexity) than without it (136–149). Hui, Dube, and Chebat (1997) also found that, no matter the valence of the background music played, people preferred to wait with music rather than without. People did prefer positively valenced music, however, and exhibited more approach behaviors toward the business with positively valenced music playing (87–104). One interesting aspect of this study was that it supported a previous finding by Kellaris and Kent (1992) that listening to music one likes actually makes wait time seem longer. Most people would assume this to be a negative thing, but the subjects in the study did not mind the seemingly extra wait because it was made more enjoyable by the music (365–376).

11. Tom (1990) compared the use of hit music, parodies of hit music, and originally scored music for product advertisements and found that original music was more effective for memory

purposes than either hit music or parodies of hit music. Parodies of hit music were found to be more effective than hit music (49–53). Yalch (1991) found that music enhanced memory for and retrieval of advertising slogans when the slogans were put to music (a jingle or song) as compared with slogans that were simply shown or spoken (268–275).

12. Kellaris, Cox, and Cox (1993) examined the effect of attention-getting background music that either supported (fit) the intended message of the advertisement or did not support the intended message. As one might expect, they found that message-congruent music had a more positive effect on ad recognition and recall than did message-incongruent music (114–125). Gorn (1982) found that people were more likely to choose to buy a product when liked music was played in the background than they were when disliked music was played (94–101).

13. Scartelli (1984) compared the effects of EMG biofeedback only, relaxing music only, and EMG biofeedback combined with relaxing music on muscle relaxation. He found that, while all three experimental conditions led to some level of relaxation, and while there was not a statistically significant difference between the results, the condition that led to the highest level of relaxation was the combined biofeedback/music condition (67–78).

14. Miluk-Kolasa, Obminski, Stupnicki, and Golec (1994) investigated the impact of music on the physiological responses of patients prior to surgery. One group of patients was given information about their upcoming surgery without musical intervention. The other group listened to one hour of self-selected music immediately after being given the information. Patients not exposed to music had a 50% rise in cortisol, and their levels of stress hormones remained elevated after an hour. Those patients who listened to music demonstrated a marked reduction in cortisol, with levels returning to near-baseline within an hour (118–120). Robb, Nichols, Rutan, Bishop, and Parker (1995) examined the effect of music-assisted relaxation interventions on pediatric burn patients prior to reconstructive surgery. Subjects in the experimental group listened to relaxing music and focused on deep breathing, muscle relaxation, and imagery. The control group received standard preoperative interventions. Study

results showed a significant decrease in anxiety in the experimental group (2–21). Froehlich (1984) also found that music therapy was more effective than play therapy in reducing preoperative stress in school-age patients, 2–15, and Chetta (1981) found that a course of music therapy administered to patients aged three to eight just prior to preoperative medication led to less anxiety leading up to surgery (74–87).

15. Clark, McCorkle, and Williams (1981) found that women who participated in music therapy sessions during the last trimester of their pregnancies and then listened to the music during delivery were more satisfied with the outcome of their deliveries than women who did not participate in the program. It was also found that the more the women in the experimental group practiced with the music at home prior to delivery, the more satisfied they were with the results (88–100). Hanser, Larson, and O'Connell (1983) found that women who participated in a music therapy program prior to and during delivery found the music to be an effective diversion and, as a result, reported less pain during delivery (50–58).

16. Beckett (1990) had college psychology students exercise either to no music or while listening to either continuous music or intermittent music. She found that subjects walked significantly farther during either music condition than in the no music condition (126–136).

17. Chan, Chung, Chung, and Lee (2008) investigated the use of music therapy to reduce anxiety in patients in an ICU setting. They found interesting differences in the effectiveness of the therapy depending upon a variety of demographic factors. Those who responded well to the therapy (lowered blood pressure, heart rate, and respiration) made up 58.4% of all patients; this group was labeled the "high therapeutic effects of music" group, which consisted of more females and older people. This group also had, on average, more experience with using a ventilator. The other group (41.6%) was labeled the "low therapeutic effects of music" group; this group consisted of more males, more young people, and more highly educated people (1250–1257).

Interlude

About Chapters 2 Through 8

T he next seven chapters cover different types of music to consider using during specific parts of your teaching day (see table below). If you're looking at the table and thinking we're suggesting you use music for most of your teaching day—you'd be right.

We believe that, other than during direct instruction (when music would be distracting); every moment in your classroom could be enhanced by having the right sound track. Having said this, please understand that we would not expect you to begin using all of the types of music suggested in this book right away, especially if you have been using little or no music in your classroom. Start slowly and build up your comfort level over time.

Transitions	Direct Instruction	Student Processing
Entering and exiting the classroom, moving between activities	Lecture, teacher modeling, teacher-led whole class discussions	Individual activities, small group discussions, partner or team work, recall strategies
Feel-good music (Ch. 2) Calming music (Ch. 3) Pump-up music (Ch. 4) Management music (Ch. 8)	No music	Background music (Ch. 5) Music behind activities (Ch. 6) Music to teach content (Ch. 7)

Be aware that each of these types of music have different characteristics and need to be used in particular ways. For example, with calming music, you have to be careful not to put your students to sleep; whereas with pump-up music, you have to be careful not to get them overstimulated. The following seven chapters are structured to help you understand why and how to use each type. They all include sections on

- ♪ What it is
- ♪ Why it works
- ♪ How to use it
- ♪ What to avoid
- ♪ How to get started
- ♪ Inside a classroom (case studies from teachers)
- ♪ Our Top 40 (suggested tracks to be used in the classroom)

2

So Happy Together

Using Feel-Good Music to Manage Student Mood

Music produces a kind of pleasure which human nature cannot do without.

—Confucius

Ah, music—a magic far beyond anything done here.

—J. K. Rowling

Music is the sound track of your life.

—Dick Clark

What It Is

When we hear a feel-good song, we get a rush of dopamine in the pleasure/reward centers of our brains. This is the feeling you get when your favorite song comes on the radio—it's like taking a giant bite of chocolate or the first sip of your favorite latte or parking all day without feeding the meter and not getting ticketed or . . . anything else that makes you feel good! It's an instant shot of pleasure.

You may know this from your own subjective experience, but experiments have also proven that music actually affects our physiology—heart rate, respiration, and blood pressure.[1] There is considerable research looking at the ability of music to elicit the physiological reaction commonly known as *chills*—you know, that shiver that starts at the base of your neck and radiates over your scalp, down your spine, and outward toward your extremities, often accompanied by goose bumps.

Chills are actually a rather complex physiological reaction of the autonomic nervous system (ANS) to strong emotion, and they often occur in response to emotionally powerful stimuli such as gruesome pictures, frightening sounds, or evocative smells, in addition to music. However, while many nonmusical chill experiences are negative (for example, occurring in response to surprise, shock, or fear), studies have shown that chills experienced while listening to emotionally powerful music are invariably viewed as positive.[2]

The ability for songs to deliver an emotional lift is one of the main reasons that music is one of the constants of the modern human experience—why we spend our lives literally surrounded by music.[3]

The best thing is that this powerful, positive effect is available to anyone. You don't have to be an experienced musician or an expert on musical theory to enjoy the emotional benefits of listening to music. In fact, studies have consistently shown that, while musicians may be better at identifying and discussing the elements of musical structure, they are no better at determining the *emotional* qualities of music than nonmusicians.[4] Put another way, the emotional benefits of music are egalitarian; they are available to anyone with a radio, a CD player, an MP3 player, or a computer.

Why It Works

If we're going to use this effect in teaching, we need to understand what makes a feel-good song work. With some categories of music in this book, the characteristics of the music that lead to its effect are pretty clear-cut. But it's not so simple with feel-good music. Certainly, genre is not a determining factor. Some people have feel-good favorites that are hard rock—or country, or classical, or jazz, or rap, or . . . well, you get the point. Instead, a number of factors combine in complex ways to create songs that make us feel good. Some of these factors are out of our control; for example, the association factor attached to a couple's "song" (it was playing the first time they kissed). However, many are within our control (see Table 2.1), meaning we can deliberately select songs with the greatest probability of creating a feel-good effect on our students.

Table 2.1 Characteristics of Feel-Good Music

Factors We Can Control	Factors Outside Our Control
Complexity—We tend to prefer music of medium complexity **Familiarity**—We tend to prefer music we have heard before **Musical Elements**—Most feel-good music is in the major mode, with a faster tempo and strong beat **Emotional Peaks**—Some songs include specific structural characteristics that create emotionally powerful and pleasing effects **Lyrics**—We prefer some songs because the lyrics are witty, poetic, or meaningful	**Association**—We prefer some songs because of their associated memories **Opinions of Others**—Our musical tastes are influenced by the opinions of those we respect, be they parents, teachers, or DJs **Personal Values and Identity**—We tend to like the same music as our peers, with listening to music acting as an important bonding process

Complexity

Complexity goes a long way toward determining whether we like a piece of music or not. The "optimal complexity model" predicts that people will least enjoy music at either extreme—low complexity or high complexity—and will tend to prefer music of medium complexity. The relationship between liking and complexity can thus be graphed as an inverted U-shaped curve, and there is a good deal of research to support the truth of this model. Of course, complexity is only complexity if one can discriminate the patterns of musical elements that make up a piece of music. Young children are not very good at doing this, so they tend to like just about any music they hear. As children develop, their ability to identify musical complexity grows. As a result, older children become more discriminating in their musical tastes (they become pickier), and the "optimal complexity model" becomes more applicable.[5]

Familiarity

While we have all fallen in love with a song upon first hearing, research has also shown that the more times we hear a song (up to a certain point), the more we tend to like it. There is another theory to explain this phenomenon—the "theory of optimum response"—and it explains why we tend to grow to like a song more as it becomes more familiar. There is a point, however, at which we reach our optimum appreciation of the song, and after that point we get diminishing aesthetic and emotional returns from each repeated listening. In other words, it gets old and we look for new favorite songs.[6] Before we reach this point of diminishing returns, however, we become very fond of and attached to our favorite songs—so much so, in fact, that studies have shown that most people consider any version of a favorite song that is in any way altered from the original as being "wrong" and much less pleasing.[7]

Structural Elements

Researchers have identified some consistent effects of certain musical elements (mode, melody, harmony, rhythm) on human physiology. For example, the most consistent musical effect is that of the major versus the minor mode. Experiments from the 1930s on have confirmed that music played in the major mode tends to convey and engender in the listener positive feelings such as joy, playfulness, and excitement, while music in the minor mode tends to convey and engender feelings of sadness, tenderness, or sentimental yearning.[8]

The effects of other musical elements are less clear-cut. Firm rhythms, for example, tend to convey vigor or dignity while flowing, less-accented rhythms tend to be seen as graceful or tender; but these effects are only evident when the rhythmic element is supported in certain ways by other elements. Similarly, complex or dissonant harmonies tend to be exciting and agitating, while simple and consonant harmonies tend to make people feel happy, serene, and lyrical; but again, these effects only become evident when found with the right mix of other elements. And the rising or falling of the melodic line has been shown to have little consistent effect on listeners whatsoever.[9]

So, attempting to isolate specific musical elements under experimental conditions can only tell us so much. Far more important than the effect of any single musical element is the effect created by the *combination* of all of the elements in a piece. After all, we don't hear elements such as melody, harmony, and rhythm in isolation, and when we start combining elements in different ways, things get complex very quickly. For example, we can feel pretty confident in saying that a piece of music in the major mode with a quick tempo, strong beat, and simple, consonant harmonies will produce feelings of excitement and happiness in most listeners. However, change a single element, and that piece of music can suddenly produce a very different effect on listeners.[10]

Emotional Peaks

We talked earlier about music eliciting positive chills. Research shows that chills usually occur when certain structural elements appear in the music, especially if these changes violate the listener's expectations—that is, if the changes are novel. Examples of such changes that reliably produce chills are new or unexpected harmonies, the first entrance of a solo voice or choir, the contrast or alternation between a solo instrument and the full band or orchestra, a gradual increase in volume, or a rise in register.[11] Composers who know what they're doing often build in more of these elements as a song progresses, building the emotional intensity up to a climax at or near the end of the song.

Physiologically, it appears that the surprise or intensity of such peak moments in music activates the pleasure pathways in our brains, creating a feeling of euphoria similar to that elicited by food, money, sex, and drugs such as cocaine. Studies have identified blood flow changes and dopamine release in brain areas involved with pleasure such as the caudate (in anticipation of a pleasurable event) and the nucleus accumbens (in response to an actual pleasurable event) when listening to pleasurable music.[12]

Lyrics

Some songs become favorites because the lyrics themselves are enjoyable in some way. They may be clever, funny, or touching or say something of importance to the listener, something he or she identifies with.

Associations

Sometimes, a song becomes a favorite through its *association* with a positive memory—the "our song" phenomenon. In this case, it's not the song itself that makes us feel good but its positive associations. Obviously, these associations will differ greatly from person to person—a factor we cannot control for when selecting feel-good songs.

Opinions of Others

Also outside our control, musical preferences are affected by the attitudes and preferences of other people.[13] A number of research studies have shown that we often allow the opinions of others to

color our own perceptions of music. For example, when fed bogus information about teacher, disc jockey, music critic, or peer opinions concerning the quality (good or bad) of a musical selection prior to hearing it, students at various age levels (midelementary grades to college age) tended to adopt the opinions of others as their own compared with those not fed the information in advance.[14] And it's not just the opinions of others that affect our enjoyment of music, but our own preconceived attitudes and beliefs. In one study, for example, college students listened to the exact same performance of an instrumental piece twice, but were told prior to one presentation that the performer was a professional pianist, while they were told prior to the other presentation that the performer was a college music student. They were then asked to rate the performances. Study subjects consistently rated the "student" performance as being of lower quality than the "professional" performance, even though the performances were in fact the same (Duerksen, 1972).

> Nothing separates the generations more than music. By the time a child is eight or nine, he has developed a passion for his own music that is even stronger than his passions for procrastination and weird clothes.
>
> —Bill Cosby

Personal Values and Identity

Finally, research has also shown that people's preference for certain kinds of music and specific artists and songs often has much to do with their personal identity and values. That is, people—especially adolescents—often meet others through music and form bonds with like-minded others around their musical experiences. The music becomes a powerful element bonding people to each other socially.[15] And since youth is a time of powerful emotions generally, as well as a time of identity formation, and since music is both a carrier of strong emotion and one element contributing to one's sense of identity, it is no wonder that research shows that most people prefer and remain attached to the music of their youth throughout their lives.[16]

How to Use It

As teachers, we can use this powerful tool in our classrooms to modulate mood and energy. In fact, judiciously using feel-good music is one of the fastest and easiest ways to energize students, engage them, and create classroom community. If there exists such a thing as a "magic bullet" for quickly improving the mood and raising the energy level of a group of listless students on a rainy Monday morning, that magic bullet is music!

So, how can you harness and employ the power of feel-good music to achieve your educational goals? Well, obviously, you're not going to play this kind of music while you are doing direct instruction or while students are working on an academic task of any sort. While having such music on might make students feel good about being there, it would also seriously distract them from learning. So the best time to use feel-good music is during transitions—when students are coming into class, getting materials out or putting them up, transitioning between tasks, and leaving the room.

INSIDE A CLASSROOM

Opening Music for Weekly Assemblies

Christy Sheffield
Educational Consultant, Middle School and High School
Great Expectations Oklahoma
Ames, Oklahoma, USA

"Our school athletic teams are the Raiders, so our weekly assemblies for all students in Grades 7 to12 are aptly named Raider Roundup. We use these sessions for announcements, honoring successes, showcasing talents, building a sense of school community, and presenting awards. Since students migrate from all over the school premises to arrive at the gymnasium for these assemblies, we have found it remarkably beneficial to select music to play in the auditorium as students arrive and as they depart for their next classes.

"Without music playing, student voices can create a jolting hubbub. This is especially true when a teen crowd is moving into and out of an auditorium for an assembly. They are free from obligations at the moment and choose to talk to friends, call out to classmates clear across the area, or even hurl inappropriate insults at others as they pass. Since adding music as students enter the auditorium, we have found that students can still speak to one another, but their conversations become more contained in their immediate area and are spoken more softly. In addition, some students who have yet to become confident in their own interpersonal skills are more apt to speak with others when their comments are 'covered' by music.

"Beyond acting as a sort of crowd control, the music is a powerful mood setter for the day. The target mood varies from week to week, depending on what events are on the docket, but generally the music for the arrival time is strong and upbeat; it serves to raise the spirits of everyone. The music for departure is usually calmer and is often an elegant piece of classical music that sends students out on a grand note to fulfill the high expectations we have for them."

Advice to Teachers: "Music can have a tremendous impact on your students' emotions. Use it to elevate the students' moods, to start a class session in a happy and joyful frame of mind, to calm students and relieve stress, or to pump up their enthusiasm and motivate them to step up to the challenges you place before them. Give some thought to the soundtrack you are providing for your school day!"

Suggested Songs: "We rotate many songs through our play list. We are diligently on guard against using any music that might have objectionable lyrics, since our goal is to call students to high standards of character. As we choose music for our Raider Roundup occasions, we give some thought to matching selections with students' tastes, but we also work to shape their tastes with music that spans generations, musical genres, and ideals that fit our school creed."

At the Beginning of Class

Imagine the following two scenarios. In Scenario 1, no music is playing as students come into class. What are they thinking about? Whatever was running through their heads out in the hallway on the way to class. Maybe someone called them a name, or they passed their reflection in a mirror and saw that their hair isn't looking so hot today, or they're wondering what's for lunch. Who knows? Whatever it is, their minds are generally distracted and not focused on coming to your class and learning. Unless you do something about the situation, students are going to continue to turn these thoughts over in their heads, and it takes much longer to get them focused on task.

In Scenario 2, as students approach your classroom, they have the same thoughts revolving in their heads, but in this case, something is different. As they walk through the door, they are greeted by a song that they enjoy. Immediately their thoughts go to the song and the pleasurable associations they have with it. They start bopping along as they head to their seats in the midst of a dopamine rush. The bell rings and you let the song play for a few more seconds as you take roll. Then you suddenly cut the music off and call the class to attention. There are some grumbles and pleas to hear the rest of the song, but you gently switch their focus to the day's lesson. Because the song switched their focus from their *outside* of the room concerns to *inside* the room, they are much easier to refocus than the group in Scenario 1, and because of the extra dopamine in their systems, they are now in a much better mood to tackle the subject matter of the day's lesson. It truly is a magical thing—and all you had to do was put on a song just before they came in!

At the elementary level, of course, students are usually not moving from room to room and teacher to teacher, but there is still the opportunity to use feel-good music at the beginning of the school day as students first enter the classroom to set the tone for the day ahead. And any time students leave the classroom (for recess, special subjects, lunch, etc.) and return, there is once again the opportunity to use feel-good music at the beginning of each of these chunks of the school day.

Within a Class Period

You can also play feel-good music during the multiple transitions that take place *within* your classroom during instructional time. In the elementary grades, even within self-contained classrooms, there are

---

INSIDE A CLASSROOM

First Day of Class

Darcy Mellsop
Self Defense and Violence Education
Wellington, New Zealand

"I teach a self-defense class. When people first come in to begin a course in how to defend themselves from violence, there is often an understandable element of nervousness prior to starting. I use music to relax attendees as they are filling out the usual forms and waiting for the course to start.

"Before I started using music in my teaching, I always made an effort to be bubbly and welcoming when people came into the venue, but it took lots of energy for me to juggle talking to everyone individually, introducing them to each other. Since I started using music, it has been an astounding change. The whole precourse atmosphere has changed. I still greet participants and introduce them to each other, but now it's much easier, and the attendees are so much more relaxed. They no longer fear speaking at normal volume in a quiet room because the music covers their voices. It's much more relaxing for everyone."

Advice to Teachers: "Music definitely has a place in the classroom. If your choice of music is appropriate for the task, it will work like nothing else. For me, it took everything to a whole new level. Come along and experience it for yourself."

Suggested Songs: "For my self-defense course, I use songs that are pretty aggressive, such as 'The Monster Is Loose,' by Meat Loaf; 'Sabotage,' by the Beastie Boys; and songs by artists such as Rage Against the Machine and Silverchair. Such selections work well for a self-defense class for Grades 11 and 12, but may not be appropriate for use in a more typical kind of school setting or in lower grades."

---

transitions from beginning-of-the-day routines to the first subject-area content of the day, from the tables to the carpet area for read-aloud time and back, from one learning center or station to another, and so on. And each of these transitions offers another opportunity to use feel-good music to manage the mood of the group.

And at all grade levels, there are the necessary classroom procedures that create transitions in the flow of learning: when students need to get out materials to prepare for an activity; when students change seating arrangements from individual work to group work to pairs; and when students need to clean up the area at the end of an activity or class. Again, these transitions offer excellent opportunities to use feel-good music.

At the End of Class

Again, think about two scenarios. In Scenario 1, the end of the class period or school day is approaching and you ask students to start putting things away. There is no music playing during this time. Things are more than a little chaotic as students put away class materials, stuff books and papers into backpacks, and talk to others around them about afterschool plans. When students are dismissed, there is a wild rush for the door. Sound familiar? The question is— What will students remember about these few minutes if and when they remember them later? Probably just the general sense of chaos.

Now, imagine Scenario 2. Again, it is the end of the class period or school day, and again you instruct students to begin preparing to leave. But this time you put on some feel-good music to accompany this activity. What happens? The cleanup activity itself is less crazy, as students pay at least partial attention to the music as they pick up. You see heads bobbing and, bodies swaying, and you may even hear a few students humming or singing along. In addition, the music puts students in a better mood, and that dopamine rush is coursing through their bodies as they leave. What will students remember about these few minutes later? They will probably remember the general good feeling they had as opposed to the chaotic feeling from Scenario 1. And when they head toward your room the following school day, that memory will trigger those good feelings again. If you repeat this ritual consistently, they will begin to anticipate that good feeling and associate it with your classroom. This means they will enter class each day in a better mood than they had in the past. And, as we all know, getting students in a positive mood for learning is half the battle, right?

Guidelines for Using Feel-Good Music

♪ You don't have to use whole songs. You only have to play as much of a song as needed to cover the transition period, and this is often less than a minute. If you use an MP3 player, you can actually set music files to begin at a particular point in the song instead of the beginning, if you choose. So, if the chorus of a particular song is the part you want to use, you can set the selection to begin there.

♪ It doesn't matter if you use instrumental songs or songs with lyrics. As long as the general effect of the song on most students is a positive mood inducer, it doesn't matter. For most students, the songs that are familiar to them and that they consider feel-good music will be songs with lyrics, but that shouldn't stop you from experimenting to find some instrumental tunes that will have the same positive effect. A good mixture is always nice.

♪ When the transition period is a longer one such as at the beginning of the school day, you may play several feel-good songs back-to-back. When this is the case, you can make use of something often called the ISO principle or the vectoring effect in the music therapy field. We just call it *ramping*. By ramping, we mean that you start where you expect students to be when they first hear the music, and you then move them toward the ideal target state. So, for example, if students generally straggle into your classroom one or two at a time over a fifteen-minute period at the beginning of the school day, you have time to play three to five average length songs. If your students tend to be fairly lethargic, start your feel-good music with a tune that, while upbeat, is not as energetic as some. Then gradually ramp up the songs, choosing progressively more up-tempo and upbeat selections as you go, until you end up with the last song before starting class being one that best matches the state you would like your students to be in when class starts.[17]

♪ Don't worry about using music that your students are not familiar with. If they got to choose, they would *always* choose music they know, but it's good to stretch them a little and broaden their horizons. Remember that they will often come to like music as they become more familiar with it.[18] Try music from different time periods and different genres; as long as they meet most of the criteria laid out in this chapter, they should work for most students. And if you work with teenagers, you can ignore their complaining about your music choices to some extent. Remember that, being teenagers, they see it as part of their job to disapprove of and make fun of your musical selections. Very often this is just bluster. You will probably be able to tell if they are just putting up a front or if they really do dislike a choice. Obviously, since the point of this type of music is to make students feel good, if they truly dislike a selection, don't use it again.

What to Avoid

Earlier, we said that the use of feel-good music was not as clear-cut as some of the other uses we will cover in this book, and that's certainly true. So, let's step back for a minute and talk about some of the challenges of using feel-good music in the classroom.

Music and Direct Instruction Don't Mix

The first caveat, as stated in the previous section, is that *feel-good music should never be played during instruction or in the background during learning activities* such as reading, writing, project work, or group discussions. To learn something, one must first get it into working memory, which means one must pay *attention* to it. In this case, if students are attempting to listen to the teacher, or focusing on what they're reading or writing, or trying to understand a point a group member is making in a discussion, they need to be able to bring their attentional focus to bear on that task, and they don't need to have that focus distracted by a feel-good song playing in the background. After all, there are few things as distracting as a well-known and well-loved song; it virtually cries out for our attention!

Consider Avoiding Controversial Music Selections

A second warning concerns what genres of music might or might not be appropriate for the classroom. While we all hate to have the specter of censorship hanging over our heads, and while our first, gut reaction to any hint of censorship might be to push back against it, we can probably all agree that, while a song may be just fine for listening to at home or while out at a club with adult friends, it might not be the best choice for school.

But this does bring up some tricky issues. While there are some songs from every musical genre that can be useful in certain classroom situations, we must admit that some genres are considered more generally acceptable for classroom use than others. Most parents of school-age students have absolutely no problem with you using classical music in your classroom. Easy listening and contemporary jazz will probably not raise any eyebrows, either. But when we start talking about pop, rock, R&B, soul, and blues music, things begin to get fuzzy, and the lyrics of the individual songs we use begin to be much more important. Sure, the kids might love the current Lady Gaga chart-topper, but will some of your students' parents have issues with you using it in class? Possibly. And when we start talking about heavy metal and rap music, the number of songs that many parents consider objectionable rises significantly. We may not agree with it. We don't have to like it. But that's the way it is.

For the record, we believe the dangers of listening to certain songs or certain genres of music are often overblown. The popular public perception is that if kids listen to music that has a harsh sound to it such as hard rock, heavy metal, and rap, or if they listen to music with lyrics that discuss or even glorify sex, drug use, violence, or suicide, the music will affect the listeners, causing them to be more likely to participate in similar behaviors. In fact, there has been a good deal of research into this issue, and the results don't support the music-leads-to-deviant-behavior hypothesis. Studies have shown that heavy metal listeners are *not* angrier than fans of other musical genres,[19] that juvenile male felony offenders who are fans of rap music self-report virtually *no connection* between their music listening and their deviant behavior,[20] and that listening to heavy metal music does *not* lead to higher incidence of suicidal thoughts and behaviors (such listening has actually been shown to *reduce* suicidal behaviors in female listeners).[21]

As a matter of fact, the research points in exactly the opposite direction of popular belief. While research over the past two decades does show that certain patterns of problem behavior are correlated with listening to certain types of music, it also clearly shows that children and young adults with problems tend to listen to music that *reflects* the issues they have and helps them to cope with those issues. That is, the problems exist *prior to* the music listening; the listening does not *cause* the problems.[22]

Regarding the issue of the content of musical lyrics driving behavior, a number of studies have shown that students often have very poor recall of the lyrics of even their favorite songs and often completely miss or misinterpret references to sex, violence, and drug use. Rather, children and young adults seem most often to take away from a song more of a *gestalt*, a very general sense of its tone and attitude, than any specific information from its lyrics.[23]

That said, the smart educator must always balance the usefulness of a song in a lesson with the concerns of students and their parents. If even one of your students' parents is likely to object to the use of a certain song, artist, or even entire genre of music in your classroom, it might be best to seek an alternate approach.

Beware of Negative Associations

A third issue has to do with those tricky associations we mentioned earlier. A song that the majority of students love might make another student break into tears because that was the song playing when her boyfriend broke up with her. There's just no way to know everyone's personal associations with a song, and no way to predict such reactions. You will just have to make your feel-good selections using your best judgment, and then adjust based on student reaction.

To Offer Choice or Not to Offer Choice—That Is the Question

One final issue concerns the element of student choice. In our experience, it's almost impossible to find even a single song or artist that everyone likes, much less a number of them to use for variety, so you can't expect to please everyone with your song choices. The best you can hope for is to find a number of songs that most of your students like and keep them rotating. You can, however, be sure that at least *one* student likes a selection—if you allow him to select it! We have found that letting students choose some of the songs to be played during transitions is one of the best ways to improve relationships between teacher and students and build classroom community.

But you have to be careful with student choice. While younger students will generally not select songs that are objectionable in any way, if you work with older students, you might need to institute some type of nomination and screening system to check songs for appropriateness. Students can nominate songs and turn them in to you for prelistening. You can listen to them at home and, if they're OK to use, play them in class. If they're not acceptable, just return the song to the student and perhaps have a little talk about appropriateness.

Getting Started

So, with these caveats in mind, where do you start? We recommend putting together a playlist of songs that you think have nearly universal appeal as your starting place. We have found, surprisingly, that a lot of 1960s music still works well today, as the kids have heard many of these songs on TV commercials and on movie soundtracks. Or you might start by gathering together some greatest hits collections representing different genres and time periods. The reasons these songs were hits was because a large percentage of people liked them, so they are a pretty safe bet for feel-good music. You can also check out our Top 40 list below, as well as our expanded list of feel-good music found in Appendix A, and even more suggestions on our website, www.rockandrollclassroom.com.

Once you have your starter list ready, begin using it as described above for transitions and observe the kids. The key to becoming good at using feel-good music—and any other use of music in the classroom, for that matter—is *kid-watching.* You will be able to tell if they like a song or not by how they react. If most of the kids don't like a song, cross it off your list and don't use it again. If most of them like it, use it again. Keep experimenting over time and tweak your list. Soon you will have a collection of songs that work like a charm.

INSIDE A CLASSROOM

The Power of Music

Kenny Mulkey
6th Grade Teacher
McDowell Middle School
Hondo, Texas, USA

"I started the year off by playing music as the students walked into the room. This seemed to energize them and set the tone for the day. One morning, after several weeks of this, I was not able to get to my room in time to set up my iPod, so there was no music playing as the students entered. I noticed that as they began to walk into the room, most of their faces dropped and they became very quiet. There was some whispering and finger pointing, but for the most part, no one said a word. The children simply walked in, grabbed their supplies, and sat at their desks to answer the morning's warm-up question.

"I went through my typical morning routine, not really paying any attention to the fact that they were unusually quiet and somber. As I began to start my lesson for the day, I suddenly realized how out of character the kids were acting. Finally, one young lady got up the nerve to ask me what was wrong. I told her nothing, that everything was fine. She then asked what they had done to get in trouble. I explained that they were not in trouble, and couldn't figure out why she thought they were. She seemed to accept my explanation, and we continued with class. Then, after about five more minutes, she spoke up again and said, 'Well, if we're not in trouble, and there's nothing wrong with you, then why isn't there any music?' I realized at that point the impact music had had on my students, and from that day forward, I made a point to include it in every lesson somehow."

Our Top 40 Feel-Good Songs

The following songs are some of our feel-good favorites. Keep in mind that this list was generated by a couple of White, American males of a certain age. There's nothing magical about this list, and we certainly wouldn't expect you to agree with most of our choices. We simply provide it to show you the variety of music that might be considered feel-good music by many people. Most of these songs have vocals, but we have also listed some instrumental selections. These songs are *not* ranked; they are listed in alphabetical order (in an attempt to reduce arguments).

1. "ABC," The Jackson Five
2. "Bang the Drum All Day," Todd Rundgren
3. "Brown Eyed Girl," Van Morrison
4. "Celebration," Kool and the Gang
5. "Don't Worry, Be Happy," Bobby McFerrin
6. "Feelin' Good," Nina Simone
7. "Fireflies," Owl City
8. "Girls Just Want to Have Fun," Cyndi Lauper
9. "Green Onions," Booker T. and the M.G.s
10. "Here Comes the Sun," The Beatles
11. "Hey Soul Sister," Train
12. "I Gotta Feeling," Black Eyed Peas
13. "I Got You (I Feel Good)," James Brown
14. "Jailhouse Rock," Elvis Presley
15. "Jessica," The Allman Brothers Band
16. "La Bamba," Richie Valens
17. "Linus and Lucy," Vince Guaraldi
18. "Love Shack," The B-52s
19. "Margaritaville," Jimmy Buffett
20. "My Favorite Things," Julie Andrews
21. "My Maria," Brooks and Dunn
22. "New York, New York," Frank Sinatra
23. "Oye Como Va," Santana
24. "Peaceful Easy Feeling," The Eagles
25. "Proud Mary," Credence Clearwater Revival
26. "Respect," Aretha Franklin

27. "Stand By Me," Ben E. King

28. "Stayin' Alive," The Bee Gees

29. "Sweet Home Alabama," Lynyrd Skynyrd

30. "Take Five," Dave Brubeck

31. "Thank God I'm a Country Boy," John Denver

32. "The Weight," The Band

33. "Three Little Birds," Bob Marley and the Wailers

34. "Tiny Dancer," Elton John

35. "U Can't Touch This," M.C. Hammer

36. "Walking on Sunshine," Katrina and the Waves

37. "Werewolves of London," Warren Zevon

38. "What a Wonderful World," Louis Armstrong

39. "Who Let the Dogs Out?" The Baha Men

40. "Y.M.C.A.," The Village People

Notes

1. Krumhansl (1997) had subjects listen to music selected to induce various emotions. The selections were chosen to represent happiness, sadness, and fear. Results showed not only that subjects were able to accurately determine the appropriate emotion from the music, but also that physiological reactions such as heart rate and amplitude, respiration, blood pressure, and skin conductance were affected by all music selections and varied consistently with the musical selection (336–353). Lundqvist, Carlsson, Hilmersson, and Juslin (2009) also showed varied physiological reactions to happy music versus sad music. Happy music generated more zygomatic activity (the muscles used to smile), greater skin conductance, and lower finger temperature as compared with sad music (61–90).

2. Grewe, Katzur, Kopiez, and Altenmuller (2011) were able to induce chills in test subjects in a variety of ways—through aural, visual, tactile, and gustatory stimulation. Some people were even able to produce chills through self-stimulation—thinking about an intense emotional event. Chills in response to nonmusical sounds and pictures were mostly produced by

sounds and pictures with a negative valance (scary or surprising sounds, gruesome or sad pictures), but virtually all chills produced by music were judged to be of positive valence (pleasurable) (220–239).

3. In a study by Hargreaves and Hargreaves (2004), 346 people who owned a mobile phone were sent one text message a day for 14 days. Upon receiving the text, participants completed a questionnaire about any music in their surroundings at the time or any music they had heard since the last message. Results showed that music was frequently in the environment, that music was heard most when respondents were alone, that pop music was heard most frequently, that music was heard most often in the background, and that music was most often heard in the evenings and on weekends (41–77). Several other studies support the ubiquitous nature of music, but also emphasize the uses to which people put music. In a study by Juslin and Laukka (2004), 141 listeners between the ages of 17 and 74 recorded their daily listening activities in diary and questionnaire forms. This study showed that people generally use music to enhance or change their moods (to relax, to arouse, to comfort) or to evoke emotional memories. Overall, positive emotions dominated in people's responses to music (217–238). Another study, by Ter Bogt, Mulder, Raaijmakers, and Gabhainn (2011), found that people in general use music for mood enhancement, coping with problems, and defining personal identity. Even people whose involvement with music was low listened to music frequently and used it as a mood enhancer (147–163).

4. Madsen, Byrnes, Capperella-Sheldon, and Brittin (1993) conducted five different studies designed to assess the aesthetic responses of musicians and nonmusicians to classical music selections. They found that musicians and nonmusicians did not differ in either the magnitude or the frequency of their responses to music (174–191). Robazza, Macaluso, and D'Urso (1994) also found that musicians and nonmusicians ascribed similar emotions to pieces of music (939–944).

5. Hargreaves and Castell (1987) had people of different ages (four- and five-year-olds up to adults) listen to familiar real-life tunes (nursery rhymes and carols), unfamiliar real music (folk music), and "statistical approximations to music." Four- and

five-year-olds liked all selections the same. Six- and seven-year-olds preferred the familiar music to the unfamiliar music and the statistical approximations. By the age of ten, subjects preferred the familiar music most and preferred the folk music to the statistical approximations. Groups from age thirteen up to adults also preferred familiar music most and the folk tunes next, and their liking for the statistical approximations dropped off dramatically. These data suggest that not only do people prefer more familiar music, but that they become more discriminating over time concerning what is considered "real" music (65–69).

6. Getz (1966) found that junior high school music students came to like originally unfamiliar musical selections in music class the more they heard them. Liking rose after a couple of weeks and reached a peak between the sixth and tenth week of class (178–192). That familiarity leads to liking has also been shown in a variety of other ways. Teo, Hargreaves, and Lee (2008) examined how culture and education impact familiarity with musical styles, and thus liking. Adolescents from Singapore and the United Kingdom were asked to judge their familiarity with and preferences for Chinese, Malay, and Indian music. Singaporean girls showed greater preference for, and familiarity with, the Chinese and Malay styles than did girls from the United Kingdom. Both groups rated Indian music lowest on familiarity and preference ratings (18–32). In a recent study, Daltrozzo, Tillmann, Platel, and Schon (2009) have even been able to identify, using EEG technology, the brain waves that occur when we recognize a tune as being familiar. These waves peak at about 400 milliseconds after recognition of a familiar tune (1754–1769).

7. Furman and Duke (1988) determined that people are very particular about having their favorite popular tunes altered in frequency or tempo. Subjects consistently chose the unaltered versions as their favorites and judged the altered selections to be "wrong." Results showed, however, that people were not nearly as particular about having the frequency or tempo of instrumental music altered (220–231).

8. Hevner (1935) had subjects listen and respond to two different versions of ten original musical compositions. The only difference between the two versions was that one version was

written in the major mode and the other was written in the minor mode. Subjects found that the selections written in major mode created feelings of joy and excitement, while the minor mode selections produced feelings of melancholy (103–118). Infante and Berg (1979) had subjects view several video clips showing happy, neutral, and sad faces and pleasant or unpleasant situations. In the background during viewing, they played music in either the major or minor mode. It was discovered that neutral faces were perceived as happier when music in the major mode was playing. Also, sad faces didn't seem "as sad" when major mode music was playing. Similarly, music in the major mode caused the unpleasant situation to be perceived more pleasantly (135–148).

9. Hevner (1936a) had subjects listen to music in which elements such as mode, rhythm, harmony, and melody were varied. Subjects responded to the music by choosing from a list of descriptive adjectives to describe their feelings. Through this method, Hevner found that the interactions of the different elements were complex, but that in general the mode (major or minor) was the most significant element in producing the music's effect. Rhythm and harmony were judged as secondary in their effects, and the rising and falling of the melody produced no consistent effect (246–268).

10. Hevner (1936b) is careful to point out that music produces only general mood effects, although if the composer is knowledgeable, those mood effects can be produced rather reliably. Assigning specific *meanings* to a piece of instrumental music, however, is "ridiculous," as those meanings come from the life experiences and associations of individuals, and thus their interpretations will vary greatly. Hevner also points out that the major mode does not always produce feelings of happiness. It is only interpreted as happy *in comparison to* the same piece composed and performed in the minor mode (186–204). Webster and Weir (2005) asked 177 college students to rate musical excerpts on continuous happy/sad scales, and their finding supported Hevner and other previous research, finding that music in a major key, with nonharmonized melodies and faster tempos, was consistently rated as "happier" (19–39).

11. In a study by Sloboda (1991), eighty-three listeners recorded their physical reactions to emotional music selections. Eighty

percent experienced reactions such as shivers, laughter, tears, and a "lump in the throat." The shivers were evoked most often by new and unexpected harmonies (110–120). Grewe, Nagel, Kopiez, and Altenmuller (2007) had thirty-eight subjects listen to classical, rock, and pop music and report their feelings. Feelings and arousal occurred most often at the first entrance of a solo voice or choir and at the beginning of new musical sections (774–788). Guhn, Hamm, and Zentner (2007) examined chills and other physiological responses during music. They found that the passages that caused chills also caused a large increase in skin conductance in participants experiencing chills (473–483).

12. Blood and Zatorre (2001) used PET scans to study blood flow changes in the brain during highly pleasurable music listening leading to chills. They found blood flow changes in brain regions associated with reward, emotion, and arousal (11818–11823). Also using PET scans, Salimpoor, Benovoy, Larcher, Dagher, and Zatorre (2011) identified dopamine release in the striatum (in the brain's reward system) during peak emotional responses to music (257–264). Further proof that dopamine is involved in pleasurable music listening comes from Goldstein (1980), where listeners were given either naloxone (an opiate receptor antagonist) or a saline solution (placebo) intravenously. In 30% of listeners who received the naloxone, the experience of chills was virtually eliminated (126–129).

13. LeBlanc (1982) developed a hierarchy that describes the complex factors that affect musical preferences. The hierarchy is represented as a flow chart with eight levels and a number of factors at each level. The entry level of the hierarchy (Level 8) shows nine factors that affect our reactions to music at the very outset. Four of the nine factors at this level are family, peers, educators and authority figures, and media (28–45).

14. Radocy (1976) fed bogus information to college students about the alleged performers or composers of different selections and found that the students were influenced by the information (119–128). Alpert (1982) studied the effect on fifth-grade students of bogus approvals of different types of music attributed to disc jockeys, peers, and music teachers. Specifically, student approval of classical music was increased due to bogus

disc jockey and teacher approvals (173–186). In another study, Silva and Silva (2009) found that college students had their attitudes change as a result of reading an essay about the artist or listening to a critic praise the song (181–194).

15. Schafer and Sedlmeier (2009) found that people showed great variety in the strength of preference they reported for their favorite music, but that the one criterion most closely related to the strength of preference was the potential of music to express people's identity and values and bring them together (279–300).

16. Schulkind, Hennis, and Rubin (1999) found that older adults responded most strongly to songs of their youth and remembered more about these songs (948–955). Bartlett and Snelus (1980) also found fairly accurate, very long-term memory of music in older adults. In addition, they found that subjects recalled at least some of the lyrics better if they were cued by the melody than if they were cued by being given the title of the song (551–560).

17. Shatin (1970) explains this effect and proves that people's mood can definitely be moved along a continuum using this approach. While he warns that people are individual in their reactions to the same songs, he also points out that "there is certainly a common or modal type of mood response which is predictable for various pieces of music" (81).

18. In one study, Mull (1957) found that college-age subjects increased their liking of two unfamiliar, nontraditional classical performances (Schoenberg's String Quartet III, op. 31, first movement and Hindemith's String Quartet IV, op. 32, second movement) through repeated listening (155–162). In a study of preschool children, Peery and Peery (1986) found that students who were exposed to weekly, forty-five minute classes in appreciation of classical music liked classical music significantly more than a control group after the ten-month course (24–33).

19. A study conducted by Gowensmith and Bloom (1997) did not support the common perception that heavy metal fans were more aroused or angrier than fans of other types of music. Heavy metal music was found to be arousing for *all* listeners, not just heavy metal fans, and heavy metal fans did not show higher levels of anger than nonmetal fans (33–45).

20. Gardstrom (1999) found, in a sample of male felony offenders, that rap music was the overwhelming favorite genre. She found also that 72% believed that music influenced them at least some of the time, but that only 4% believed that there was any connection between their listening and problem behavior. Most subjects stated that they listened to music that reflected their lives, but that it was not a causative agent in their actions (207–221).

21. Lacourse, Claes, and Villeneuve (2000) examined a number of differentiating characteristics of adolescents who preferred heavy metal music, including family relationships, attitudes, drug use, and suicide risk. When controlling for other factors, they found that suicide risk was not higher among those who worshipped heavy metal music and artists. In fact, girls who listened to such music for vicarious release were found to have a *lowered* risk for suicide (321–332).

22. Mulder, Ter Bogt, Raaijmakers, and Volleberg (2007) divided Dutch youth aged twelve to sixteen into groups based on their music listening profiles and compared these with their social-psychological functioning based on self-reports. They found that different profiles were at risk for different problems. For example, youth who listened to rock exclusively were at risk of both internalizing problems such as withdrawn behavior and problems with social relationships and externalizing problems such as aggressive behavior. Elitists and omnivores, who tended to listen to the music of their parents, tended to have more withdrawn behaviors, while urban and rock-pop groups demonstrated more aggressive behaviors. The middle-of-the-road group that preferred happy-go-lucky Top 40 hits showed little in the way of behavior issues (313–324). Schwartz and Fouts (2003) also showed that adolescents with eclectic tastes were less likely to have problems and conjectured that they were probably more flexible at using music according to mood. These studies once again point out that these risk factors are correlations, and that the music is not the *cause* of the problems but rather an indicator to look for (205–213). Finally, Took and Weiss (1994) compared adolescents who preferred rap and heavy metal with those who favored other musical genres. Not surprisingly, those who favored rap and metal had more problems with behavior, sexual activity, drug and alcohol use, and arrests than those who preferred other

musical types. Interestingly, however, when gender was controlled, the researchers found only one issue remained significant: below-average elementary school grades and problems in elementary school. It seems that many students get on a downward trajectory early and then choose music that relates to their angst and frustration (613–621).

23. It seems that parents for generations have worried about explicit lyrics their children might be exposed to. In the 1980s, this worry turned into a full-scale crusade with the rise of groups such as the Parents Music Resource Center who advocated for a rating system for rock albums. But is this a legitimate concern? Rosenbaum and Prinsky (1987) cite findings that less than a third of high school students could provide accurate interpretations of popular songs. In their own study, they found that teenagers identified only 7% of the songs they listened to as having anything to do with sex, violence, drugs, or Satanism (79–89). Wanamaker and Reznikoff (1989) found that students did not score higher on hostility after listening to a song with aggressive lyrics in comparison with one with nonaggressive lyrics. They concluded that "the findings are congruent with other investigators' reports that subjects do not pay attention to rock lyrics" (561). Hansen and Hansen (1991) found that subjects took away from heavy metal songs "theme-relevant content," but not specific, detailed content (373–411).

3

Calming the
Restless Natives

Using Music to Reduce
Excess Energy and Stress

Music has charms to sooth a savage breast, to soften rocks, or bend a knotted oak.

—William Congreve

Music is the language of the spirit. It opens the secret of life, bringing peace, abolishing strife.

—Kahlil Gibran

What It Is

Many people use calming music as a means of self-medicating when feeling stressed after a hard day's work. If putting on certain music is part of your unwinding ritual when you get home, you are already using calming music as an intrinsic part of your life.

As briefly explained in Chapter 1, calming music has long been used as a highly successful treatment tool in the healthcare sector. The field of music therapy had its beginnings over two hundred years ago, with specifically designed music playing a part in the treatment of serious conditions such as anxiety, depression, and posttraumatic stress disorder for many years.[1] Music has also been shown to be effective in pain reduction following surgery and child birth, and it has been found to be helpful in relaxing intensive care patients, especially women and older patients.[2] For stress reduction, music has been shown to be one of the very best methodologies, reducing blood cortisol levels (a stress hormone that plays a key role in the fight or flight response) by a whopping 66%.[3] Calming music has also been shown to be effective in reducing anxiety and increasing client-counselor interactions in counseling sessions,[4] and it has been shown to work effectively in combination with other relaxation techniques and cognitive therapy,[5] including one treatment program where this combination of music and therapy was used to reduce teacher burnout![6]

The William Congreve quotation at the beginning of this chapter is often misquoted as "Music has charms to soothe the savage *beast*," instead of the "savage *breast*." As teachers, we all have moments when the term *beast* fits our charges quite well—and the beast-to-teacher ratio seems to be about a hundred to one. At such times, we could all use a little help to calm the natives so they can get down to the process of learning. That's where calming music comes in. Congreve is right—music *does* have a seemingly magical power to calm us down when we are wound up a bit too tight or when we are just a bit overexcited.

As teachers, we have many opportunities to make use of this calming effect. For example, research shows that, for students who have issues with test or performance anxiety, calming music reduces anxiety if listened to before the start of testing[7] or during testing.[8] Calming music has also been shown to be one of the most effective ways for students to de-stress after a grueling exam.[9]

Why It Works

There are two important physiological and psychological mechanisms behind the effect of calming music.

- ♪ **Entrainment**—Human rhythmic processes synchronize with the beat of the music, enabling slower tempo music to slow our heart rate and breathing.
- ♪ **Preference**—Music we like can have an even more calming effect on our physiology than entrainment.

Entrainment

As a simple, broad definition, *entrainment is a phenomenon in which two or more independent rhythmic processes synchronize with each other.* This type of synchronization can occur in objects as well as in living organisms. For example, the process of entrainment was first discovered and identified by the Dutch physicist Christiaan Huygens in 1665. Huygens discovered that when two pendulum clocks were set on a common support and the motion of one pendulum was disturbed so that they were not swinging left-to-right in a coordinated fashion, the pendulums of the two clocks would slowly synchronize and would be swinging in unison again within half an hour.

There are also many examples of living systems entraining to their environments. For example, fireflies often sync up to match the flashing patterns of those around them. Human beings don't flash, but we do oscillate in many ways. We have obvious biological rhythms such as our heartbeats, respiration, and brain waves. But we also respond to rhythms that are much longer in their cycles such as circadian rhythms (the biological cycles such as sleepiness and wakefulness, that entrain to the daily rhythms of light and dark) and ultradian rhythms (shorter oscillations such as the waxing and waning of appetite and the roughly 90- to 120-minute energy and alertness cycles that we experience during the day). Even when we sleep, we do so in a rhythmic pattern, moving through different stages of lighter and deeper sleep. On a social level, we also tend to entrain our speech patterns to those with whom we are speaking.

Similarly, when two or more people sing or play music together, they must synchronize to a beat in order for the performance to be pleasing. This entrainment, the "getting on the same page" with the other musicians, makes making music pleasing as a social activity as well as an artistic pursuit. If each performer kept his or her own beat, the result wouldn't be pleasing at all!

But most important for our purposes in this book, entrainment also occurs when people *listen* to music. In this situation, we have two rhythmic processes interacting: (1) the beat and other characteristics of the music; and (2) the physiological responses of the listeners—and one of the processes (the physiological processes of the listeners) changes to more closely match the other (the music).

This concept is widely supported by research. Humans do clearly respond physically to music, though the type and amplitude of responses recorded has varied greatly from study to study due to a variety of factors, including the type of music used in the study and whether the music was selected by the experimenters or the subjects. One of the most consistent research findings is that human respiration is quite sensitive to the effects of calming music, slowing down gradually as we listen.[10] Our bodies respond in a variety of other ways, as well, with changes in blood pressure, skin conductance, and finger temperature often being documented.[11]

Another physiological measure that clearly responds to calming music is heart rate. The resting human heart rate is generally between 60 and 80 beats per minute, with most people falling into the 70 to 80 beats range. Interestingly, a great deal of Western music is composed to be played at this tempo, which the casual listener perceives as moderate. Thus, a number of studies have shown that if we play music with a tempo below the moderate rate, heart rate often does drop.[12]

MUSIC & RHYTHM
FIND THEIR WAY INTO THE
SECRET PLACES OF THE SOUL
- Plato

Preference

A number of studies have shown that the *psychological* feeling of relaxation and reduced anxiety can occur even without the concurrent *physiological* changes mentioned above. In fact, some studies have documented subjects feeling more relaxed (reduced subjective tension) while physiological measurements showed no change, or in some cases actually showed *increased* autonomic arousal and muscular tension![13] How can this be?

It appears that preference is an even more crucial factor involved with our relaxation response to music than entrainment. In a number of studies, subjects listened to music precategorized as either relaxing (generally slower and calmer) or stimulative (generally faster with more structural changes and a stronger beat) while physiological measures were taken. In addition, subjects were asked which pieces of music they preferred and which they did not, or their responses to self-selected, preferred music were compared with their responses to experimenter-selected music. The results showed that how much the subjects liked the music was an influential factor (sometimes the *most* influential factor) in whether they felt more relaxed during and after listening—and this tendency for subjects to *feel* more relaxed psychologically when listening to preferred music was found to be true whether the physiological data showed that their *bodies* were more relaxed or not![14]

Characteristics of Calming Music

Not surprisingly, the importance of preference can make using calming music complicated. The research clearly shows that different people often respond differently to music due to a variety of factors. One study showed that, when asked to judge whether music was calming or not, college music therapy majors often categorized music differently than did nonmusic majors.[15] And another study showed that even the physiological responses of different people varied a good deal in response to the same music.[16]

This doesn't mean that we can't formulate good guidelines for choosing calming music—we can. There are certain characteristics of music that *generally* correlate with a calming response for the *average* person. However, we must always keep in mind the unique responses of individuals when making musical selections for our classrooms. With those caveats in mind, here are some general characteristics to look for when selecting calming music:

- **Tempo**: In general, music that is below the resting heart rate is likely to cause an entrainment effect to slow respiration and heart rate. For most people, music at or below 60 beats per minute is ideal.
- **Instrumentation**: Generally, the less instrumentation there is in a piece, the more calming it is. For this reason, many people use solo piano and solo acoustic guitar pieces or pieces by small acoustic groups such as string quartets. Also, certain instruments tend to be more calming, such as strings and woodwinds (minus sax), while others tend to be more arousing, such as brass and electric instruments.
- **Calm Emotional Tone**: While this is hard to describe, you know it when you hear it. Some adjectives that describe the kind of tone often conveyed by calming music are lyrical, leisurely, serene, quiet, soothing, dreamy, and tender.[17]
- **Beat**: A less pronounced beat is usually more calming than a heavy one.

♪ **Volume**: Low to medium volume tends to work best for creating a calming effect. The music must be loud enough to be heard, but if it gets louder than medium volume, it will begin to have an arousing effect.

♪ **Vocal or Instrumental**: Either can be calming as long as most of the characteristics in this list are present.

When most of the characteristics listed above are present, and especially if your students *like* the music, they will find the listening experience pleasant and relaxing.

INSIDE A CLASSROOM

Calming Music to Begin the Day

Holly Osborne
Primary Teacher, Year 4 (equivalent to 4th Grade in the US)
Bosvigo Primary School
Truro, Cornwall, Britain

"When the children enter the classroom in the mornings, they are often very loud and boisterous. I use a calming, relaxing CD, which calms them at the beginning of the day. I put the music on as I leave the classroom to go outside to collect the children so that it is on as we enter. I turn it down for the register, but it is still playing in the background.

"Since introducing music into the classroom, I have noticed that the children have been much more forthcoming with group discussions. I also have been able to introduce them to a range of music that they may not have had the benefit of listening to at home. The children enjoy having the music on and are now regularly asking for their own tracks to be played; one child's self-esteem rocketed once we had played his CD during register time. Before introducing music, the children were less inclined to focus during the morning as they were creating the sounds themselves, but now with the music on, they already have sound in the background, so they are quieter when coming into the classroom."

Advice to Teachers: "I would highly recommend using music in the classroom, either as a sound level indicator (if it's loud, they are allowed to talk loudly or vice versa), as well as encouraging the quieter members of the class to participate, as they are not the only sound in the room, which helps their confidence. The use of an iPod would be very helpful, but I find that using a CD player is just as great; I have created a few shuffled track CDs, which work brilliantly!"

Suggested Songs: "I like 'Good People,' by Jack Johnson, which, in addition to being calming, creates a more friendly, happy atmosphere for the start of the morning."

How to Use It

How can we use this type of music successfully in our classrooms to manage mood and energy levels? The first step is to identify those predictable times when the students are going to be a bit crazy. What are those times in your classroom? Right after recess? Right before lunch? Before and after an assembly? Friday afternoons? It varies from class to class, but most teachers have a pretty good idea about when those times are for their classes. The key is to be proactive and have some calming music cued up and ready to go at these times.

Like feel-good music, calming music is best used *during transitions.* But in this case, your goal is quite different. Whereas, with feel-good music, you are trying to raise mood (which often carries with it a rise in energy), with calming music you are actually trying to *reduce* the amount of energy your students are displaying (without affecting mood negatively).

At the Beginning of Class

Let's say you are an elementary teacher, and your group is generally crazy right after recess. Have some calming music on as they come in. Let it play at low to medium volume as they settle in and get out materials. The music will slowly "bring them down" and will allow you to turn it off and transition them into the next academic task.

If you have the time, you can also teach your students to use some nonmusical calming strategies during such transitions. One such calming technique is closing the eyes, sitting with a straight back, and breathing deeply from the diaphragm several times while focusing on and counting the number of breaths. Or you could include progressive muscle relaxation techniques or some slow, gentle group stretching or brain gym movements. If you employ any of these techniques (or anything similarly aimed at calming students down), make sure that you have calming music playing in the background, as it will intensify the calming effect and bring your students to the right state for transitioning back to learning more quickly.

INSIDE A CLASSROOM

Calming Down After Recess

Zoie Moody
Key Stage One Coordinator, Year 2 (equivalent to 2nd Grade in the US)
St. Dennis Primary School
Cornwall, England

"After playtimes, before the children come into the classroom, I put on a gentle, calming piece of music. This is known as the 'calm down time.' On entering the class, the children come to the carpet and sit down. I or another child then lead the children in relaxing breathing in time to the music. We use gentle yoga/ brain gym movements (staying seated), and follow the same pattern of movements each time so that the children know it by heart. In the last 30 seconds of the music, the children are allowed to create their own movements (staying seated) in time to the music. When the music stops, the children know to be still, quiet, focused, and ready to learn.

   "Before I used calming music in my classroom, after playtimes could be quite hectic, and reentry into the classroom could be noisy and time-consuming. I would often have to repeat myself loudly to get the children to sit down and focus for learning. Since introducing music, the children come into the classroom calmly and quietly. The deep breathing helps calm them down, and the gentle movements and brain gym actions help focus their attention."

Suggested Songs: "I use gentle, mellow tracks with a steady beat. The track I use for calming down, relaxing, or quiet time is 'Sunset,' by Nitin Sawhney."

Within a Class Period

You can also use calming music for transitions *during* a class period (putting materials away, getting materials out, changing groupings, changing activities, rotating to learning centers). If you use calming music during these times, you will notice that students move more slowly and calmly about the room.

Now, let's be clear here. Whether or not you employ calming music for transitions during class completely depends on your goals for the transition. We've already mentioned that you can use feel-good music during these same transitional times. If you use feel-good music, your main goal will be to raise students' mood. In the next chapter, we will talk about how you can use up-tempo music (what we call pump-up music) to speed students up during transitions, so if you want transitions to be snappy, calming music is not appropriate! On the other hand, if your goal is to calm students down and have transitions that are quieter and more controlled, then calming music would work well. Just realize that there is a trade-off; your transitions will be calmer, but they will generally take longer.

At the End of Class

You can also use calming music for that last transition of the class period or the school day, as students are preparing to leave your room. We've already talked about sending students out of the room with feel-good music and how this strategy can lead to a positive feeling about your class in your students' minds. But if these end-of-class or end-of-the-school-day transitions are often too wild and crazy for your taste, with students grabbing book bags and talking loudly, you can use calming music as a way to slow them down and bring them under control. Don't count on calming music to do the whole job by itself, though. The end of a class period, and especially the end of the school day, are naturally arousing times for kids, so you will probably have to implement some type of structure or policy for calm, safe transitions out of the classroom, in addition to using calming music as an aid for keeping a lid on the combined energy level in the room.

Guidelines for Using Calming Music

♪ Don't get caught in the *genre trap*. By the genre trap, we mean preconceived ideas about certain genres of music being best for certain situations. For example, many people have heard that classical music is the best kind (genre) of music to use for calming music or for background music. But the truth is that there is no *one* kind of music that always works for calming. A classical piece like Pachelbel's Canon or almost any adagio movement would probably work, but the "Overture" from *Carmen* (a very fast-paced and exciting classical piece) is just going to make students more excited. So, you really can't think in terms of genres; you have to listen to each song and judge it on its own merits. Yes, there are going to be some classical pieces that work as calming music. But a lot of smooth jazz and new age music will fit the bill, as well, in addition to certain individual songs from many other genres.

♪ Don't be afraid of songs with lyrics. Just as with feel-good music, as long as you are using calming music outside instructional times, the words of the song will not interfere with academic work. There are many excellent calming songs with vocals, and many calming instrumentals, as well.

♪ Use the ramping technique. When you have longer stretches of time to calm students down, start with a song that is at a moderate tempo and maybe slightly arousing. Follow that song with one that is a bit slower and calmer, and follow that one with another one that is calmer still. Over a period of ten to fifteen minutes, you will see students gradually relax. This is a good technique to use at the beginning of the school day, or in any situation where students drift into class one or two at a time over a number of minutes (such as returning from lunch). Studies have shown that the entrainment effect to calming music increases over time.[18]

♪ Make use of preference. Calming music doesn't have to be familiar to your students, as long as a number of the characteristics listed earlier are present. However, since the research has noted that people tend to relax more to music they like, it's a good idea to find some calming music that most of your students enjoy and use these selections frequently. The fact that the songs are familiar and enjoyable will only add to their effectiveness.

What to Avoid

Turn Music Off for Instruction

First of all, *never use calming music* (or any other kind of music for that matter) *while you are doing direct instruction.* You need to have students' full attention during these times, so you don't need to be competing with the music. If you have had calming music on while students were transitioning from the previous task, make sure you turn it off before starting your next instructional chunk.

Too Calm to Learn

The major issue you have to watch for when using calming music is that you can get students *too* calm. You may be thinking that you could go for a little bit of "too calm" in your classroom, but the fact is that if you notice kids yawning and beginning to look sleepy, you need to get some music on that's a little more up-tempo. Sleepiness is not a good state in which to learn! The best level of arousal for learning seems to be a state of "relaxed alertness," so that's a good guideline to keep in mind.

Beware of Prepackaged "Relaxation Music"

Beware of taking at face value the claims of all of the many products out there that claim to have been composed specifically to have a calming effect. Our experience is that *some* of the pieces from these collections work well for calming, while others do not. In fact, some research studies have looked into this issue and have found that some music marketed for its calming effect actually causes *higher* tension levels in some listeners.[19]

INSIDE A CLASSROOM

Music During Lunch Break

Kim McArdle
K–6 Support Teacher, Assistant Principal
Warren Central School
Warren, New South Wales, Australia

"To provide the opportunity for children who would rather do quiet activities during lunch break, I run our 'Billabong Room,' where the children can play with construction games, color, read, complete puzzles, etc. During this time, I use music as a settler and for their enjoyment, selecting CDs that may be familiar, but not those heard regularly via media.

"'Billabong' is very popular, and before I used music, the room at times became quite noisy (contrary to the purpose of the room). Since introducing music, there is a more settled atmosphere, and the children like to sing along when they recognize songs; they also play in a more relaxed and friendly manner when music is playing."

Advice to Teachers: "Music certainly lightens the mood of all, including the teacher, and results in a more positive and productive learning environment."

Suggested Songs: "We use songs from *The Great Australian Songbook*, Volumes 1 & 2. Some particular Aussie favorites include 'Give Me a Home Among the Gum Trees,' by Bob Brown and Wally Johnson; 'Redback on the Toilet Seat,' by Lazy Harry; and 'My Island Home,' by Neil Murray."

Authors' Note: This example shows that music can accomplish more than one goal at a time. The music used here is probably best categorized as feel-good music, but since no academic activities are occurring during the period described, and since the music is familiar and obviously enjoyable for the students, it also has a calming effect.

Getting Started

While standing by our "buyer beware" proviso, we will admit that many of those collections marketed as calming or relaxation music can actually be a good place to start your search for calming music. A decent percentage of the pieces in those collections will probably work for you. Just be aware that you have to judge each piece *individually*. If you decide to try a track in class, make sure you watch students' reactions. If the vast majority of students seem to relax in response to the piece, keep it in your play list. If it doesn't seem to work so well, don't use it again.

You might also start by browsing music files in certain genres using a music service such as iTunes. Yes, we just warned you about the genre trap, and that warning still goes. But just because you can't think in terms of *whole* genres when selecting pieces to use in your classroom, that doesn't mean that some genres aren't more *likely* to have more calming music in them than do other genres.

For example, if you go to the iTunes store and use the browse function to look for music, you will be given a list of genres. From this list, certain genres are obviously better candidates for calming music than others. For example, you might want to dig a little deeper into genres such as classical, easy listening, instrumental, jazz, new age, and soundtrack, but probably not into genres such as Latin, country, dance, fitness & workout, or rock.

And when you dig deeper, you can fine-tune your search even more. For example, by clicking on the jazz genre, you will be given a list of subgenres. Some of these subgenres will be better candidates for your search than others. When looking for calming music, it might be fruitful to search subcategories such as contemporary jazz, cool jazz, and smooth jazz, but not so fruitful to browse big band, Dixieland, hard bop, mainstream jazz, or ragtime (all of which will yield mostly music that is too fast or that has too many changes in it). You can then click on one of the subgenres and listen to portions of tracks by different artists within that subcategory. Searching for calming music this way can be time-consuming, but it can also be a lot of fun!

iTunes also provides other ways for you to get ideas for calming music. Once you've found one or more good selections that fit the criteria, download them into your iTunes music library. You will then be given suggestions for similar songs in the iTunes sidebar. You can sample these songs and quickly find new artists and songs that fit what you're looking for.

Other useful sources are internet radio sites like Pandora (www .pandora.com). When you enter the name of an artist whose music is typically considered calming such as new age pianist George Winston, the site will deliver to your computer a list of similar artists that you can look into. You can then take this approach a step further by having Pandora create a "station" of similar music. Pandora has done a great deal of work to categorize thousands and thousands of songs through its Music Genome Project. When you choose a song and have Pandora create a station around that song, the site plays full-length songs with similar characteristics to your original choice. All you have to do is listen and take note of songs you want to use in class.

We hope this has given you some good places to start. For more calming music ideas, see our Top 40 suggestions below and our expanded list in Appendix B—all of which have tempos around the 60-beats-per-minute (bpm) mark.

A Note on Beats Per Minute

Which brings us to an important question when it comes to selecting calming music: How do you figure out a song's bpm? Sadly, this is not readily available information. Currently, you have three options:

- ♪ **Low tech**—Listen to thirty seconds from the middle of the song (use a stop watch or the iTunes counter) and count how many times you tap your foot (or hand, or nod your head) to the music. Double this number is your bpm. Don't start from the beginning, as the intro is sometimes faster or slower than the main body of the song.
- ♪ **High tech**—If you aren't too crazy about sitting around counting beats to determine the tempo of every song in your music library, you can find software that will do the job for you. For example, at the time of the writing of this book, we are using a program called beaTunes (www.beatunes.com) that works with iTunes to analyze your music library in a number of ways. This software can do things such as suggest songs with similar attributes that can be combined to create playlists, but it can also count the beats per minute of the songs in your library and insert this information into a column in iTunes. Even if you have thousands of songs in your library, this program can do the entire job in a few hours, saving you many hours of toe-tapping.

Warning: There are a few drawbacks to such programs. Since these programs are not human, they lack human judgment. As a result, the bpm number they assign to a particular song is sometimes way off. This can happen for two main reasons:

♪ Some songs are constructed so that the drums play on every eighth note (twice for every beat), others on every quarter note (once per beat), and still others on every other count. Now, we're human, and we can figure out what's going on and determine what the real beats per minute of a song is, but software (at least at its current level of sophistication) can't do this so well. What happens, then, is that the software will often report that a song is either only *half* as fast (60 bpm instead of 120, for example) as it really is, or exactly *twice* as fast (120 bpm instead of 60) as it really is. If the software program is a good one, the developers understand this issue, and there will be a built-in fix for this problem. In beaTunes, for example, you simply highlight the song and click on "Halve BPM" or "Double BPM" in the Edit menu, and the software automatically changes the bpm number in both the beaTunes interface and your iTunes music library.

♪ The software has trouble establishing an accurate bpm count for music that lacks a clear, discernible beat. This includes solo piano pieces, solo guitar pieces, and music primarily played by string instruments, since they have no drumbeat for the software to pick up on. Instead, the software has to try to find some regularly repeated, stressed notes in the music itself, and the results tend to be very inaccurate. Again, your software may have a built-in way to address this issue. For example, in beaTunes, right clicking on a song offers you the "Tap Beat" option, allowing you to play the song in question and, using your computer's mouse, tap your finger to the beat that you hear. As you do so, the software keeps track of your tapping, averaging your beats as you go. Tap to the beat as long as you think necessary to establish the correct bpm for the song; then click "OK." The software then changes the number in both the beaTunes interface and iTunes automatically to the tempo you tapped out. This is a very neat feature, but it is quite time-consuming if you need to tap out the beats of hundreds of songs. Unfortunately, if you have a big music library, this is exactly what you will probably have to do; then again, since the software will probably give you a correct number for two-thirds to three-fourths of your music library right off the bat, it's still a huge time-saver if you want to establish the bpm of all the songs in your library.

♪ **Ask us!**—This book has an associated website, www
.rockandrollclassroom.com, with resources and services for
teachers using music in their classrooms. E-mail us through the
site and we will let you know the bpm of any song.

We hope this information is helpful to you as you look for music
to match the different tempo recommendations we make in this book.
Keep in mind that tempo is only one factor to consider when looking
for the right kind of music for a particular classroom use, though it is
often the most important one. Happy listening!

Our Top 40 Calming Songs

The following are some of our favorite calming songs. Again, there's
nothing magical about this list. The goal here is just to show you the
kinds of music that might fit under the label of *calming music*. While
this list leans toward classical, jazz, new age, pop, and standards,
keep in mind that a specific song from just about any musical genre
could have a calming effect, as long as it embodies most of the
characteristics discussed in this chapter.

1. "Air," David Garrett

2. "All at Sea," Jamie Cullum

3. "Angela (Theme from *Taxi*)," Bob James

4. "Arioso," Johann Sebastian Bach

5. "As Time Goes By," Steve Tyrell

6. "Blackbird," The Beatles

7. "Blues for the Night Owl," Ramsey Lewis

8. "Blue Skies," Dena DeRose

9. "Bombay," Ottmar Liebert

10. "Charlie Brown Theme," David Benoit

11. "Come Away With Me," Norah Jones

12. "Don't Ever Leave Me," Keith Jarrett and Charlie Haden

13. "El Farol," Santana

14. "Emma's Song," Rick Braun

15. "Forever in Love," Kenny G

16. "Georgia on My Mind," Ray Charles

17. "Happiness," David Benoit and Al Jarreau

18. "I Cover the Waterfront," Joe Pass

19. "I Left My Heart in San Francisco," Tony Bennett

20. "Largo," from *Winter,* Antonio Vivaldi

21. "Little Star," Jim Brickman

22. "Memories," Joe Sample

23. "Misty," Erroll Garner Trio

24. "Moon River," Ed Gerhard

25. "Morning Has Broken," Cat Stevens

26. "Nimrod," from *Enigma Variations,* Edward Elgar

27. "Pachelbel's Canon," George Winston

28. Piano Concerto No. 2, Adagio Sostenuto, Sergei Rachmaninoff

29. Piano Concerto No. 15 in B Flat, Wolfgang Amadeus Mozart

30. Piano Sonata No. 8 in C Minor, opus 13 (*Pathetique*), Ludwig van Beethoven

31. "Put Your Head on My Shoulder," Michael Buble

32. "Shenandoah," Bill Frissell

33. "Sleepwalk," Larry Carlton

34. "Somewhere Over the Rainbow/What a Wonderful World," Israel Kamakawiwo'ole

35. "Soulville," Ben Webster

36. "The Girl from Ipanema," Stan Getz and Astrud Gilberto

37. "The Saturday Race," Johnny Smith

38. "With You I'd Believe," Euge Groove

39. "Your Song," Elton John

40. "You've Got a Friend," James Taylor

Notes

1. Heller (1987) gives a succinct history of the music therapy field in his article "Ideas, Initiatives, and Implementations: Music Therapy in America (1789–1848)."

2. Chan, Chung, Chung, and Lee (2008) analyzed the effects of a music therapy intervention on people confined to the intensive care unit. The researchers found that different people reacted differently to music. While one group of patients—characterized

as mostly male, young, and more educated—showed only
small positive effects in response to the music, another
group—characterized as mostly female and older—showed
"statistically significant reductions in all physiological
outcomes," meaning that their heart rate, respiration, and
blood pressure all responded to the music, resulting in a
highly therapeutic calming effect (1250–1257).

3. This statistic comes from Svoboda (2009), who also mentions
   a study conducted by doctors in Japan's Osaka Medical
   Center, who found that when they played calming music to
   patients undergoing colonoscopies, the patients' cortisol
   levels rose less than that of patients who underwent the same
   procedure in a quiet room (95–98).

4. Prueter and Mezzano (1973) studied the effects of different
   kinds of background music and silence on client-counselor
   interactions and found that soothing background music not
   only caused clients to open up and talk more, but that their
   interactions with counselors were more effective, as well
   (205–212).

5. In a meta-analysis of twenty-two quantitative studies, Pelletier
   (2004) found that music-assisted relaxation techniques
   significantly decreased arousal (192–214).

6. Cheek, Bradley, Parr, and Lan (2003) compared the effects of
   two programs designed to help teachers deal with stress. One
   group received cognitive/behavioral interventions, and the
   other group received the same cognitive/behavioral program,
   with the addition of calming music. The teachers in the group
   with music reported significantly lower burnout symptoms
   than the group without music (204–218).

7. Stanton (1975) tested students in three situations: silence,
   calming music on as students entered the testing room (but
   not as students tested), and calming music on throughout the
   test. Students scored highest in the condition where music
   was on as they entered the room and got ready for the test
   (80–82).

8. Knight and Rickard (2001) found that students placed in a
   stressful situation (preparing to give an oral presentation)
   were much calmer when working with calming music on in
   the background than when working in silence (254–272).

9. Labbe, Schmidt, Babin, and Pharr (2007) found that listening to classical or self-selected music following a stressful test reduced negative emotional states and physiological arousal (163–168). Khalfa, Dalla Bella, Roy, Peretz, and Lupien (2003) found that cortisol levels (which had increased during testing) ceased to increase following the test when in the presence of calming music, while cortisol levels continued to increase for thirty minutes following testing for those not exposed to music (374–376).

10. Iwanaga, Ikeda, and Iwaki (1996) found that heart rate and respiration did not change when listening to stimulating music, but both measures decreased gradually while listening to sedative (calming) music (219–230). Lovell and Morgan (1942) had subjects listen to a repetitive, oscillating sound, and found that respiration entrained to the sound (though heart rate didn't), and that this entrainment had a calming effect (435–451). Haas, Distenfeld, and Axen (1986) found that, not only did respiration entrain to match the rhythm of music, but also the tapping of one's toes to the beat increased the effect by cancelling out other signals from higher neural centers (that is, it kept subjects' attention more focused on the beat, which amplified the beat's physiological effects) (1185–1191).

11. Watkins (1997) reviews the research literature on physiological responses to calming music and cites examples of music reducing the stress response, including decreased anxiety levels, decreased blood pressure and heart rate, and changes in plasma stress hormones (43–50). Krumhansl (1997) conducted a very detailed study, measuring subjects' psychophysiological responses to happy, sad, and fear-inducing music on twelve different dimensions. She found that all three types of music significantly affected all twelve measurements, and in the same direction (though the amplitude of the changes varied from one musical type to another). Effects were seen on heart rate, respiration rate, blood pressure, skin conductance, and finger temperature (336–353).

12. Iwanaga and Moroki (1999) had subjects listen to either sedative (slow-paced) music or excitative (fast-paced) music and recorded heart rate, blood pressure, and respiration. Respiration and blood pressure remained at low and stable levels while subjects listened to the sedative (calming) music,

and heart rate slowly dropped by several beats per minute over the six-minute listening period (26–38).

13. Hanser (1985) reviewed the research literature on this issue and found that when both psychological and physiological responses were studied, results were often contradictory. She quotes several studies (Hanser, Martin, & Bradstreet, 1982; O'Connell, 1984) in which subjects reported feeling significantly reduced anxiety while listening to calming music, while the physiological data showed no relaxation effect (193–206). Davis and Thaut (1989) had subjects listen to preferred (self-selected) relaxation music and found that, while state anxiety decreased and relaxation increased, the physiological data actually showed an arousal effect (168–187).

14. Iwanaga and Moroki (1999) found that subjects listening to preferred music felt less tension, regardless of the music's properties, compared with subjects listening to nonpreferred music (26–38). Stratton and Zalanowski (1984) found that, when they had subjects listen to five types of music, four of these types led to a relaxation response. The only musical type that led to increased tension was atonal music. It was hypothesized that, because this type of music is unfamiliar to most people, it was the least-liked type, and this negative reaction led to higher levels of tension. Their overall conclusion was that "the single factor most closely related to relaxation was degree of liking for the music" (189–190). Davis and Thaut (1989) allowed subjects to select their own music for relaxing. Subject-selected music covered a wide variety of genres (classical, rock, hard rock, folk, Christian, and jazz) and varied greatly in tempo and volume, and more than half of the choices contained lyrics. Nevertheless, all subjects showed reduced subjective tension, even though the physiological data often showed that their bodies were more aroused. Taken together, the data shows that listening to music that one enjoys is often relaxing (at least psychologically), no matter what type of music it is. This data also calls into question any rigid definition of "calming" music based on musical characteristics (168–187).

15. Hadsell (1989) had music therapy majors and nonmusician student volunteers rank a variety of musical selections according to how sedative or stimulating they were. The

results between the two groups varied greatly, with the variation being greatest with the musical selections precategorized as sedative. Neither group agreed consistently with the precategorized labels (106–114).

16. Stratton and Zalanowski (1984) point out that people often have different past experiences with different types of music, and that these experiences and associations color their reactions to the music. Thus, music precategorized as relaxing might not work for everyone equally well (184–192).

17. Hevner (1936a) pioneered an approach to musical response that used a "wheel" of adjectives divided into eight categories. The adjectives best describing calming music are found in Categories 3 and 4 ("dreamy, tender, sentimental" are from Category 3; "lyrical, serene, tranquil, and soothing" are from Category 4). The adjectives that would best describe the opposite kind of music (stimulating) would be found directly across the wheel, in Categories 7 and 8—adjectives such as "soaring, dramatic, passionate, exciting, vigorous, robust, and majestic" (246–268).

18. Rider (1985) found that spinal cord injury patients in a music therapy program responded best to an entrainment and ramping approach, with the music starting out as less pleasant and moving to more pleasant over time (183–192). Smith and Joyce (2004) found that relaxation increased not only when listening to the right kind of music (they found Mozart's *Eine Kleine Nachtmusik* to be very effective), but when listening to the music multiple times over several days (215–224).

19. Taylor (1973) sounded a cautionary note about taking at face value the claims of music to be relaxing or stimulating. He found that listeners often responded differently than expected to such precategorized music—both psychologically and physiologically (86–94). Logan and Roberts (1984) found that one type of music, composed by Steven Halpern specifically to induce a state of relaxation, actually *raised* tension levels in listeners (177–183).

4

They Like to Move It (So Let Them)

Using Pump-Up Music to Energize Students

Music is an outburst of the soul.

—Frederick Delius

In music the passions enjoy themselves.

—Friedrich Nietzsche

What It Is

Just as there are times in any classroom when students are overly energetic, there are also times when they are sleepy, lethargic, or even apathetic. At such times, it can feel like you're working your tail off just to get students to pay attention. The answer to your problem may be as close as your iPod or CD player. The right kind of music has the power to change such states within minutes, sometimes even seconds. Adding some up-tempo pump-up music into the environment, especially if combined with some vigorous movement, gives students a jolt of adrenaline and adds instant energy to the classroom—energy that you can then redirect to a learning task.

71

Why It Works

We've all experienced first-hand the stimulation of a fast-paced, rousing tune. But the question is *why* we respond the way we do, and the answer to that question is, just as it was with feel-good and calming music, "it's complicated."

Entrainment, Arousal, and the Orienting Effect

To begin to tease out the different factors that contribute to the stimulating effect of pump-up music, let's flash back to the previous chapter, where we talked about entrainment, and the natural tendency of human beings to synchronize physiological rhythms such as heart beat and breathing to music.

What is it about music that causes people to respond physically? Is it the beat? The mode? The rising and falling of the pitch? Research has found that the *tempo* of the music is the most important factor driving entrainment. Sometimes we entrain to music consciously. For example, people listening to music while exercising tend to match their movements to the beat of the music and use it as a pacing mechanism,[1] which allows them to work harder and leads to more satisfying and enjoyable workouts.[2] But a person doesn't have to be working out to entrain to a beat. Research has shown that the respiration of stationary listeners will entrain to a steady beat, even if no music is present. On the other hand, a bare beat does not affect mood; that takes other musical elements—mode, melody, and harmony (Khalfa, Roy, Rainville, Dalla Bella, & Peretz, 2008).

In the previous chapter, we saw that if the beat of the music is below a person's current heart rate, that person's heart rate and respiration will tend to slow down in an attempt to match the beat. And we might reasonably expect the converse to be true. Research certainly shows that music with a faster beat than the listener's heart rate causes *some* physiological factors to increase in an attempt to entrain with the music. For example, up-tempo music has been shown to cause an arousal effect that manifests itself as increases in skin conductance, blood pressure, and respiration—especially if the fast beat is reinforced by other musical characteristics deemed "emotionally powerful" such as those discussed in Chapter 2.[3]

However, this is not always true of heart rate. One would think, following our entrainment discussion in the previous chapter, that music with a tempo faster than the resting human heart rate (60 to 80 bpm) would cause heart rate to speed up. In fact, while some studies have demonstrated heart rate acceleration in response to stimulating music, others have actually shown *deceleration,* while still others have shown no change.

Why would our heart rate sometimes drop when listening to up-tempo music? After a great deal of discussion in the research literature, a consensus seems to be emerging that the drop in heart rate sometimes observed in subjects listening to up-tempo music has to do with something called the *orienting response.* When first orienting and attending to a new sound in the environment (such as a song), a variety of automatic, temporary physiological changes take place, one of which is a reduced heart rate. These changes appear to be designed to enhance sensory processing of the stimulus (more than likely, to assess the situation for any sign of danger). If the sound disappears, or if it continues in a repetitive fashion (such as a steady beat in a song), the listener habituates to the situation, and the orienting response disappears.[4] At this point, the arousal effect of the music may override the initial deceleration and cause heart rate to return to, or even rise above, baseline. This conflict between the orienting response and the arousal effect appears to explain why some studies show heart rate deceleration, some show acceleration, and some show no change in heart rate in response to stimulating music. Overall, however (even if heart rate decelerates), stimulating music causes a variety of physiological changes that indicate arousal.

Movement Accentuates Arousal

So yes, stimulating, up-tempo music does clearly cause arousal, as measured by respiration, skin conductance, and blood pressure, along with less consistent effects on listeners' heart rates. But playing stimulating music isn't the only way to energize students. Another powerful way to wake up their bodies and minds is to get them up and moving around the room, as movement leads to the same physiological arousal effects as stimulating music. And the combination of physical movement *plus* pump-up music is a surefire way to energize sluggish students.

This connection between movement and music actually begins very early in life. Research has shown that, even as infants, we prefer to move to a beat. In fact, if there is sound in the environment but no clearly discernible beat, infants will *impose* a structure on the sound and move to that imposed beat![5] And not only do we feel the need to move to music, we also clearly *enjoy* doing so, especially if the music is faster and/or louder.[6] When it comes to combining music with exercise, studies have shown that using slower-paced music while doing submaximal exercise (walking, slow jogging, etc.) helps increase endurance,[7] while using faster-paced music while doing more intense exercise helps to raise heart rate and respiration to meet the challenge. It appears that listening to music that matches our movement goals is a highly effective strategy.[8]

THOSE WHO HEAR NOT THE MUSIC THINK THE DANCERS MAD

INSIDE A CLASSROOM

Energizing Students for Learning

Erik B. Smith
5th Grade Teacher
Fay Galloway Elementary
Henderson, Nevada, USA

"I think it's very important to periodically create a state change that energizes students' bodies, while simultaneously altering their cognitive dispositions. The resulting release of positive neurotransmitters enhances the students' disposition to learn and to engage with the task at hand.

"To do this, I first set a large visual, computer-based timer for 90 seconds on the overhead LCD projector. I then give a brief instruction to take 11 to 15 large steps in any direction and stop. Next, I ask each student to take their pulse to determine their resting heart rate. I then ask the students to immediately begin a variety of cardiovascular exercises or movements such as jumping jacks, kangaroo hops, lunges, or in-place pogo jumps, which are to be conducted at a maximum level of physical exertion upon hearing the music. I encourage students to create their own form of physical activity. They are to maintain this movement until the timer expires and the music stops. At this time, each student recalculates his or her pulse. Upon conclusion, I typically give students a glucose booster such as a gummy bear, jelly bean, or M&M when returning to their desks.

"Prior to implementing this activity, I primarily relied on using an upbeat song, 120 beats per minute or higher, while the students walked around the room to a specific instruction such as touching 25 specifically colored objects or high-fiving as many people as possible before returning to their seats. The results were consistently positive. Yet, I was still interested in 'raising the bar' to achieve even more dramatic physiological effects that would significantly change students' learning states as supported by the latest cognitive research. Since introducing this musically based aerobic activity, I have observed the following benefits: (1) reduction in off-task behavior; (2) a heightened level of cooperation; (3) improved mood such as elevated calmness or alertness; and (4) extended periods of increased ability to stay mentally engaged."

Advice to Teachers: "I believe any educator, trainer, or teaching professional should seriously consider the enormous benefits of a musically driven learning atmosphere. The research is clear that utilizing the appropriate beats per minute and matching it with the corresponding physical or mental task can have beneficial physiological effects that can improve a learner's overall mood. Enhanced mood levels can lead to increased cognitive performance, elevated levels of cooperation, and stronger feelings of joy and excitement about being in the learning environment, and the novelty of the activity creates a sense of uniqueness about being in your classroom that permeates the learner's disposition toward being in school—something that's becoming rarer and rarer in today's schools. It creates a win-win situation for both teachers and students."

Suggested Songs: "Unchained," by Van Halen; "Jerk It Out," by the Caesars; "Wanna Be Starting Something," by Michael Jackson.

Extra Adrenaline = Better Learning

Increased heart rate and respiration are not the only physiological changes that take place when listening to pump-up music (or moving); they are just the most easily noticed. Less obvious is the fact that for the heart rate to speed up, extra adrenaline must be released into the bloodstream. This is important to teachers because adrenaline (in moderate amounts) also has positive effects on learning.

For one thing, extra adrenaline equals more arousal, and more arousal equals better attention. And, as molecular biologist John Medina (2008) points out in his book, *Brain Rules: 12 Principles for Surviving and Thriving at Work, Home, and School,* "The more attention the brain pays to a given stimulus, the more elaborately the information will be encoded—and retained" (p. 74). A number of research studies support this conclusion by demonstrating that up-tempo music leads to higher arousal, and that this higher level of arousal (especially if augmented by positive mood) leads to better cognitive performance.[9]

In addition, extra adrenaline in the system has been shown to act as a long-term memory "fixative." That is, when more adrenaline is present in the body and brain, we more easily encode information in the hippocampus, the part of the brain primarily responsible for long-term memory storage.[10] Bottom line? When we have extra adrenaline in our systems, we're more alert, we pay better attention, and we learn more easily. And having up-tempo music in the learning environment is one of the easiest ways to start this positive cascade of events leading to learning.

Characteristics of Pump-Up Music

Most people believe they know pump-up music when they hear it, and they are probably right. However, let's try to define this type of music as clearly as we can to differentiate it from the other types of music discussed in this book. Here are some general guidelines to support your search for stimulating music to use in your classroom:

♪ **Tempo:** Pump-up music needs to fall in the 120- to 160-beat-per-minute range—meaning, pretty fast. Think "Bandstand Boogie" by Les Elgart. This is not to say that music that is a little slower (say, 80 to 120 bpm) can't also have a stimulating effect; it can, and in fact, we will talk about that tempo of music in a later chapter. It is also important to point out that some music is probably *too fast* for use in the classroom—even as pump-up music. Once you get above about 160 bpm, you may be engendering a frenzied state in your students. While a little extra adrenaline in the system is good for learning, too much can lead to a lack of focus.

♪ **Instrumentation**: Whereas the music used for calming students often uses minimal instrumentation, music used to stimulate students is just the opposite. Pump-up music usually employs rich instrumentation and attention-getting instruments like trumpets, saxophones, and electric guitars.

> Music is the shorthand of emotion.
>
> —Leo Nikolaevich

♪ **Exciting Emotional Tone**: Pump-up music is generally exciting, and while it's hard to define *exciting* exactly, some other adjectives that might fit the bill include *soaring, dramatic, passionate, vigorous, robust*, or *majestic* (Hevner, 1936a).

♪ **Beat**: Pump-up music usually has a strong, pronounced beat.

♪ **Volume**: Pump-up music works best when played at a medium-loud volume. Obviously, students must be able to hear the music for it to have its intended arousing effect, and a little extra volume adds to that effect.

♪ **Vocal or Instrumental**: Since you will be playing pump-up music during transitions, it doesn't matter if the music has lyrics or not. There is a great deal of excellent pump-up music available of both types.

♪ **Overlap With Feel-Good Music**: Pump-up music and feel-good music often overlap, and this is an important point for teachers to be aware of. A song can be a feel-good song for a number of reasons (see the characteristics listed in Chapter 2) without being arousing. For example, there are many good feel-good songs with tempi well below 120 beats per minute (some of our favorite feel-good tunes are ballads). These songs can still be somewhat arousing if other characteristics are present (a strong beat, attention-getting instrumentation, played at a loud volume, for example), but if the goal is to energize students, such songs may not do the trick, even though they might serve to raise students' moods. On the other hand, not all pump-up music is going to necessarily improve mood. A song may be up-tempo and arousing without necessarily being enjoyable. Having said all of this, there are many songs that have characteristics of both feel-good and pump-up music, which is great because, if your goal is to energize your students, it can't be a bad thing to use the music to put them in a good mood at the same time. Two birds, one stone, and all that.

When a number of these characteristics are present in a song, the chances are good that it will work well to energize your students. Fortunately, there is a great deal of music available in almost every genre that will serve this purpose.

How to Use It

First, identify the best times to use it. Are there certain predictable times in your teaching day or week when your students tend to be sleepy, listless, or lethargic? Monday mornings or after lunch are usually good candidates, as are days when the weather is gloomy. You will know what those times are in your own classroom. The trick, as always, is to anticipate these situations and be prepared.

At the Beginning of Class

As with feel-good music and calming music, the best times to use pump-up music are during transitions. For example, if you know that your students tend to drag into class first thing in the morning or at the beginning of specific class periods, you can combat this problem by having some pump-up music cued up and ready to go as students come in. Play it at medium to medium-loud volume as students enter the room. You will notice that some students immediately brighten up and start bopping to the music. Some of the more reserved students may look at the more energetic ones and laugh, or at least smile, and perhaps begin to bob their heads or tap a foot to the beat. It's all good, and helps to add energy to the classroom—energy that can then be used for learning.

Within a Class Period

You can also use pump-up music during those smaller transitions during class time (getting materials out, putting things away, switching from individual seat work to group work). When you play pump-up music during these transitions, you will notice that students move more quickly about the room instead of dragging. Transitions get done more quickly as a result, saving you instructional time.

You can even ratchet up the management potential of this use of music by using the same up-tempo song for a particular kind of transition for a period of time. Tell the students that you are going to play forty-five seconds (or whatever is appropriate) of the song, and that they need to be done with the transition and ready for the next activity by the end of that piece of the song. You can use the chorus or any piece of the song, but use the same piece each time so that students can anticipate when the piece is getting ready to end. You will notice that your students will speed up even more just toward the end of the selection so they can be finished transitioning before the song ends.

At the End of Class

And don't forget the final transition, at the end of a class or the end of the school day. Playing up-tempo music as students leave sends them out on a positive, energetic note. When they walk toward your class the next day, they will remember that feeling, and they will bring that energy back with them for the start of a new day of learning.

Again, don't use this music in the learning environment while you are actually teaching. You may be getting tired of hearing us say that, but we feel that we can't stress this point too much. Having music on while doing direct instruction would only interfere with learning, not enhance it, which is your goal. You *can* play music while students read or write, or while they participate in any number of other individual or group processing activities, and that use of music (background music) is the subject of the next two chapters.

Guidelines for Using Pump-Up Music

♪ Avoid the genre trap. When most people think about pump-up music, certain genres come to mind immediately—primarily rock and roll, hard rock, hip-hop, and dance music. But you can find at least some songs that fit the characteristics described in this chapter in just about any musical genre. While genres such as hard rock and dance music contain a high percentage of pump-up music almost by definition, you can find excellent pump-up selections from genres such as jazz, R&B, country, and even classical. In fact, some interesting research has found that when subjects listened to rock music and classical music with similar pump-up characteristics, the classical music selections actually were significantly more arousing than the rock music![11]

INSIDE A CLASSROOM

Tidy-Up Time

Zoie Moody
Key Stage One Coordinator, Year 2 (equivalent to 2nd Grade in the US)
St. Dennis Primary School
Cornwall, England

"At tidy-up time, I play the same piece of music each time to signal that it is time to start tidying things away. It is quite fast-paced without being too hectic, which generates a purposeful atmosphere. The children know the music so well that they know when it is nearing the end and position themselves on the carpet ready. We often sing along and dance a little (while staying on task tidying), which helps create a sense of fun and a relaxed, happy place to be.

"Before I used music in my classroom, tidy-up time would take forever, with some children opting out while others did all of the work. It was often a noisy, hectic time, and I would often have to repeat myself lots of times to get the job done. Since introducing music, everyone joins in. There is a calm, happy, purposeful atmosphere, and the class is usually tidy in the three minutes it takes for the music to end. Sometimes we might have a little 'shimmy' with the person next to us, which creates a feel-good vibe and a sense of fun. I rarely have to repeat myself or remind people what they should be doing, and there is a lovely sense of teamwork."

Advice to Teachers: "Do it! It helps to make your classroom a fun place to be. Use the same tracks for specific routines so that the children get used to how much time they have to complete the task."

Suggested Songs: "It doesn't matter what music/song you use, as long as you use the same one each time. I use a funky track so that we can have a little dance along the way should we so choose!"

♪ Vocal or instrumental selections work equally well. Most people are probably more familiar with pump-up music with vocals, but there are also many great instrumentals that would serve as well, and it might be good to broaden your students' musical horizons a bit by including instrumental pump-up songs in your mix.

♪ Use ramping to build energy over longer stretches of time. When you have ten or fifteen minutes to play several musical selections back-to-back, you can use the ramping technique to take your students from a low-energy state to a high- (or at least higher-) energy state. Say, for example, that your students tend to drag into class a few at a time on Monday morning. Have a medium-tempo and medium-energy song on as the first students enter. Follow that with a higher-tempo song, and follow that song with one with higher energy still. You will notice that your students' body language demonstrates increasing energy over time. In fact, the rationale behind Muzak programming grew out of studies done by the U.S. Army in the 1960s, demonstrating that when popular selections were sequenced in order of ascending energy, workers became more alert and attentive (Rosenfield, 1985). If you time it right, you will have your students energized for learning just as class is ready to start.

♪ Don't mess with popular favorites. A number of studies have shown that most people generally favor up-tempo music to slower-tempo music,[12] so your students will probably by and large enjoy your periodic use of pump-up music. However, research has also shown that people get very attached to their favorite songs,[13] so if you decide to play a cover version of a student favorite, just realize that you do so at your peril. You will probably get complaints.

Follow the guidelines laid down here, and you will soon have those sleepy students awake and in a great mood for learning. As always, watch how your students react and adjust. Slowly over time you will build a whole list of songs that work well for you.

What to Avoid

In addition to the previously mentioned warning about not playing pump-up music (or any music, for that matter) while doing direct instruction, here are a couple of other caveats to keep in mind.

The Danger of Overstimulation

While pump-up music is wonderfully effective for arousing students when they are in low-energy states, you have to be careful that you don't take things too far and overstimulate them. Moderate levels of arousal are optimal for learning. Too little arousal, and students don't bring enough attention to bear on the task at hand; too much arousal, and they can start acting crazy or silly—again, not a good state for learning.

Teachers sometimes get in trouble in this regard when they anticipate that students will be in a low-energy state, but this turns out not to be the case. The teacher who plays pump-up music when his or her students are already aroused runs the risk of sending them over the edge. The key here (as usual) is kid-watching. If you anticipate a low-energy state at a certain time and plan to use pump-up music for the occasion, you need to observe your students prior to turning the music on to make sure that your assumption was correct. If you find that your students are already energized enough to learn, you should forgo the use of the planned music, perhaps substituting less-arousing background music in place of the pump-up selection.

Chaotic and Unsafe Movement

As previously mentioned, the arousing effects of pump-up music can be further amplified by having students move around the classroom. In general, it's a great combination—students get an extra shot of energy, and the movement activity gets done quicker than it would have otherwise. But again, be sure to observe your students before you give your directions for the activity and turn on the music. If they are already somewhat aroused, the double shot of adrenaline could lead them to move too quickly around the room, possibly leading to unsafe conditions. Some of the danger can be mitigated by teaching students in advance what safe movement looks like in your classroom and establishing safe movement procedures. But even if you have stressed safe movement, you have to be careful. When students get pumped up, those routines sometimes magically disappear from their heads (we're sure you're shocked!). If you have planned to play pump-up music behind a movement activity, but you see that your students are already in a high-energy state, either tone down the music by switching to a less-energizing piece, or tone down the movement you ask them to do.

Getting Started

An obvious starting place is to use tracks from collections designed to be energizing—for example, compilations of dance music, collections marketed specifically as "energizing" music, or the ever-popular Jock Jams collections that are often used to pump up fans at athletic events. The chances are most of the songs found in these collections will exhibit many of the characteristics of pump-up music discussed in this chapter.

In addition, you can use the browse function on your favorite online music source to find music that fits the bill. Now, we know that we already warned you against assuming that *all* songs found in certain genres will automatically work for pump-up music, and that warning still stands, but that doesn't mean that making some initial assumptions isn't a good way to *start* your search. For example, in iTunes, you can start by browsing genres such as dance, electronic, fitness & workout, hip-hop/rap, Latin jazz, and rock. When you click on some of these genres, menus of subgenres open up that allow you to refine your search. Sample selections from a number of artists, and you will find more good choices than you will ever be able to use in class.

For more ideas to get you started, see our Top 40 list below, our expanded list of pump-up selections in Appendix C, and the other suggestions found on our website, www.rockandrollclassroom.com.

Our Top 40 Pump-Up Songs

Following are some of our favorite pump-up songs. As you can see, you can find good pump-up songs from a variety of genres and time periods, both lyrical and instrumental. Our intention with these Top 40 lists is to give you ideas so that you can get off to a quick start. Certainly you will have your own tastes and favorites. Also, we would like to remind you that pump-up music and feel-good music often overlap, so some of the songs found here may serve the dual purpose of energizing your students while simultaneously raising their moods. Have fun with it!

1. "Accidental Mambo," Mambo All-Stars

2. "Any Way You Want It," Journey

3. "Bandstand Boogie," Les Elgart and His Orchestra

4. "Beer Barrel Polka," Lawrence Welk

5. "Best Years of Our Lives," The Baha Men

6. "Boogie Woogie Bugle Boy," Bette Midler

7. "Born to Be Alive (Club Version)," Patrick Hernandez

8. "Brassman's Holiday," Arturo Sandoval

9. "Bumble Boogie," B. Bumble and the Stingers

10. "Cancan," Jacques Offenbach

11. "Cool Affair (Eric Kupper Remix)," Black and Brown

12. "El Tropicana," The Socka Boys

13. "Friday Night Shuffle," Larry Carlton

14. "Fun, Fun, Fun," The Beach Boys

15. "Get Ready for This," 2 Unlimited

16. "Hot, Hot, Hot (Radio Edit)," Buster Poindexter and His Banshees of Blue

17. "House of Tom Bombadil," Nickel Creek

18. "I Got My Mojo Working," The Paul Butterfield Blues Band

19. "I Like to Move It," from *Madagascar*, The Party Cats

20. "In the Mood," Doc Severinsen

21. "It Don't Mean a Thing," Ella Fitzgerald

22. "I've Been Everywhere," Johnny Cash

23. "Jumpin' at the Woodside," Count Basie and His Orchestra

24. "Main Squeeze," Chuck Mangione

25. "Mickey," Toni Basil

26. "Outa Space (Single Version)," Billy Preston

27. "Punchdrunk," Bela Fleck

28. "Rock and Roll Part 2," Gary Glitter

29. "Sabre Dance," from *Gayane*, Aram Khachaturian

30. "Sandstorm," Darude

31. "Seventy-Six Trombones," from *The Music Man*, Ensemble

32. "Shake a Tail Feather," Ray Charles

33. "Southbound," The Allman Brothers Band

34. "Strike It Up," Black Box

35. "The Final Countdown," Europe

36. "Toss the Feathers," The Corrs

37. "Turn the Beat Around," Gloria Estefan

38. "Twilight Zone," 2 Unlimited

39. "William Tell Overture, Finale," Gioacchino Rossini

40. "Yackety Sax," Boots Randolph

Notes

1. Safranek, Koshland, and Raymond (1982) had subjects complete a motor task with no rhythmic background, with an

even beat, and with an uneven beat. With no rhythmic background, subjects demonstrated a consistent personal rhythm. With a steady beat, however, subjects adjusted their movements to match the beat, and their movements became smoother (161–168).

2. Waterhouse, Hudson, and Edwards (2010) had subjects cycle while listening to music of different tempi. They found that speeding up the music increased work output and raised heart rate. In addition, subjects reported liking the faster music significantly more than the slower music selections (662–669). Wininger and Pargman (2003) found that subjects rated satisfaction with the music listened to while working out as the most important factor in exercise enjoyment (57–73).

3. Bernardi, Porta, and Sleight (2006) exposed subjects to six different music selections while measuring physiological factors. Breathing rate, blood pressure, and heart rate all increased with exposure to faster tempi and simpler rhythmic structures, demonstrating a clear arousal effect (445–452). Van der Zwaag, Westerink, and van den Broek (2011) had subjects listen to pop and rock songs while conducting an office task. Increased tempo was found to raise arousal and tension (250–269). Rickard (2004) demonstrated that, when musical characteristics identified as "emotionally powerful" were combined with a faster tempo, they significantly increased arousal (371–388).

4. Stekelenburg and Van Boxtel (2002) had subjects perform a reading task. Novel sounds were introduced into the environment, and subjects exhibited an orienting response to the sounds that included heart rate and respiratory deceleration. When the stimulus sound was presented repeatedly, subjects habituated to it and the orienting response ended (707–722). Gomez and Danuser (2004) showed that heart rate appears to lag behind other physiological responses when arousing music is played, with skin conductance and respiration demonstrating an arousal effect to thirty-second musical excerpts while heart rate remained the same (91–103). Graham and Clifton (1966) hypothesized that heart rate would decelerate when orienting but accelerate when the stimulus elicited a startle reaction or was judged to be dangerous. This hypothesis appears to be confirmed by subsequent research (305–320).

5. Phillips-Silver and Trainor (2005) designed an experiment where infants were bounced on either every second beat or every third beat while listening to a rhythmic pattern with no clear accents. Later, the infants that were bounced on every second beat preferred to listen to a rhythmic pattern with accents every two beats, and those bounced every third beat preferred to listen to a rhythmic pattern with accents every three beats. These results indicate a clear connection between movement and musical preference starting early in life (1430). Phillips-Silver and Trainor (2007) then extended these results by repeating the experiment with adults. They found that adults, too, prefer to move in response to music and that they will interpret an ambiguous rhythm to be the same as one that they have moved to previously. That is, adults who bounced previously in march time (every two beats) preferred to bounce in march time to music with an ambiguous rhythm, while adults who bounced previously in waltz time (every three beats) previously preferred to bounce in waltz time to an ambiguous rhythm (533–546).

6. Edworthy and Waring (2006) had subjects listen to no music, fast/loud music, fast/quiet music, slow/loud music, or slow/quiet music while exercising on a treadmill. Subjects preferred exercising to music rather than no music, and fast/loud music was found to lead to optimal exercising (1597–1610). Karageorghis, Jones, and Low (2006) had subjects listen to different tempi of music while exercising at different intensities. They found that people preferred medium-tempo music to slow-tempo music at all exercise intensities, and that they preferred fast-tempo music when exercising at high intensity (240–244, 246–250).

7. Both Copeland and Franks (1991, 101–103), and Birnbaum, Boone, and Huschle (2009, 50–57) found that subjects exercising at slow speeds worked out most efficiently when listening to similarly-paced music. When moving slowly, listening to up-tempo music caused physiological arousal and led to lowered cardiac efficiency.

8. Simpson and Karageorghis (2006) found that subjects running 400-meter sprints ran much more efficiently when listening to synchronous music (music that matched the pace they wanted to run) than when not listening to music (1095–1102).

9. Husain, Thompson, and Schellenberg (2002) had subjects complete a spatial task while listening to four versions a Mozart sonata, created by editing the file to produce slower and faster versions, and to create versions in both the major and minor modes. Results indicated that subjects did better when the tempo was faster, leading to arousal, and when the music was in the major mode, leading to improved mood (151–171). Schellenberg, Nakata, Hunter, and Tamoto (2007) also found that subjects performed better on an IQ test after listening to up-tempo music as compared with slower-tempo music (5–19).

10. Ahmadiasl, Alaei, and Hanninen (2003) had two groups of rats negotiate a water maze. Rats who exercised an hour a day for ten days during the testing period were compared with rats who did not exercise during the testing period. Rats in the exercise group showed higher levels of epinephrine in their hippocampi and had superior maze-swimming times to the no-exercise group, indicating increased spatial learning (106–109).

11. Dillman-Carpentier and Potter (2007) demonstrated that subjects were more aroused when listening to fast-paced music as opposed to slower-paced music—no surprise there. But when they looked at how genre interacted with measures of arousal, they found that subjects were significantly more aroused when listening to fast-paced classical music compared with fast-paced rock music. They hypothesized that the rock music did not arouse subjects because they were more familiar with the genre, while most of the subjects were not as familiar with faster-paced classical music, and thus they attended to it better, leading to higher levels of arousal (339–363).

12. Holbrook and Anand (1990) found that subjects generally prefer music with a medium tempo, but that the more aroused they are, the more they prefer faster-tempo music (150–162).

13. Geringer and Madsen (1987) investigated pitch and tempo differences on subjects ranging from fifth grade through college age. They found that subjects consistently preferred the original versions of popular tunes to versions altered in any way (204–212).

5

Music to Work To

Using Background Music to Increase Focus on Individual Work

Music washes away from the soul the dust of everyday life.

—Berthold Auerbach

Music is the wine that fills the cup of silence.

—Robert Fripp

What It Is

Background music is an important support to learning during student input activities such as silent reading, and output activities such as writing, doing worksheets, or working on math problems. Its goal is to put a soft pad of sound over the room to cover up irregular environmental sounds such as a student tapping a pencil on a desk or a foot on a chair leg, or a teacher walking down the hall having a conversation. These kinds of noises are distracting for learners, and you will see students' heads popping up and turning (orienting) to the sound to see what's going on. Every time students do this, they lose focus on the learning task and then must get back into the flow of the

task when they turn back to it. Added up, these small distractions cause a great deal of lost learning time across every school day. Used correctly, background music covers these distracting sounds so that they do not rise to the level of consciousness. As a result, students remain on task and are better able to concentrate on the material, leading to better learning. Done correctly, background music can be one of the most powerful tools a teacher can use to increase learning.

Why It Works

Interpreting the research into why background music works takes us into a minefield of disagreement. One study claims that playing background music delivers great gains in focused attention, time on task, and learning, while the next claims that background music serves only to distract students and decrease learning.

Why have the results of background music research been so inconsistent? The answer is that no two studies are designed alike,

and teasing out the truth from the results takes a bit of detective work. You have to dig into each study individually and look at how it was conducted. Here are some of the key questions to ask when evaluating the results of a study:

- Who were the subjects? How many were there? How old were they?
- What was the task they were asked to complete?
- What kind of music was played in the background while they completed the task (genre, tempo, mode, vocal or instrumental, familiar or unfamiliar, preferred or not)?
- At what volume was the music played?
- Was there a control group in the study, and if so, what were the control conditions?

Once you have all of this information, you can ask the most important question of all: *How do the results of this study translate (if they do at all) to a classroom situation?* All too often, the answer is: *Not particularly well.*

For example, take the control condition used in many background music studies: *silence*. What, exactly, does this word mean in the context of a particular research study? Well, in some studies it means that subjects completed the task(s) in a laboratory room with others working on the same task(s) with no music playing—a condition somewhat similar to a "quiet" classroom, though our guess is that a lab setting during testing with (typically) young adults as subjects is quite a bit more silent than even the quietest classroom full of school-age kids. In other studies, silence means something even more controlled—for example, having the members of the control group perform the assigned task(s) (reading, working math problems, taking a portion of an IQ test, etc.) in a room by themselves, with external sounds limited or eliminated altogether by means such as soundproofed walls or by having the subjects wear headphones to block out any ambient sounds.

In a way, it makes some sense that, when conducting an experiment on the effects of background music, you would want to use a control group that completes the task at hand under conditions as different as possible from the experimental group(s) to get more pure distinctions. But we have just one question: *In the real world (especially in a school environment), is total silence really an option?* When was the last time your classroom (with students in it) was so quiet that you thought to yourself, "Man, this absolute lack of sound is kind of creepy?" It's much more likely that, even when all of your students are engaged in a quiet task such as silent reading, little sounds constantly pop up to intrude upon the quiet.

The fact is, in a school setting, the choice isn't between background music and silence, as it is in many studies. Silence, unfortunately, is not really an option. The choice, rather, is between students working in a room with normal ambient sounds and students working in a room in which background music is played to cover those ambient sounds. And when the effect of background music has been studied in conditions more closely resembling a classroom setting (where performance with background music is compared with performance with different types of ambient noise in the environment instead of being compared against results obtained in silence), the effects of background music on performance have almost always been found to be very positive.[1]

INSIDE A CLASSROOM

Music as a "Sound Pad" to Cover Multiple Activities

Maureen Stolte
Special Education Reading Teacher, Grades 6–8
Brandon Middle School
Virginia Beach, Virginia, USA

"In my reading classroom, small groups of students rotate to different activities such as independent reading, small group instruction, and computers. I use instrumental classical music as a 'sound pad' during each 20-minute session. Classical music is the perfect choice because there are no lyrics. Therefore, the students who are reading, thinking, discussing ideas, or working on online activities can concentrate on the task at hand. The music serves as a buffer in an active classroom, so the students can focus on improving their skills.

"Before I used classical music as a sound pad in my classroom, my students were easily distracted by the instruction and discussion taking place at the small group table, as well as by students reading into a microphone as they worked on fluency evaluations through the computer software. Since introducing classical music, my students remain on task because the music creates a soothing atmosphere conducive to learning. Classical music playing in the background has enabled my students to focus on independent reading and complete skill-building activities while others in the room are reading aloud or participating in small group instruction or discussion. An added bonus has been that my students have learned to appreciate and enjoy listening to classical music.

"Recently, my students took a standardized reading assessment. After I read the directions, I asked the class if anyone had any questions. To my surprise, a young man raised his hand to request listening to Handel's 'Water Music Suite' while testing! According to the results of the assessment, my students made significant improvement. I attribute this growth to effective use of classroom time as well as successful delivery of a research-based reading program enhanced by music."

Advice to Teachers: "Classical music can transform a busy classroom into a magical environment where students strive for academic success by focusing their effort on improving skills. Since not all classical music is alike, and since some classical music sets a tense tone, my advice is to carefully preview pieces and select relaxing classical music. In addition, be prepared for the students to complain when you first introduce this genre to your classroom routine. Remember that some students have not had exposure to classical music, so they might not have developed an appreciation of this genre. With a little encouragement, students will embrace listening to classical music while working."

Suggested Songs: "As stated above, I use a lot of relaxing classical music in my class. Some of my favorites are Water Music Suite in F Major, Suite in D Major, Suite in G Major, and "Arrival of the Queen of Sheba" by George Frideric Handel (performed by Bela Banfalvi and the Budapest Strings); Cello Suite No.1 in G Major, "Prelude" by Johann Sebastian Bach (performed by Yo-Yo Ma); Sonata in D for Cello and Piano, opus 4, Allegro by Dmitri Shostakovich (performed by Yo-Yo Ma); Andante Cantabile for Cello Solo and String Orchestra, opus posth. by Tchaikovsky (performed by Yo-Yo Ma, with Lorin Maazel and the Pittsburgh Symphony Orchestra); and Oboe Concerto in C Major, Minuet by Antonio Vivaldi (performed by Burkhard Glaetzner, with the New Bach Collegium Musicum Leipzig)."

We believe that, once you take into account some of the serious design flaws in many of the studies that have been conducted, you are left with some pretty clear guidelines about how to use background music effectively.

Distraction—The Enemy of Focused Attention

Studies have shown that we automatically orient to novel, irregular sounds in the environment—sounds such as someone using the pencil sharpener, whispering to a neighbor, or sneezing—and that when we do so, our performance on the task at hand suffers. But these studies also show that, when a sound is repeatedly presented, or when the sound continues in a more or less steady state (such as an instrumental song), we habituate to the situation, and the sound no longer calls for our conscious attention.[2]

What we are talking about here is a battle between two types of attention: (1) stimulus-driven attention and (2) focused attention. Extensive studies by cognitive scientists in recent years have found that the two types of attention do very different jobs and that they are directed by different parts of the brain.[3]

♪ When using ***stimulus-driven attention*** (sometimes called our "alerting network"), we constantly scan the environment, looking for any change in conditions. Whenever our senses present us with data concerning any appreciable change in our environment—something moving across our field of vision, or a sudden change in temperature or air pressure, or some new sound that we notice—we immediately orient toward that stimulus. This is our built-in danger detector at work, and since the brain's number one job is to ensure our survival, this whole stimulus-driven attention and orienting system is both automatic (meaning that it works unconsciously without us telling it to) and very powerful.

♪ In contrast, ***focused attention*** (sometimes called "controlled attention" or the "executive network") is a process whereby we consciously direct our attention toward a specific part of our environment. Some scientists call this type of attention *spotlight* or *flashlight* attention, as it can be focused like a beam of light on selected parts of a person's surroundings or internally on the contents of working memory, and we can shift the beam of our focused attention to other data at will. This type of attention allows us to engage in activities such as setting priorities, planning a course of action, completing a task, and controlling impulses.

When we ask students to engage in an academic task, we are asking them to bring the beam of focused attention to bear on the task. But we must also be aware that the environment surrounding the task (the context) may contain elements that call out to our students' stimulus-driven attention systems. And when stimulus-driven attention wins the battle, focused attention suffers. Once students orient to the stimulus and determine that it is no danger to them, they are free to reestablish focused attention on the task—but precious learning time has been lost in the meantime.

Students (as long as they're awake) are always paying attention to *something*; it just may not be what we would like them to be paying attention to. And that's where background music comes in. The primary impediment to good, focused attention is distraction, in the form of all of those novel, ambient sounds in the environment that call out to our stimulus-driven attention system. The goal of using background music is to cover these novel sounds so that they do not alert the stimulus-driven system to orient toward them, thus allowing focused attention to remain on task.

Other Issues—Arousal, Task Difficulty, Personality Types, and Mood

If all we had to consider when selecting and implementing background music in our classrooms was the issue of covering distractions to maximize focused attention, things would be pretty straightforward. But unfortunately, there are other factors that interact with attention, and chief among these is arousal. In fact, arousal can be viewed as a third type of attention in its own right. Whereas the other two types of attention discussed above are directed toward a particular aspect of the environment, arousal is our more general *background* (nonselective) level of attention—that is, how wakeful or alert we are. We can raise our level of arousal with stimulants such as caffeine, or (as discussed in the previous chapter) by moving around vigorously, or by listening to some energizing music.

We talked in the previous chapter about how arousal generally leads to better learning. But raising arousal isn't necessarily always a good idea. We may not think very well when our arousal level is too low (bored, tired, sleepy), but neither do we do so when we are *too* aroused (nervous, anxious, or hyped up).

Determining the perfect level of arousal for high-quality learning has been the subject of many studies over the past century. As far back as 1908, two psychologists, Robert Yerkes and John Dillingham Dodson, formulated a "law" that explained the impact of arousal on performance. This law—now known as the Yerkes-Dodson Law—is generally represented graphically as an inverted U shape (see Graph 5.1), with performance being low under conditions of both low arousal and high arousal, and with medium arousal leading to peak performance. This state of optimal arousal has been described by education experts Renate and Geoffrey Caine (1991) as "relaxed alertness" (p. 70). So, for our students to perform optimally, we not only need to make sure that we eliminate or mask distractions, but also need to work at getting our students in that sweet spot of medium arousal.

Moreover, several other factors also come into play when we attempt to create the optimal level of arousal in the classroom. One factor that must be accounted for is task difficulty. One often overlooked, yet highly important, aspect of the Yerkes-Dodson Law is that the research shows different optimal levels of arousal depending on the difficulty of the task. For difficult tasks, performance begins to drop off rapidly with higher levels of arousal (the inverted U-shape curve mentioned above), but for simple tasks, higher levels of arousal continue to enhance performance.[4] That is, for simple tasks, and especially for tasks that demand stamina or persistence, the curve of performance rises as it moves from low arousal to medium arousal, but then flattens out and remains high beyond this point (see Graph 5.2). In fact, for the most simple or boring tasks of all, such as vigilance tasks where subjects have to steadily watch a monitor for changes, research has shown that performance is best when highly arousing background stimulation is used to keep subjects alert.[5]

In addition to task difficulty, your students' personality types also come into play. A good deal of research has shown that introverts and

Graph 5.1   Yerkes-Dodson Law (Wikipedia)

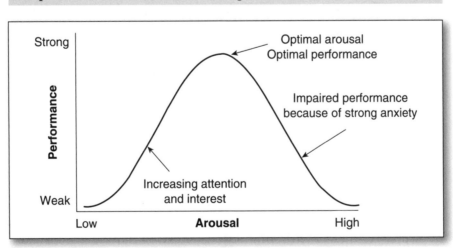

Graph 5.2 Arousal and Performance (Wikipedia)

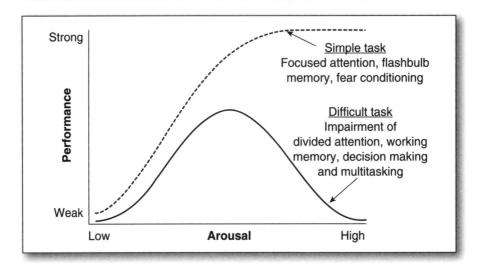

extroverts differ in their arousal responses. While extroverts tend to perform better with higher levels of stimulation (whether that stimulation is in the form of background music, white noise, or a television playing in the background), introverts tend to work much better under lower-arousal conditions (closer to silence).[6] And if you have students with ADHD (attention deficit hyperactivity disorder) in your classroom, you need to be aware of the fact that these students (apparently due to lower dopamine levels) need an even higher level of stimulation to reach that optimal level of arousal (think of them as "*extra*-extroverts").[7]

Finally, we need to consider the impact of mood on performance. In Chapter 2, we talked about how feel-good music could elevate students' moods, and we discussed a number of characteristics of that kind of music that were responsible for creating positive affect in students. Chief among these characteristics was the positive emotional effect of music played in the major mode. Not many studies have looked into the interactions between mood and performance under background music conditions, but those that have done so clearly show that background music in the major mode leads to higher productivity than background music in the minor mode.[8]

What all of this amounts to is that there is a complex interplay between the difficulty of the task, the personalities of the students completing the task, the mood they're in, and the level of distraction/arousal of the background context surrounding the task. With all of these "moving parts," there is little wonder that the research results appear so confusing, with some studies showing that a more arousing background enhances task performance[9] while others show just the opposite.[10] It all depends on how the research study was designed and the exact mix of all of these elements that were used. Only when you look at the exact conditions of each study (the kind of task performed, the personality types of the subjects, the characteristics of the background music used, etc.) can you begin to see patterns in the data with any clarity. Armed with this information, a teacher who knows his or her students well and keeps the overall goal in mind (to have as many students as possible in the optimal, medium-arousal state while eliminating distractions that would activate the stimulus-driven attention system) can begin to make conscious, well-informed decisions about what kind of music to use in the background as students work.

Characteristics of Background Music to Use Behind Individual Work

At this point, you may be beginning to wonder if this whole idea of using background music in your classroom isn't too complicated to be worth the effort. Don't worry, it's really not that difficult—in fact, it's very doable. The goal of the previous section was not to make you despair; we just wanted to make sure you are aware of all of the issues, so you can make informed choices. To help you do that, here are the basic characteristics of good background music:

♪ **Moderate Tempo**: We've talked in previous chapters about entrainment and the physiological changes (heartbeat, respiration, blood pressure, etc.) that speed up or slow down in an attempt to match a repetitive environmental stimulus such as the beat of the music. And since in most cases we don't want students to speed up *or* slow down when reading or writing, but rather to remain in a steady, focused state, we generally want to use music that matches the resting human heart rate, which tends to be between 60 and 80 beats per minute. This is medium-slow to medium speed, if you don't want to count beats when selecting your music. You can usually tell by watching your students if it's too slow (they will start getting drowsy) or too fast (they will start getting twitchy in their seats or start tapping their feet to the beat or some similar behavior).

♪ **Instrumental *Only*:** For music used during transitions, when no teaching or academic work is taking place, it doesn't really matter if you use instrumental music or music with vocals. But in the case of background music, since students are invariably either inputting and processing words (reading) or generating words (writing, thinking), it is not a good idea to introduce any other words into the environment at this time, as research shows that doing so will interfere with thinking and reduce task performance.[11] The only possible exception to this admonition is if you play a song that is being sung in a foreign language that none of your students speak (Enya singing in Gaelic, for example, or Josh Groban singing in Italian). The voice in such situations could be viewed as simply another instrument. But there is some doubt about whether even this is a good idea,[12] so the safe bet is to stick with instrumental music only.

♪ **Repetitive**: Remember, your whole goal here is to cover up sounds that call attention to themselves (and away from the learning task). If the music calls attention to itself in any way, it is simply a different kind of distraction and learning will be impeded, not enhanced. What you're shooting for, then, with background music, is music that *doesn't* call attention to itself in any way. You want tunes that repeat the same musical phrase throughout with only minor variations. You *don't* want music that gets louder and softer, or music where the instrumentation suddenly changes (a saxophone suddenly comes wailing in, for example), or music that speeds up or slows down. You want the music to be like white noise that covers other sounds but gets tuned out by the brain as if it wasn't there (habituation).

♪ **Fairly Simple Instrumentation**: The more instruments involved, the more complex and arousing the music tends to be, and the higher the chance that something in the instrumentation will call attention to itself (and away from the work). We have found that while the music doesn't have to be as stripped-down as calming music often is, the best background music still tends to be on the spare side—but certainly, more instruments can be involved if most of the other characteristics on this list are being met.

♪ **Unfamiliar to Your Students**: As stated above, you don't want music that calls attention to itself, so it is important to choose music that you think none of your students will recognize. If they recognize the tune, they will start bopping to it, or humming along. This means it has gotten their attention, which means that their attention is *not* on their work! You may find a wonderful rendition of Pachelbel's Canon that perfectly matches all the other criteria listed here, but if you use it, we can pretty much guarantee that you are going to have students who recognize it. They might not be able to name the piece or where they heard it (probably on TV or at a wedding), but it will nonetheless distract them from their task. The same goes for instrumental versions of popular songs that your students know (which is why we don't recommend Muzak as background music). If they recognize the tune and already know the words, they may begin to play the words as a soundtrack in their heads, or worse, they may begin to actually sing along with the song! If you want the academic work to get done, avoid these choices.[13]

♪ **Major Mode:** Just because background music is not supposed to call conscious attention to itself doesn't mean that it is completely ignored. The characteristics of the music will still exert a (mostly unconscious) influence on students. And, as we've pointed out several times, people respond positively to music in the major mode. So, by choosing background music in the major mode, you can positively influence your students' moods while helping them focus—a win-win!

♪ **Low Volume:** Studies have shown that louder music is more arousing and attention-getting than softer music, as you would expect.[14] Since you don't want students to be aroused or to pay attention to the music in this case, you want to keep the volume low. And since little or no talking should be taking place in the learning environment while background music is playing behind individual seatwork, the music can be played quite softly and still achieve the desired effect. Again, all you're trying to do is cover up (usually) soft, irregular environmental sounds that could be distracting. Play the music just loud enough to achieve this goal.

If you choose music according to the guidelines above and use it as suggested in this chapter, we think you will be very happy with the results. While most of the research cited in this chapter was conducted in laboratory conditions, the results of the (admittedly fewer) research studies that have been done in real classroom situations has been quite favorable.[15] Just keep your goal in mind—covering environmental noise with music that is not in itself distracting so students can stay focused and on task—and watch for evidence that the music you are using is or is not achieving that goal. If a piece is not working, reflect on why and adjust your choices.

How to Use It

Whenever you ask students to read, do processing activities, practice skills, or write, you expect them to do the work with good effort and focused concentration. But sometimes the classroom environment is a challenge. Background noise can come from many sources, such as the air conditioning or heating kicking on, or interruptions from the intercom, or a group of students walking by your classroom door talking noisily. In addition, students by and large like to be social, and when you are not on stage demanding their attention, some students see an opportunity to talk instead of work. As we've discussed in this chapter, all of these distractions call out to your students' stimulus-driven attention systems. But you don't have to let the distractions win. If you plan ahead and have some good background music (matching the characteristics listed above) cued up and ready to go immediately after you give your directions and get students started on their individual seatwork, you can provide a pad of sound that works to filter out the distractions and allows your students to focus.

Reading

In our experience, it makes sense to subdivide individual seatwork into two categories: (1) reading (input) and (2) writing (output). Of the two situations, students are generally more distractible during silent reading than during writing—or during any other activity, for that matter. This makes sense when viewed from the perspective of *cognitive load*. When reading, students are trying to understand the thoughts and words of someone else, which can be very challenging. To comprehend well, they need to bring a great deal of concentration to the task, and any extra distractions in the environment tend to quickly overload their working memory capacity and interfere with processing. As we've discussed previously, medium arousal is the optimal arousal level for a task of medium difficulty, but as the difficulty of the task rises, higher levels of arousal cause performance to drop off steeply. As a result, we recommend keeping your background music toward the low-arousal end of the spectrum while students are reading silently. Good background music for reading, then, tends to be around 60 to 70 beats per minute, with spare instrumentation and a highly repetitive structure, and played at very low volume.

INSIDE A CLASSROOM

Music Behind Writing, Completing Worksheets, or Test Taking

Shari Rindels
1st Grade Teacher
Catalina Ventura School
Phoenix, Arizona, USA

"Music is a vital part of my classroom. I use music in many ways—as a starting point for specific activities, as background music, as a signal to pack up to go home, or to change the tone of the classroom. Visitors who come to my room do take notice and comment on the high engagement they witness as a direct result of the music playing. I find, too, that music adds a level of fun and energy as well as providing good background for thinking/working/test taking. Students seem to stay on task longer, focus more intently, and are less distracted by others.

"Before I used music in my classroom, time seemed to slowly drag on, whether it was time on task completing a worksheet or activity, or just think time. During creative writing time, ideas and thoughts seemed to take longer to take form and get written on paper. During independent practice, worksheets seemed to take forever to get done, and every little noise in the classroom became completely annoying and distracting. Students were often off task, fidgety, or just sitting there doing nothing, looking bored and disinterested or stressed and overwhelmed.

"Since introducing music, student engagement has increased 100%, academic performance has improved greatly due to increased focus, writing assignments get completed with less complaining, I find fewer students just sitting there without producing anything, pack-up time is smooth and less harried, and best of all, students smile and enjoy what they are doing. How do I know? They tell me so! And if I forget or am not fast enough to get the music going, they let me know and will say, 'It's too quiet to work, Miss Rindels! We need the music…pleeeeze?!' As a teacher, I find that music is a nice rest for my vocal chords, a good chance to take a quick drink of water, and a huge boost for my patience level. Just as children need a break from my voice, so do I!"

Advice to Teachers: "As Nike says, just do it! You will see a phenomenal increase in student engagement, enjoyment, and increased focus. Plus, your school day will seem to fly by! Give it a try; you will never be without it again! And as you use music in the classroom, you'll find more and more songs out there that fit your routines, lessons, and activities. Music truly is the universal language; enjoy it and have fun with it!"

Suggested Songs: "During writing journals/creative writing time, I use Gary Lamb's piano CD titled *A Walk in the Garden*. I always start with the song 'Shumiko and Mary (Two Ballerinas),' which has a very upbeat tempo. It gets the kids focused and working quickly. I reserve this song just for any activity that involves writing; they get used to it and know that when the song starts, it's writing time. I also use Gary Lamb's CD titled *Productive Flow*, which works well as background music during writing, worksheets, or testing time. It has the perfect tempo to keep the students on task and motivated."

Writing

When students are engaged in output activities—when they are putting their own thoughts into words through writing or into some graphic form by creating a graphic organizer, or when they are problem solving—our experience is that the optimal level of arousal needs to be a bit higher than when students are reading. For one thing, since students are doing their own thinking as opposed to trying to understand the thoughts of another, the cognitive load is generally not quite as high. In addition, due to pens and pencils scratching and papers shuffling, there is usually a little more ambient noise in the classroom when students are writing, working on math problems, or creating a graphic organizer than there is during silent reading. As a result, we recommend using background music during output activities toward the higher-arousal end of the background music spectrum: 70 to 80 beats per minute, a little more instrumentation, a little more noticeable beat, and played at low volume (but a little louder than you would use behind silent reading).

Guidelines for Using Background Music Behind Individual Student Work

In addition to the suggestions above, here are a few more guidelines for using background music effectively in your classroom:

- ♪ Concerning tempo, 60 to 80 beats per minute is the right range most of the time. But if the majority of your students are underenergized (sleepy, lethargic), you might want to raise the arousal level of your background music a bit, into the 80- to 100-beats-per-minute (bpm) range (the kind of music we will be recommending in the next chapter for group work) to simultaneously wake them up a bit while covering distracting sounds. On the other hand, if your students are a little wild and crazy, you might want to resort to some instrumental calming music in the 50 to 60 bpm range to simultaneously calm them down and help them focus.
- ♪ If you regularly ask students to do long stretches of individual seatwork, you might consider using the same background music over and over. This approach has a couple of advantages. First, you don't have to have a 200-song collection of background music—twenty good songs might do it. Not needing so many songs makes it a lot easier to find just the right collection of songs that works like magic for your students. Second, we

have found that students get used to having the same songs on during certain activities. For example, if you have students write for thirty minutes every day and you use the same background music each time, students quickly come to see this music as their writing music. You will find that, if you try to switch it up after this point, at least some of your students will complain. Also, having a consistent set of background songs allows the music to act as a management cue—you will notice that, as soon as the first song comes on, students will usually settle down quickly and get to work. Now, we know that this idea of using a consistent set of background songs runs counter to the idea of not using familiar music as background music, stated earlier, since your set of background songs quickly becomes familiar. However, while it's true that students come to recognize your background set as familiar, for some reason this music is treated differently than, say, instrumental versions of popular songs your students know from outside of school. You will simply have to weigh the advantages and disadvantages of using the same set of songs for your background music and make your own decision.

♪ Every group of students is different, so you always have to take the personalities of your students into account when choosing your background music. Remember that introverts tend to be more easily distracted by background music (or anything else, for that matter), while extroverts tend to enjoy it and work better when the background music is more arousing. So think about the students you work with and adjust accordingly. For a group with a majority of introverts, use background music that is closer to calming music in its characteristics. If you have a large number of extroverts, use background music that is closer to the upper (more arousing) end of the background spectrum. What if you have some of both? Well, the best you can probably do is to shoot for the middle and differentiate, if needed, for individuals (for example, if you have an extreme introvert, move him or her as far from the sound source as possible, or give him or her ear plugs or headphones to wear).

What to Avoid

If you follow the guidelines in the section above, you should have a very good experience using background music in your classroom most of the time. But there are a few dangers you will need to avoid, as well.

Again, Avoid the Genre Trap

One of our biggest challenges in talking with teachers about background music is getting past a lot of the misinformation out there. For example, many people (as a result of the out-of-control Mozart effect movement a few years back) have heard "You should use classical music for background music," or more specifically, "You should use baroque music," or even *more* specifically, "You should use Mozart music for background music." Wrong, wrong, and wrong! Classical music in general and even Mozart's music in particular are *far* too varied to be used categorically. Classical music is probably the most varied of all musical genres, from extremely slow classical funeral dirges to spritely tunes that can reach 200 beats per minute, from stately string quartet music to a thundering full orchestra. You can't just say, "Use classical music." Many teachers who have tried classical music in their classrooms have put on pieces that did not have the proper characteristics for background music, and then wondered why it didn't work for them. *Some* classical music works well for background music, *some* baroque music works well, and *some* Mozart music works well, but then so does a lot of smooth jazz, new age, and world music. It's not the *genre* that's important, but the *characteristics* of each specific piece of music.

Too Calm and Too Aroused Are Both Bad for Learning

As we've already stated, most of the time you want to use medium-paced music for your background music. Some teachers make the mistake of using calming music behind individual seatwork, and they end up with a classroom full of sleepy students. Other teachers go too far in the other direction and use music that is too arousing, and they end up with students who are hyper and can't focus. Remember to always read your students' energy level and then choose your music carefully to get them into that sweet spot of optimal arousal.

Don't Turn Over Control to Someone Else

Make sure that *you* are in full control of the music in your classroom environment. We have seen some teachers who use the radio as their source of background music. This is a very bad idea. Even if the station you use generally plays selections of music that match the guidelines for background music that we've laid down in this chapter, there will be certain songs that don't, and they will tend to be distracting. And then there are the commercials; nothing is as distracting as a voice suddenly coming out of nowhere to intrude on one's train of thought! Even if you were to use a music service like Pandora.com that is to some extent "programmable," you are left at the mercy of the site as far as what specific song is delivered to your classroom at a particular time. And never allow students to use MP3 players like iPods with earphones—unless you have created the playlist they will be listening to and can ensure that they are *only* listening to that playlist. We will go into more depth on these issues in the final chapter.

Getting Started

Find a couple of good artists who intentionally create music intended to be used as background music. For example, Gary Lamb specifically composes music in the 60 to 80 bpm range ideal for background music. On his website, you will find this statement: "Educators and other professionals discovered the tremendous benefits Gary's music had for the mind. With its ideal tempo and composition, Gary's music found its way into many classrooms and other settings where there is a high premium on relaxed alertness." We have used a lot of his music for background music, as have many other teachers we know, and we've found most of it to work very well. If you look at Gary's website (www.garylamb.com), you will see that he has a six-CD set of music called "Music for the Mind" (also sold through the website of the educational publisher Kagan at www.kaganonline.com). This set of CDs includes songs designed to create the state of relaxed alertness that we want our students in when they do their individual seatwork. It's definitely worth checking out.

Of course, as we've mentioned before, you can also start your search by browsing through certain genres at your favorite online music store. If you go to the iTunes store, for example, good genres to start with include classical, easy listening, instrumental, jazz, new age, soundtrack, and world music. Some of these genres, when you click on them, produce lists of subgenres. Again, some of these subgenres are more likely to contain good background music selections than are others. You simply have to explore a bit.

Another option is to let an online radio station such as Pandora (www.pandora.com) do the work for you. Just create a "station" using one of your favorite background songs or one of your favorite background music artists as the starting point. Pandora will then deliver to you a constant stream of similar music. Just kick back, listen, and take note of new songs and artists that fit the criteria. Before long, you will have a long list of great background music to use in your classroom.

INSIDE A CLASSROOM

Practicing Art Skills With Background Music

Chris Elvy
Grade Three Teacher (equivalent to 3rd Grade in the US)
St. Mary's Catholic School
Penzance, England

"I play background music (Mike Oldfield's 'Tubular Bells') while the children—30 seven- and eight-year olds—practice a new skill in art. Once I have made expectations clear, modeled the day's art skill, and gotten all of the resources ready, the children know that they have around 20 minutes (the time it takes for one side of the CD to play) to practice the skill taught. Once the music finishes, the children carry on, but they can then talk if they wish.

"Before I used music in my classroom, I found it difficult to get the children to concentrate on the skills being taught. They would lose focus and talk when they should be working. Since introducing music, it has helped concentration and stopped off-task chatter. In addition, the children now produce more work of a much higher quality."

Advice to Teachers: "It can work, but you have to find the right music to produce the results you want. Wrong music, no result."

Suggested Songs: "Tubular Bells," by Mike Oldfield

Our Top 40 Individual Work Background Songs

Below we list some titles and artists that we have found to work well for background music. You may not recognize many of the titles and artists. That's OK. You're looking for music that works for a very specific purpose, and that's all that counts. By the way, it's also important to realize that you don't have to *like* the music you choose for background music. It just has to *work* for learning. (Of course, it's a bonus if you like it, as well.) Also, note that several different musical genres are represented in this list. Again, genre is not what counts— it's the specific characteristics of each piece that count. That said, we strive for as much variety in these lists as possible in order to give you some leeway within which to express your own tastes.

For this chapter, you will also notice that we have made a slight modification to our usual Top 40. Since we have discussed subdividing this category into two subcategories based on task difficulty and arousal, we offer twenty selections for "Reading" and twenty selections for "Writing" below. These are pretty fine distinctions, though, and really, just about any song on this list should work for either purpose.

Reading

1. "All the Pretty Little Horses," Harry Pickens

2. "Body and Soul," Coleman Hawkins

3. "Close to Home," Bela Fleck

4. Concerto in C Major for Flute, Harp, and Orchestra, Wolfgang Amadeus Mozart

5. "Embraceable You," Miles Davis (with Charlie Parker)

6. "For All We Know," Keith Jarrett and Charlie Haden

7. "Friendship," Gary Lamb

8. "Home Again," Scott Wilkie

9. "It Never Entered My Mind," Pierrick Pedron and Mulgrew Miller

10. "Largo," from *Winter,* Antonio Vivaldi

11. "Music Box Dancer," Tim O'Neill

12. "Poem for Eva," Bill Frisell

13. "She Was Too Good to Me," Dave Peck

14. "Song for Monet," David Lanz

15. "The Secret, the Candle and Love," Andreas Vollenweider

16. "The Quiet Ambient," All India Radio

17. "The Water Is Wide," Steven Sharp Nelson

18. "Traumerei," Robert Schumann

19. "Valentine to Tagore," Deepak Chopra and Adam Plack

20. "Watermark," Enya

Writing

1. "Angela (Theme from *Taxi*)," Bob James

2. "Autumn Sky," Lao Tizer

3. "Celestial Soda Pop," Ray Lynch

4. "Crazy Love," Peter White

5. "Emma's Song," Rick Braun

6. "Ethno-Dimensions," R. Carlos Nakai

7. Fireworks Music, "Bourre," George Frideric Handel

8. "Harlem Nocturne," Kofi

9. "His Name," Joe McBride

10. "HoppIpolla," Vitamin String Quartet

11. "Hymn," Liz Story

12. "I'm Confessin,'" Lester Young

13. "Maui-Waui," Chuck Mangione

14. "Movin' On," Earl Klugh

15. Orchestral Suite No. 3 in D Major, BWV 1068: *Air*, Johann Sebastian Bach

16. "Share My Tears," Jackiem Joyner

17. "Spring Vibes," Echophlekz

18. "Terrible Thing," Booker T. and the MGs

19. "Whistle," All India Radio

20. "Your Story," Gil Goldstein and Bob Mintzer

The selections listed here should get you off to a good start. And don't forget the larger list in Appendix D, as well as more selections on our website, www.rockandrollclassroom.com.

Notes

1. Martin, Wogalter, and Forlano (1988) compared the effects of background speech and music while subjects completed a reading comprehension task. They found that when speech was present in the background (as you often find in a "quiet"

classroom setting where students sometimes whisper to each other, or where talking in the hallway or the classroom next door can be heard), it was much more disruptive to reading comprehension than was background music (382–298). Cassidy and MacDonald (2007) compared the impact of high-arousal music, low-arousal music, "everyday" noise, and silence on subjects taking cognitive tests. They found that performance was best in silence (which, as we've pointed out, is not really an option in a real classroom), but they also discovered that low-arousal music (like we recommend for background music in this chapter) led to better scores than either high-arousal music or everyday noise (517–537). The findings of Jancke and Sandmann (2010) are also interesting in light of the present discussion. They compared results on a verbal learning task under four music conditions and one "noise" condition and found no advantage of music as compared with noise, but their noise group completed the task with "brown noise" in the background, not "everyday noise," as was used by Cassidy and MacDonald (2007) (1–14). Brown noise (similar to white noise but at a lower frequency) is a much more steady-state, artificially produced noise condition to which the brain appears to more easily habituate than irregular, everyday noises, so it appears not to be as distracting.

2. Stekelenburg and Van Boxtel (2002) measured subjects' physiological responses during a reading task when unexpected sounds were presented. Subjects demonstrated orienting responses, including eye movements toward the sound source, heart rate deceleration, and respiratory and skin conductance changes. However, when the researchers presented the sounds repeatedly, subjects habituated to the sound (707–722).

3. Two areas, one in the parietal lobe and one in the superior part of the frontal lobe, are responsible for focused attention, while two other areas are responsible for stimulus-driven attention—one at the border between the parietal lobe and the temporal lobe and the other a little farther down the frontal lobe than the frontal area used for focused attention. For an in-depth explanation of the different types of attention, see Klingberg (2009), Chapter 2.

4. Sanders and Barron (1975) conducted two studies to assess how distraction impacted performance. They found that distraction (in the form of environmental sights and sounds

not directly tied to the task) raised arousal levels and impaired performance on complex tasks, but that the raised level of arousal ("drivelike effects," to use their terminology) actually raised performance on simple tasks (956–963). Oldham, Cummings, Mischel, Schmidtke, and Zhou (1995) measured the performance of office workers who either were allowed to listen to music on headphones for four weeks while they worked (experimental group) or were not allowed to listen to music (control group) (547–564). It must be pointed out that the music the experimental group listened to was self-selected music, which better fits our definition of feel-good music than background music. Nevertheless, those workers doing simple jobs dramatically increased their job performance when listening to music. This outcome could be explained variously as a result of raised mood, relaxation, or raised arousal. Those workers holding more complex jobs, however, suffered performance declines when listening to music, which indicates that the arousal-inducing qualities of the music interacted negatively with task difficulty (547–564). And it appears that most people are pretty good judges of whether their present level of arousal is a good match for the task they are working on. In a study conducted by Arkes, Rettig, and Scougale (1986), it was found that subjects performing an easy sensorimotor task preferred to have complex music in the background, while subjects performing a difficult sensorimotor task preferred more simple music in the background (51–60).

5. Davenport (1974) had subjects perform a continuous visual vigilance task under one of four background music conditions: (1) continuous music, (2) music with a fixed-interval schedule (regular on-off cycle), (3) music with a variable temporal schedule, and (4) music with a random temporal schedule. Subjects performed best in the most disruptive, arousing condition—the random schedule—and worst under the schedules easiest to habituate to—continuous music and the fixed interval schedule (51–59). Corhan and Gounard (1976) replicated Davenport's findings concerning schedules of background stimulation and added another element: musical genre. They found that subjects performed better on a visual vigilance task with more arousing music (rock music) in the background than with less arousing music (typical background-type instrumental music) (662). Fontaine and

Schwalm (1979) added yet another element to the discussion: familiarity. They found that familiar music was more arousing (and thus better at maintaining the level of arousal needed for a vigilance task) than was less familiar music (71–74). Thus, all of the arousing, distracting elements that we usually try to limit in a typical background music situation become our allies when the goal is to maintain high arousal and vigilance for an extended period of time.

6. Furnham and Allass (1999) had introverts and extroverts complete reading comprehension, observation, and memory tasks in the presence of either complex or simple musical distraction. They found that, as musical distraction went up, extroverts' scores went up, while introverts' scores went down (27–38). Belojevic, Slepcevic, and Jakovljevic (2001) had subjects perform a mental arithmetic task under quiet and noisy conditions (recorded traffic noise). Extroverts performed significantly faster in noise, while introverts reported concentration problems and fatigue (209–213). Furnham and Strbac (2002) had subjects carry out three tasks—reading comprehension, prose recall, and mental arithmetic—with background noise (either background "garage music" or office noise) and found that extroverts performed better with noise than did introverts on all three tasks (203–217). Ylias and Heaven (2003) had introverts and extroverts take a reading comprehension test either in silence or with noise from television in the background. They found that extroverts performed better than introverts in the background noise condition (1069–1079).

7. Abikoff, Courtney, Szeibel, and Koplewicz (1996) had boys with ADHD and boys without ADHD complete an arithmetic task under three conditions: (1) silence, (2) with speech in the background (considered a low-stimulation condition), and (3) with background music (considered a high-stimulation condition). They found that, while the non-ADHD students performed equally well in all three conditions, the boys with ADHD performed significantly better in the high-stimulation (music) condition (238–246). Soderlund, Sikstrom, and Smart (2007) had subjects (with and without ADHD) complete a variety of cognitive and memory tasks either in silence or with distracting white noise in the background. The "normal"

subjects performed worse in the noise condition, while the ADHD subjects performed better (840–847). These and similar studies suggest that, for optimal arousal and performance, students with ADHD need a higher level of arousal.

8. Blood and Ferriss (1993) had subjects hold conversations with either minor mode or major mode music in the background. Subjects were asked to evaluate their satisfaction with their conversations using the Interpersonal Communication Satisfaction Inventory. Subjects consistently rated their conversations with major-mode background music as more satisfying than those with minor-mode music (171–177).

9. Mayfield and Moss (1989) evaluated the effect of music tempo on task performance by having subjects calculate stock prices while listening to fast-paced music, slow-paced music, or no music. Women performed better than men, and performance overall was significantly higher in the fast-paced music condition than the slow-paced music condition, even though subjects reported feeling more distracted with the fast-paced music (1283–1290). Kallinen (2002) had subjects read news stories (on a pocket computer) in a crowded cafeteria setting. They read with no music, slow music, or fast music in the background. Reading rate was significantly lower in the slow-music condition (537–551). Potter and Choi (2006) had subjects listen to eight different radio messages with differing levels of complexity. Results showed that the more complex messages led to higher self-reported levels of arousal and better attitudes toward the messages (395–419). Day, Lin, Huang, and Chuang (2009) had subjects complete a decision-making task with background music of varying tempos. Subjects made more accurate decisions with faster background music than with slower background music (130–143).

10. A number of studies over the years have found that background music, when it is too stimulating, leads to distraction and lower performance. Wakshlag, Reitz, and Zillmann (1982) studied the effects of background music on educational television programs. They found that programs with fast, appealing (more arousing) background music were viewed considerably longer than those with slower, less arousing music. Unfortunately, they also found that subjects paid less attention to the content of the shows and learned less when the music was more stimulating (666–677). Several studies

have looked into the effects of stimulating music on driving performance. North and Hargreaves (1999b) found that subjects engaged in a computer racing simulation had slower lap times when listening to arousing music. The hypothesis is that the music distracts from attention to driving, and thus from performance (285–292). Brodsky (2001) found that simulated driving performance suffered when listening to stimulating music, leading to more reckless driving and more virtual traffic violations (219–241). Many studies in educational settings have also shown detrimental effects of more arousing music, as compared with slower, less-stimulating music. Smith and Morris (1977) found that stimulating music, in comparison with calming music, increased worry scores and interfered with concentration (1047–1053). Kiger (1989) examined the effects of low information-load background music (less attention-getting structural features) versus high information-load music (more structural complexity, thus more arousing) and found that subjects performed better with low information-load music (531–534). Hallam, Price, and Katsarou (2002) found not only that ten- to twelve-year-old students had their performance on a memory task disrupted by highly arousing music, but that they demonstrated a lowered level of altruistic behavior after listening to the arousing music, as well (111–122). Cassidy and MacDonald (2007) reported lower performance on a variety of cognitive tasks when high-arousal music was played in the background (517–537).

11. In studies where "irrelevant speech" in the environment was one of the experimental conditions, it has consistently been found to be detrimental to cognitive performance. Boyle (1996) found that irrelevant speech reduced recall of word lists on a memory task (398–416), while Banbury and Berry (1998) found that office noise with speech was more detrimental to memory and mental arithmetic tasks than was office noise without speech (499–517). And the speech doesn't even have to be coming from a live human to be disruptive, as numerous studies have shown that background speech coming from television is also detrimental to performance. For example, Armstrong and Sopory (1997) found that background television had negative effects on working memory (459–480). This distracting quality of environmental speech is one of the main reasons for using background music in the first place—to cover up such speech in the environment. But what about

speech that is *embedded* in a song (that is, lyrics)? A multitude of studies have shown that music with lyrics is distracting and causes decreases in performance. Anderson and Fuller (2010) tested the reading comprehension of seventh- and eighth-grade students under two conditions: in silence and with popular (lyrical) music playing in the background. The music with lyrics had "a pronounced detrimental effect" on reading scores compared with silence (178–187). Perham and Vizard (2011) had students attempt a memory task while in the presence of vocal music that they either liked or disliked. The results showed that (again, in comparison with results obtained in silence) whether the music was liked or not didn't really matter—both types of vocal music had a negative impact on performance (625–631). But as we've pointed out, a "silent" condition is really not realistic in a school setting, so what about studies that compare task performance with instrumental background music versus performance with vocal background music? Alley and Greene (2008) found that performance on a working memory task was negatively affected by both speech and vocal music. Performance with instrumental background music was significantly better than with vocal music and varied little from results obtained in silence (277–289). And having lyrics in the background has detrimental effects on performance, no matter the musical genre. Mulliken and Henk (1985) found that reading comprehension was much better with classical instrumental music in the background than it was with rock music in the background, (353–358), and Chou and Tze (2010) found the same effect when comparing instrumental classical music with hip-hop music (36–46).

12. Jones, Miles, and Page (1990) found that recall of information in visual lists was impaired by the presence of *any* speech-like sound in the environment, including reversed speech and speech in an unfamiliar language (89–108).

13. Pring and Walker (1994) found that, when they played instrumental versions of known songs (in this case, nursery rhymes), the background music was highly distracting and significantly impaired verbal processing and working memory (165).

14. Madsen (1997) had experienced musicians listen to a twenty-minute passage from Puccini's *La Boheme* and respond, using a digital interface, to five different musical elements: melody,

rhythm, timbre, dynamics, and "everything." The researchers found that, of the five elements, changes in dynamics (volume) were the most attention-getting (80–89).

15. Hall (1952) had two hundred seventy-eight eighth- and ninth-grade students take a reading comprehension test in a normal classroom testing environment either with or without background music. Those testing with the background music outscored those testing in "normal" testing conditions (without music). In addition, boys benefitted more than girls and struggling students benefited more than "regular" students (a result seen in many studies since). Eighty-three percent of the students, when asked, requested that background music be made a regular feature during testing, so the vast majority of students clearly liked having the music on. Interestingly, however, 37% of the students thought the music should be of another type, and these students improved only one-quarter as much as those who liked the music used, so clearly it would be good to use background music that your students enjoy, whenever possible (451–458). Phillips (2004) had college-age students complete a complex problem-solving task via computer with another (anonymous) student in a computer-lab setting. Students wore headphones and either completed the work with no music, or they listened to either classical background music or popular punk music. Those subjects who heard the classical music outscored those completing the task with no music or with punk music playing through the headphones (1–4). And it's not just academic performance that is positively affected by background music. LaCasse (2010) conducted an action research study where she observed second-grade students' behavior while they worked either in typical "quiet" (no music) classroom conditions or with nonlyrical classical and new age piano and string music playing in the background. The results showed that student behavior improved by 40% when background music was played. LaCasse observed students for fifteen to twenty minutes a day during independent work time, for a total of three weeks in the no music condition and three more weeks in the background music condition. She observed 157 examples of negative and off-task behavior during the no music period and only 119 incidences of negative and off-task behavior with the background music playing.

6

Come Together (Over Music)

Using Background Music to Facilitate Group Activities

There is nothing more difficult than talking without music.

—Camille Saint-Saëns

What It Is

This chapter examines a subcategory of background music: using music behind small group work. As we've discussed, the goal when using music behind individual seatwork is to use music that doesn't call attention to itself to cover up possibly distracting sounds in the environment. That takes a very specific type of music (60 to 80 bpm, instrumental, unfamiliar, repetitive, and simple in instrumentation) that acts somewhat like white noise. However, the goals for using background music behind small group work are a bit different, requiring a different type of music.

Let's look at the characteristics of group work. Clearly, the broad term *group work* covers a lot of situations. Students may be standing or seated; they may be working in pairs or trios or larger groups; they may be working together on an ad hoc basis or in long-standing teams; and they may be doing something as simple as a think-pair-share or group brainstorming, or as complex as a long-term, multistep project. But whatever the specific demands of the group task, you will have far more movement and noise in the room than during individual seatwork, and this means an even greater chance for distraction from the task. Nevertheless, even in such challenging conditions, the right kind of background music, used the right way, can make student interaction more effective and increase learning.

The teacher has two goals when using music in these situations: *Management* and *Energy*.

♪ **Management**—We want to put up a "wall of sound" between groups so that group members can hear each other as they talk but have difficulty hearing what is being said in other groups. Why would this be an issue? Well, have you ever had group work taking place (in a classroom without music playing) and you heard a member of one group say, "Hey, they just said _____ over there. Write that down"? Of course you have!

These situations are frustrating for teachers because they are detrimental to everyone getting his or her own work done (rather than "stealing" ideas or answers from another group). If students are listening in on the discussions of other groups, they are not doing their own thinking. Music allows a teacher to manage such situations by putting just enough sound into the environment to make it possible for students to hear their own group members—and *only* their own group members— which allows (OK, maybe we should say *forces*) students to do their own work.

♪ **Energy**—We also want to inject a little energy into the learning environment. Yes, we know that there are times when there is a little bit *too much* energy in the room (we'll talk about that later), but in the vast majority of classrooms, the opposite is the general rule—not enough inspiration, not enough attention, not enough motivation, and not enough energy devoted to the learning task. There are many reasons for this, of course, and we can't go into all of them here. But adding some mildly energizing music into the environment behind small group work often helps to lift the level of energy students bring to the task and makes them more willing to interact.[1] If that same music also filters out distractions and helps them to better focus on the task at hand, it's all good!

Why It Works

We teachers like to think that, when we are "on stage"—lecturing, or leading discussions—that students are doing a lot of learning. But the research on memory shows that our students don't actually do most of their learning while they are receiving input from us. Rather, the real learning takes place when students are given the opportunity to *process* the material themselves in some way. These processing activities might include individual tasks such as writing about the material, or summarizing it, or putting the material into some other form such as a graphic organizer. But we might also ask our students to do their processing with another student in a think-pair-share, or with an ad hoc group pulled together to discuss the material, or with a long-standing group using a cooperative learning structure. Whenever students work together to do the processing, it is important that we do whatever we can to make that processing as effective as possible. And one powerful tool we can use to make these group processing situations worthwhile is—you guessed it, music!

INSIDE A CLASSROOM

Music Makes Group Work a Powerful Learning Tool

Bo Power
8th Grade Teacher
Wesley College
Perth, Australia

"I use a playlist on my iTunes account titled 'group work' that has a rather neutral feel to it. After I have frontloaded the task for the students, I turn on the music. If I want to grab the students' attention after they have started on the activity, I raise the volume for a moment and then pause the music. The students shift from group work to focus on me with relative ease.

"Before I used music in my classroom, the students' group discussions were limited. One of two things usually happened: (1) one loud and vivacious group would dominate the room, or (2) students were afraid to talk, so the silence threatened any emerging creative thoughts. In the first instance, I would often see students in the quiet groups looking wistfully over to the group having fun, while the energy in their own group withered and died, taking with it any chance for constructive conversation.

"At times, we teachers questioned the benefits of using group discussions, as we were seeing only limited educational value from them. Since introducing music behind our small group work, though, we are now witnessing a higher level of interaction and conversation between group members. The music softens the room and creates a private space for the small groups to work independent from the noise clutter and interjections of surrounding groups. It has allowed us to use small group work as a powerful learning tool."

Suggested Songs: "Take Five," by Dave Brubeck; "Memphis" by Lonnie Mack

---

The Battle of Attention Systems, Part Two

Remember our discussion in the previous chapter of stimulus-driven and focused attention? We framed the interaction between these two systems as a kind of battle. Teachers ask their students to pay focused attention to a particular task and try to set up classroom conditions such that students are able to maintain that focus. Meanwhile, any change in environmental conditions, including unplanned sounds, calls out to students' stimulus-driven attention systems and threatens to pull them away from the task at hand. We talked in the last chapter about how teachers can use background music to cover these distracting sounds so students are not disturbed when they are engaged in an individual task like reading or writing.

In this chapter, we are looking at situations that differ in some of the particulars—group tasks instead of individual, more movement and more noise in the environment—and yet, the battle between the two attentional systems remains the primary dynamic.

For example, one of the main enemies of focused attention is human speech in the learning environment.[2] When students are engaged in group work, there is going to be a great deal more speech in the air than when they are reading or writing individually. So, it is a very challenging task for students to focus on and process the speech in their own groups while simultaneously tuning out all of the other speech in the room—especially the speech of the groups closest to them, or the groups that are loudest.

But we have an ally in this battle for focused attention: something called *habituation*. Habituation is the process whereby the brain, when repeatedly exposed to a stimulus, gradually decreases its response to that stimulus. Your students will find it hard to habituate to the speech produced by all of the conversations in the room, because (1) speech is one of the most distracting types of stimuli (because we naturally want to hear and make sense of it) and (2) because the content of that speech is always changing, and change is always attention-getting. However, they will readily habituate to music (at least the right kind of music).[3]

It might seem strange to think that adding *more* sound to what is probably already a rather noisy environment could help students concentrate on their own group's work, but that is actually what happens when you use the right kind of background music played at the right volume. First, if the music is played at the proper volume, a lot of the speech in the environment will be covered and will thus not attract students' stimulus-driven attention systems. And if that music has the proper characteristics (which we will go over in a moment), your students' brains will habituate to it, and in effect tune it out. So, paradoxically, by adding more sound (of the right kind) to the classroom, you allow your students to bring better focus to the task.

INSIDE A CLASSROOM

Music to Buffer Discussions

Jenn Currie
6th Grade Language Arts Teacher
Commodore Perry School District
Hadley, Pennsylvania, USA

"In my classroom, students work in pairs/groups often, so to help groups focus on what they are working on, and not what the other groups may be discussing, I use music in the background to buffer the conversations. Once I get the groups going on their assignments, I set soft comforting music in the background.

"Prior to using background music, I had students who were always in other groups' 'business' because it was easy to hear the discussions. Now that I'm using the music, it definitely buffers the conversations and keeps everyone on track and focused."

Advice to Teachers: "Keep the background music at a lower volume setting, as the conversations will rise to the level of the music. Louder music makes the students talk louder."

Suggested Songs: "Salsa Kenny" by Kenny G; "Little Brown Jug" by Glenn Miller Orchestra.

Characteristics of Background Music to Use Behind Group Work

So, what kind of music works best behind small group work? There are a number of similarities between this list and the one in the previous chapter, but you will also note some important differences:

♪ **Tempo**: The best tempo for background music behind small group work is generally between 80 and 100 bpm (a little faster than background music for individual tasks). In other words, we need to look for music that is slightly above the resting human heart rate so it creates a mild upward entrainment effect. This means that some small amount of adrenaline is being released into students' bloodstreams, and a slight uptick in energy will result, which is usually one of our goals in situations where we want students to interact with each other.

♪ **More Elaborate Instrumentation, More Noticeable Beat**: While a faster tempo and more elaborate instrumentation don't *always* go together, most of the time you will find that there is a correspondence. We have also found that more instrumentation and a more noticeable beat, like the faster tempo, help to add energy to the activity. If you've ever walked into a room where a live band is playing an up-tempo song, you know what we mean. It's hard to stay apathetic in such an environment; you just want to move!

♪ **Instrumental *Only***: As we explained in the last chapter, it is very important not to interject words into the environment when students are inputting (reading or listening) or generating (writing or speaking) words. Doing so will only make it harder for students to concentrate on the task at hand.[4]

♪ **Unfamiliar Tunes**: Again, the goal is to keep students' focus on their work, and any tune that is familiar will call attention to itself and pull attention away from the work. Instrumental versions of known popular songs should be avoided as well, as students who know the lyrics might be tempted to supply them either by singing them out loud or by running the lyrics through their minds as they listen, and either eventuality would lead to less attention to the academic task and poorer performance.

♪ **Major Mode**: While the mode of the music has no effect on whether or not it effectively covers distractions (volume is the key there), research has shown that music in the major mode improves mood and increases productivity (apparently due to the improved mood).[5] And since we definitely want our students to be in a good mood when working with others, why not make sure that the background music we choose for this purpose does both jobs at once?

♪ **Medium Volume**: How loud the music needs to be is determined by the task at hand and how much student-generated sound has to be covered. The farther student groups are from each other physically, the lower the volume can be. If they are seated or standing very close to other groups, the volume will have to be a bit higher. The only way to know if you have the volume right is to watch students as they work. If they can't hear their own groups talking, the volume is too high. If they can tell what nearby groups are saying, the volume is too low. As with all of the different uses for music, the key is kid-watching. Keep your goal in mind and observe what's going on; then adjust accordingly.

How to Use It

Newer Material, Harder Tasks

In the last chapter, we pointed out that when the task was less challenging, a medium-to-high arousal level was best for optimal performance,[6] but that when the task was more challenging, higher levels of arousal caused performance to drop off dramatically.[7] It is very important for teachers to keep this fact in mind when choosing music to play behind small group work.

In our list of characteristics of good small group background music above, we gave you some general guidelines: 80 to 100 beats per minute (bpm), more elaborate instrumentation (than individual background music), more noticeable beat (than individual background music), and medium volume, for example. And that list is a good starting place. But when we factor in the difficulty level of the task, we need to do some fine-tuning to those characteristics.

But before we do so, it might be helpful for you to think of this category of music as a *continuum* rather than a static list of characteristics. If you visualize this continuum (like a timeline), at the lower-arousal end you would find music that is closer to 80 bpm, that has a little less instrumentation and a little less noticeable beat when compared with the other end of the continuum (but still more than the background music for individual work discussed in the last chapter), and that is played a little more softly whenever possible. At the higher-arousal end of the continuum, the music would be closer to 100 bpm, with more instrumentation and more of a beat, and it would be played louder (but not so loud that it would interfere with student interactions).

Now, with this continuum in mind, it becomes easier to make good choices about what songs to use behind small group work in any particular situation. For example, when the task is more challenging, you might want to select music at the lower-arousal end of the continuum in order to make sure that students aren't too aroused to focus and do the work. What would make a task more challenging? For one thing, the newer the material is, the more difficult the processing of that material will be. For example, it is more difficult for a group to discuss a brand new topic (sprung on them cold, so to speak) than it is to discuss everyone's opinions about a topic after the teacher has already given some background information about it.

And of course, some tasks are just more difficult than others. For example, complex problem solving or critical thinking about a complex issue is a much more challenging task than brainstorming or reviewing a topic previously covered. So, our recommendation is that when the material is new or complex, you choose music that is closer to the lower-arousal end of the continuum, at 80 to 90 bpm, with less instrumentation and less of a beat, and that you play it at medium-low volume (or as low as you can get away with and still keep groups from eavesdropping on or interacting with other groups). Doing so will keep your groups from becoming too aroused to do good work.

Older Material, Easier Tasks

On the other hand, when the task you give your groups is less challenging, as in working with easier material or working with older material (doing a review activity), you can select music that is closer to the higher-arousal end of the continuum. Remember that the research on the interaction between arousal and task difficulty shows that for easier tasks, performance rises with higher levels of arousal. It's as if people need a little extra jolt of energy to do their best work when the task itself is repetitive or not that challenging (and especially if they think of the task as boring). In such situations, we recommend that you use music in the 90 to 100 bpm range, with more instrumentation and more of a beat (maybe even a little funky), and that you play the music a little louder (medium-loud) in order to add a little more energy to the activity (as long as you don't get it so loud that students are distracted by it). You might also find yourself enjoying the opportunity to have a little of this type of music in your classroom environment from time to time, as most people tend to enjoy music more when it is a little more upbeat. Hey, there's no law against teachers enjoying the music they use in their classrooms, right?

INSIDE A CLASSROOM

Steel Drums and Vocabulary Bingo

Maureen Stolte
Special Education Reading Teacher, Grades 6–8
Brandon Middle School
Virginia Beach, Virginia, USA

"In my special education reading intervention classroom, students play Bingo with Dolch list sight words or vocabulary words from the selections that they are reading in class. When the class plays Bingo, I play Caribbean steel drum music in the background because it is lighthearted, fun to listen to, and does not have any words that could confuse the students when they are trying to focus on finding a sight word or looking for the word that fits the definition that was read.

"Before I used music combined with Bingo in my classroom, students completed skill building worksheets, and they viewed sight word or vocabulary building as boring. After creating educational bingo cards and accenting our game time with the backdrop of steel pan music, Dolch List Bingo and Vocabulary Bingo have become so popular that students ask to play them! The music really spices up an essential learning activity for the struggling readers in my reading intervention classroom."

Advice to Teachers: "Music is a tool that can be used to turn a skill building activity into a special event. The jubilant setting that the music creates can ease the tension when students work on a task that is frustrating and difficult."

Suggested Songs: Anything by the Trinidad Steel Combo

Guidelines for Using Background Music Behind Group Work

♪ When you ask students to move from their seats to another location for a pair or small group activity, you can use music to achieve multiple goals. Here's the typical sequence: (1) ask students to stand and give them directions for how and where to move and for what to take with them (*don't* tell them anything about the activity they will be doing just yet); (2) then give them a signal to move (a command such as "Go," for example, or you could just say, "When the music starts . . .") and turn on the music; (3) depending on your students' current state and your goals, the traveling music you select could be calming music (if your students are a bit wild), or pump-up music (if they are lethargic and you want to speed them up), or feel-good music (if you just want to create or maintain a good emotional climate); (4) when students arrive at their new work spots, cut the music and get them settled in; (5) give directions for the activity (you don't want to give these directions before they move, as many students will forget them between the time you give them and the time they get settled into their new locations); (6) turn on the appropriate background music you want to play behind the small group work; (7) when the work is done, cut the background music and have students return to their original seats while you play traveling music (again, it can be calming, pump-up, or feel-good).

As discussed in the previous chapter, it is also important to consider the personality types in your classroom. If you have, by and large, an extroverted group, you might want to shift all of our recommendations in this chapter a little farther to the right (the higher-arousal end of the spectrum). That is, a group of extroverts might prefer and do better work if the background music is closer to 100 bpm on average, or even in the 100 to 120 bpm range with easier tasks, while a very introverted group may do their best work if you keep the music you use behind group work around the 80 bpm level, even for easier tasks.[8]

In addition to personality types, you need to consider the current energy level in the room. Let's say you plan to start class with some group work, and your students have just entered the room after recess or a school assembly and are all hyped up. In this situation, you might want to shift your background music more toward the lower-arousal end of the continuum to simultaneously cover distractions and calm the students down a bit—or at least not add to their energy level. On the other hand, if it's a cloudy Monday morning and your students are dragging around the room, you might want to use more arousing background music to add some energy to the room.

What to Avoid

We've already mentioned the three most common issues when implementing music behind group work, but we feel that these issues are so important that we must repeat ourselves here to make sure no one makes any of these mistakes (sorry). So, here they are, straight from the Office of Redundancy Department.

Avoid Songs With Lyrics

We've explained a number of times why interjecting words into the learning environment (whether ordinary off-topic speech or lyrics embedded in songs) leads to poorer academic performance, and we have referred to a good deal of research that proves the point. However, many teachers persist in playing vocal music behind group work. We're not really sure why this is the case; perhaps they feel their students will enjoy the activity more and be more engaged if some of their favorite popular music is playing in the background while they work. Well, they probably *will* enjoy the activity more, but are they enjoying the learning activity, or just enjoying the music? And enjoyment isn't the main goal. The main goal is to maximize the *learning* from the activity. Since music with lyrics will almost certainly be detrimental to cognitive performance (*especially* if the students are familiar with and like the music), whatever benefit you gain from enhanced mood is lost through spotty focus and less effective processing. There are many opportunities during the day to use fun, popular tunes as feel-good music, but using them behind group work is not the time.

Think "Goldilocks" When Adjusting Volume

We've already covered this topic in some depth, but it definitely bears repeating: perhaps the most important aspect of using music behind group work is getting the volume *just right*. And since a number of factors are involved with any group activity—how many students are in the room (and therefore how much talk will have to be covered), how close or far apart the students are, the introvert/extrovert mix—the only way to be sure you have it right is to *watch your students* as they get started on the activity. If you see groups asking their partners to repeat themselves because they can't hear them, or if you see them having to lean in right next to a group member in order to hear, you have the music too loud. If you notice that students are responding to comments made by members of other groups, you know that you have the volume too low (they shouldn't have been able to hear the other group's comments). It's just common sense. Observe and adjust.

Getting the Arousal Level Just Right

Again, we've talked a great deal about arousal in the previous chapters, as well as in this one. You know by now that, in most learning situations, you should be shooting for a state of moderate arousal. On the other hand, the "just right" level of arousal depends on a number of factors, especially task difficulty—for less challenging tasks, you need to amp up the arousal level so your students have the energy to stay engaged; and for more challenging tasks, you need to tone it down a bit so students can focus. Now that you know this information, you can make a pretty good guess about what musical selections would be best to play behind group work in any particular situation.

Always have a backup choice in mind, because every so often, you will find that your initial song choice (the one you put in the lesson plan) is not going to work. Perhaps your students are all atwitter over some event taking place at your school or in the community, and you hadn't anticipated this. That high-arousal song you had planned may now be too much for the situation, as students are already aroused. Or perhaps your students are down in the dumps because a planned field trip had to be cancelled due to inclement weather. All of a sudden, that moderate-arousal background song is not likely to be enough to get your students into the proper learning state. For situations like these, you must have a Plan B— some alternate music choices that you can substitute when you need to. So make a good Plan A but stay flexible and always shoot for "just right"—make Goldilocks proud!

Getting Started

Finding music for this category can be a bit challenging. Whereas it's pretty easy to find collections of music marketed as relaxation music (calming) or music for productivity or focus (background) or energizing (pump-up), the type of music we recommend in this chapter hasn't really been established as a niche in its own right; therefore, you're not likely to find collections already pulled together for you that neatly fit the criteria laid out here. So our getting-started recommendations are going to be a bit more limited.

One way to go, as always, is the browsing approach. You can start with a few likely genres, and using your favorite music service, you can follow the trail to find some good selections. Of course, to follow a trail, you need a starting point. If you use the iTunes Music Store, you might want to start with the following genres: classical, electronic, instrumental, jazz (the more up-tempo, more arousing subgenres such as big band, Dixieland, Latin jazz, or ragtime), and world. Listen to the snippets it provides and count the beats for thirty seconds and double the result. If a selection falls into the 80 to 100 bpm range, and all of the other characteristics of the tune are to your liking, download it and add it to your list. Once you've downloaded a few good group-background songs into your music library, use the iTunes sidebar recommendations to look for more music with similar qualities.

Another approach would be to use an online radio site to generate likely selections for you to listen to. If you use Pandora, for example, you can take one of the artists or one of the specific songs we recommend in our Top 40 below and have Pandora build a "station" around that artist or song. The station will select other songs and artists whose music has similar characteristics. You can listen and determine which songs and artists would work for your classroom. Spending just a little time going through this process will allow you to quickly build a great list of music to use behind your students' group activities.

Also, in addition to our Top 40, take a look at our expanded list in Appendix E. You will notice that in both the Top 40 list below and in the Appendix, we have subdivided the selections into "New Material, Harder Tasks" (lower arousal) and "Older Material, Easier Tasks" (higher arousal) categories, in case you want to really fine-tune your search. And don't forget to check out our website, www.rockand rollclassroom.com, for even more selections.

Our Top 40 Group Work Background Songs

Since we talked earlier about subdividing this category based on task difficulty, we offer twenty selections from each subcategory below. As usual, we have included a variety of genres so you can see some of the possibilities open to you.

Newer Material, Harder Tasks:

1. "Blues for Alican," Joe Pass

2. "Boom Boom," Jeff Golub

3. "Café Bohemio," Steven Katz

4. Concerto No. 1 in G Minor: Allegro, Johann Sebastian Bach

5. "Here Comes the Night," 3rd Force

6. "Hop," Viktor Krauss

7. "Last Train Home," Pat Metheny Group

8. "Mas Que Nada," Marc Antoine

9. "Mirembe," Samite

10. "Red Baron," David Benoit

11. "Shine On," ATB

12. "Sneakin' Around," Chet Atkins and Jerry Reed

13. "Sunspot," Moby

14. "Take the 'A' Train," Duke Ellington

15. "The Way I Feel Tonight," Jeff Golub

16. "Tribal Runner," Craig Chaquico and Russ Freeman

17. "Twin Guitar Special," Cindy Cashdollar

18. "Under the Sea," Digby Jones

19. "Use Me," Rick Braun

20. "You Gotta Be Real," 3rd Force

Older Material, Easier Tasks:

1. "Back Against the Wall," Euphoria

2. "Boogie Woogie Stomp," from *The Majestic*, Jim Cox

3. Concerto No. 2 in F Major, George Frideric Handel

4. "Confluence," Doug Smith and Mark Hanson

5. "Golden Soul," Lao Tizer

6. "Hayseed Strut," Cash Box Kings

7. "Hello Betty," Jeff Golub

8. "Hi-Heel Sneakers," Urban Knights

9. "In the Full Moon Light," 3rd Force

10. "Memphis," Lonnie Mack

11. "RNR," Richard Elliot and Rick Braun

12. "Rough Cut," Roger Smith

13. "She Breaks," Booker T.

14. "Spontaneous Combustion," Fishbelly Black

15. "State of Grace," Jeff Lorber

16. "The Cat," Jimmy Smith

17. "The Zodiac (2006 Digital Remaster)," Down to the Bone

18. "Together Again," Dave Koz

19. "Tuff Love," Galactic

20. "Wipeout," The Incredible Bongo Band

That should be enough to get you started. Check these out and start creating your own playlists of songs to use behind small group work. Once you get the hang of it, you will be amazed at how this simple tool helps you to keep students focused on task and raises engagement at the same time.

Notes

1. Dube, Chebat, and Morin (1995) tested the effects of background music on interactions between consumers and tellers in a banking setting. They found that people were much more likely to affiliate with bank personnel when there was pleasurable, arousing background music in the environment (305–319). Blood and Ferriss (1993) found that people rated their conversations with others as more satisfying with background music in the environment, especially when the music was in the major mode (171–177). Devlin and Sawatzky (1987) examined the effect of background music on the amount and quality of client/counselor interactions and found that clients talked more about their issues, and more in depth, with background music as opposed to silence (125–132). Overall, there is a good deal of evidence that having music in the environment makes most people more willing to talk and tends to make these interactions more pleasurable.

2. Martin, Wogalter, and Forlano (1988) found that background speech was much more disruptive than background music to subjects completing a reading comprehension task (382–398). Banbury and Berry (1998) examined the effect of background noise (without speech) and noise that included speech on the performance of office workers. They found that both prose and mental arithmetic tasks were more disrupted when speech was present in the background environment (499–517). Cassidy and MacDonald (2007) found that "everyday noise" was more disruptive to cognitive performance than background music— and that introverts were especially sensitive to noise in the environment (517–537).

3. Stekelenburg and Van Boxtel (2002) found that subjects in their study oriented toward irregular sounds in the environment during a reading task, but that subjects habituated to the stimulus when it was repeatedly presented (707–722).

4. Anderson and Fuller (2010) gave students a reading test under one of two conditions: a quiet room or a room in which lyrical music (*Billboard Magazine*'s top hit singles) was playing. They found that the vocal music had "a pronounced detrimental effect on comprehension," especially for students who claimed a preference for listening to music while studying (178–187). Alley and Greene (2008) found that college students performing a working memory task were as distracted by vocal music as they were by speech in the environment (277–289).

5. Blood and Ferriss (1993) found, not only that people engaged in conversation rated their satisfaction with the interactions more favorably when there was music in the environment, but also that, when the background music was in the major mode, productivity increased (171–177).

6. Mayfield and Moss (1989) found that college business students performed simple stock price calculations better with fast-paced (more arousing) music in the background, even though they reported feeling more distracted in this condition (1283–1290). Kallinen (2002) found that adults read business news more quickly and efficiently in a crowded cafeteria setting when fast-paced music was playing (537–551).

7. Smith and Morris (1977) found that college psychology majors reported more test anxiety and poorer ability to concentrate with stimulating music in the background (though the music used more closely resembled pump-up music than our definition of background music in this chapter) (1047–1053). Kiger (1989) examined the effect of background music on the reading comprehension of high school sophomores. He found that high information-load music (stimulating music) caused a decrease in performance compared with low information-load (background) music (531–534). Hallam, Price, and Katsarou (2002) found that the performance of 10- to 12-year-old students on a challenging memory task was disrupted when arousing music was played (111–122). Cassidy and MacDonald (2007) assessed the impact of high-arousal (pump-up) music, low-arousal music, everyday noise, and silence on a battery of challenging cognitive tasks. They found that the high-arousal music was the most detrimental condition to cognition on all tasks (517–537). On the whole, it appears clear that, as task difficulty rises, information load from other environmental

factors needs to be reduced in order for people to concentrate on their work.

8. Furnham and Allass (1999) found that extroverted students performed better on observation and memory tests with higher-complexity music in the background, while introverted students performed more poorly in the same condition (27–38). Belojevic, Slepcevic, and Jakovljevic (2001) reported that extroverted subjects performed a mental arithmetic task faster under noisy conditions (traffic noise), while introverted subjects reported more fatigue and concentration problems (209–213). Furnham and Strbac (2002) found that distraction from both background music and office noise impacted the performance of introverts more than extroverts on a variety of tasks (203–217). Ylias and Heaven (2003) tested the reading comprehension of college undergrads either in silence or with background television noise. They found that the performance of introverts was more negatively impacted by the television noise than was that of the extroverts (1069–1079).

Interlude

The Music–Arousal Continuum

A Quick (Graphic) Review of Chapters 3–6

As a further aid to adjusting music to best meet the needs of your learners, Figure I.1 considers the complex interplay between arousal, task difficulty, and personality types, using a continuum that spans all the way from calming music on one end to pump-up music on the other, with the different types of background music falling in the middle. This gives you the big picture of how music can be used to manipulate the energy level in your room to match your goals and maximize student learning.

Now, this graph is as simple as it gets, and it doesn't represent any data—it simply depicts a continuum of energy/attention states, from low arousal to high arousal. Your students might be at any point along this arousal continuum at any particular time due to a variety of factors, including what they had to eat for breakfast or lunch, how much sleep they got the previous night, and how interested they are in the subject matter currently under discussion in class (and a thousand other factors). The only factors we are interested in for our purposes are the different characteristics of the music being used in the environment to manipulate arousal.

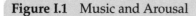

Figure I.1   Music and Arousal

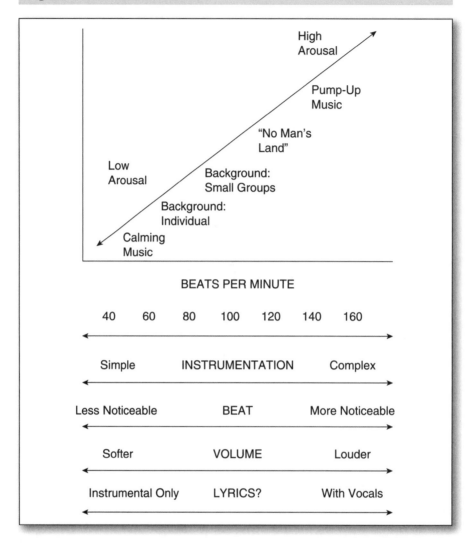

Along the line charting arousal, we list the different types of music we have discussed to this point. You will see that there is a gradual transition from calming music, to background music for individual tasks, to background music for group work. These categories, when seen strictly from a beats-per-minute perspective, cover roughly from 50 bpm to 100 bpm. There is then a gap between 100 bpm and 120 bpm that we have labeled "no man's land," as this music is tricky—too fast for background music unless students really need to be energized or unless the task at hand is really easy or boring, and generally too slow to get the strong entrainment effect you want from your pump-up music, although you will find that a lot of your favorite feel-good tunes will fall in this range. And then, we have pump-up music occupying the 120 to 160 bpm range. And yes, there is music faster than 160 bpm. In general, we don't recommend using music faster than 160 bpm, though, as it tends to be too arousing; if you use such music during a transition, you might have students literally bouncing up and down or dancing around the room—good luck settling them back down for the next learning activity after that!

Below the graph, we show the major characteristics of music that impact arousal. Each of these characteristics exists as a continuum in its own right, from low arousal on the left to high arousal on the right. You will note that the first continuum we show beneath the graph is musical tempo. This is because research shows tempo to be the most salient feature of the music as far as its effect on arousal. So, on the far left side of the line, we have music at 40 bpm (extremely slow), and at the far right side of the line, we have music at 160 bpm (the top of the pump-up range). Of course, other musical characteristics influence arousal, as well, and these other factors are represented by other continua. It is the mix of these different elements that determines how arousing the music is at any point in time.

The smart teacher takes all of these elements into account when selecting the music he or she uses in class for any particular purpose.

7

Learn It Through a Song and Remember It Forever

Using Music to Create Robust Memory of Content

Shall we begin, then, with the acknowledgement that education is first given through Apollo and the Muses?

—Plato

Words make you think a thought. Music makes you feel a feeling. A song makes you feel a thought.

—E. Y. Harburg

What It Is

The idea of using music to learn content is hardly new. One of its main functions in primitive, preliterate cultures is to embed information (especially the history of the tribe) in songs and to pass these informational songs down to future generations. These societies use songs because the brain is very poor at remembering words (semantic information) by themselves. Imagine trying to memorize the whole history of a tribe simply by listening to someone else tell it to you over and over again! But embed that same information in a song, and see how easy it is to learn and remember.

And tribal societies are not the only ones who have used this technique. During the Middle Ages, bards traveled across the European countryside, singing songs about important events and national heroes as a primary source of news for isolated villages. And what worked then still works today. This doesn't mean you have to write original songs in which to embed the content of your curriculum (though that would be both very cool and highly effective). But, when a song exists that *does* embed important content, you would be wise to use it, because it can be such a powerful teaching tool.

And, while music's mnemonic value is of primary importance when using music for learning, there are other benefits, as well. For example, using music as an instructional methodology across the content areas allows us to keep some of the fine arts in the curriculum. This is especially important in schools where the arts have been cut due to reduced school funding or the current emphasis on standardized testing (at least in the United States) in the traditional core subjects of language arts, math, science, and social studies.

Why It Works

That music works for enhancing memory is undeniable. Witness the way you can still remember and sing songs from early childhood, even though you may not have sung these songs for many years. This is why in kindergarten, most students sing "The Alphabet Song," to the familiar tune of "Twinkle, Twinkle, Little Star." However, as students get older, teachers use music like this less and less, which we believe is a serious mistake. We hope this chapter convinces you of the value of continuing to use music for mnemonic purposes throughout all the schooling years.

Embedding Extra "Hooks" for Memory Retrieval

Research suggests that music enhances the memorization process by doing two things: (1) more robustly encoding the information on the front end, thus (2) embedding additional hooks for memory retrieval at the back end. These hooks are the additional information written into lyrical form and embedded in a song—rhythm, rhyme, and melody. Information packaged like this is literally easier for us to hold onto in our memory.

> Music is the art which is most nigh to tears and memory.
>
> —Oscar Wilde

One way to make semantic information more memorable is to use rhyme, as song lyrics usually do. Rhyme helps memorization because, for example, if you can remember the first line of a rhymed couplet (two rhyming lines), but you're struggling to remember the second line, thinking about the end word of line one usually brings to mind the end (rhyming) word of line two. From that point, it is usually easy to recall the rest of the words leading up to the end of the second line, and voilà, the memory of the rhyme has allowed us to repair the lost words. Exactly *how* this works is not well understood, but it could have to do with the associations between the echo of the rhyming words in auditory memory and the meaning of the content in the lines themselves. Of course, you don't need music to have rhyme. Everything described in the previous sentences can be done by using rhymed poetry without music, and we know that cultures from prehistory onward have used poetry as a mnemonic aid. But when we add music to the equation, the effect appears to intensify.

This intensified mnemonic effect is partly due to additional structural elements added to the information—rhythm and melody. As we memorize the lyrics while listening to, playing, or singing a song, we connect, or *associate,* the words with their locations in the overall structure. That is, each word has its spot in the structure of the song—on the beat or between beats, and at a certain point in the melodic line. If we stumble over a word or phrase, all of these positional cues support the search of our associations to retrieve the lost wording.[1] This combined effect is extremely powerful. It's what you experience when the radio plays a song you haven't heard in decades. In an instant, there you are, singing along, the words coming to you effortlessly down the years!

A number of research studies have found good evidence to support this "memory hooks" hypothesis. For example, several studies have compared retention of information when listened to (read to the subject or presented via lecture) versus when it is learned through a song. The results consistently favor learning the information through a song,[2] and the value of this method is even greater for subjects who have musical experience (musicians or singers).[3] Certainly, this is old news to advertisers. For decades, research has shown that business slogans embedded in a song structure (a jingle) are better retained than the same information presented orally by a narrator.[4] Some research has even looked into the neurological basis of this enhanced mnemonic effect, finding that listening to information presented in song format activates both the right and left temporal lobes, whereas simply listening to or reading textual information typically activates only the left temporal lobe.[5] That is, when learning information presented through a song, listeners use more brain structures for the initial encoding of that information, making the memory trace more robust. Theoretically, this means that the information should be easier to retrieve later.

Rate of Presentation

Another factor that could play a major role in the mnemonic effect of music is *rate of presentation*—that is, how quickly or slowly the information comes at the listener. Obviously, rate of presentation can impact how much information we are able to process. If you've ever experienced a lecturer throwing great quantities of material at you at high speed, you'll know how difficult it is to remember what he said (the common analogy is "like trying to drink from a fire hose").

With music, the rate of presentation of information embedded in song lyrics is quite a bit slower than when that same information is input through other means, such as reading prose or listening to a lecture. For one thing, if we just look at the text only, we see that song lyrics usually use quite a bit of repetition—repeated phrases, repeated lines, even repeated stanzas (the chorus). Thus, the information in these lines is hammered home through repetition, while the repetition itself delays the introduction of new material, making for a slower presentation.

In addition, the music itself also slows down the presentation rate of the material. Most songs are sung at a slower pace than normal speech, and many songs have pauses in the lyrical presentation where the music takes center stage (such as with an instrumental solo). As a result of all of these differences, the presentation rate of information via song lyrics is usually much slower than it is through text only or speech.

And at least one study concludes that this slower rate of presentation makes a difference for learning. Kilgour, Jakobson, and Cuddy (2000) asked subjects to learn information by listening either to spoken lyrics or to sung lyrics. In their first experiment, they found all subjects had better recall of the material if it was sung rather than

INSIDE A CLASSROOM

Connecting Music and Writing: "I'm Sure They'd Not Be Missed"

Christy Sheffield
Educational Consultant, Middle School and High School
Great Expectations Oklahoma
Ames, Oklahoma, USA

"Writing is important in every curriculum area so, as an English teacher, I am always on the lookout for genuine ways to engage my student writers in diverse types of writing. One delightful way to spark some truly effective and clever writing is to ask students to rewrite lyrics for 'I've Got a Little List,' a song in the 1885 comic opera *The Mikado*, with music by Arthur Sullivan and libretto by W. S. Gilbert. The opera is set in Japan with the far-fetched, fictional premise that Ko-Ko, a citizen guilty of the capital 'crime' of flirting, has been appointed Lord High Executioner. The authorities have reasoned that he could 'not cut off another's head until he cut his own off,' and since Ko-Ko was not likely to try to execute himself, no executions could take place, and all those who engaged in flirting would be safe! In 'I've Got a Little List,' Ko-Ko names people whom he could eliminate if necessity demanded an execution because he believes society would not miss these citizens and their aggravating ways. He names categories of people rather than naming specific individuals. For example, who needs 'people who have flabby hands and irritating laughs' or 'people who eat peppermint and puff it in your face'? Traditionally, the words of this song are rewritten for specific performances with local references inserted. So that is what I ask my students to do: rewrite the lyrics to name their own categories of people who would not be missed because of their annoying characteristics.

"Before I used the lyric rewrite assignment for 'I've Got a Little List,' students were asked to write about their pet peeves about siblings or vexing behaviors of classmates. This writing task generally produced far less creative results than the request for students to rewrite 'I've Got a Little List' lyrics to fit students' own viewpoints. As a bonus, students get to practice writing in meter and rhyme, expand their cultural literacy by learning about Gilbert and Sullivan, catch the satiric humor in the original libretto, learn some new vocabulary, and showcase their writing when they and their classmates take a stab at singing their newly written lyrics! Students even gain some insight into conduct that their classmates find annoying or downright maddening. One of my classes continued to add to their list of people who would not be missed, all semester long. We all had to behave well, or some class member might be thinking of adding us and our conduct to the list!"

Advice to Teachers: "Music acts almost like an aide for you as a teacher because it helps you teach in so many ways. Music makes material memorable, inserts novelty into class periods, moves your students' bodies—even if it is only tapping toes or bobbing heads—ropes in the young music lovers in your classes, and provides a soundtrack for the learning of the day!"

Suggested Songs: "I've Got a Little List," *The Mikado*, William Gilbert and Arthur Sullivan

spoken. However, in a subsequent experiment, they slowed the spoken lyrics down and presented them at the same rate as in the sung version. When rate of presentation was controlled in this way, the researchers found that recall was just as good—in fact, even a bit better—in the spoken condition than in the sung condition. Their conclusion is that melody is not the main factor in music's mnemonic effect, but rather that the slower presentation rate of material in song form is the primary contributing factor.

The Power of a Familiar Tune

Music's mnemonic effect may also be tied to the *familiarity* of the tune in which the lyrical content is embedded. When you think about it, learning a new song is a challenging cognitive task. Not only must you learn the words, but you must also memorize the tune (melody) of the song. So, if one of these two elements (words or tune) is already familiar—and thus does not have to be learned—the "cognitive load" of the learning task will be reduced.

And research indicates that this is the case. In a study conducted by Wolfe and Hom (1993), for example, five-year-old students were asked to learn telephone numbers, some of which were spoken, some of which were sung to an unfamiliar tune, and some of which were sung to a familiar tune. The results showed that it took the subjects significantly fewer trials to learn the phone numbers sung to familiar tunes as compared with the phone numbers that were spoken or sung to unfamiliar tunes. In another study, subjects were placed in an fMRI scanner and their brains were scanned while listening to familiar and unfamiliar music. It was found that subjects' brains were much more emotionally engaged when familiar music was playing (Pereira, Teixeira, Figueiredo, Xavier, & Castro, 2011). These findings suggest that, when possible, it helps to embed content in tunes with which your students are already familiar.

INSIDE A CLASSROOM

"I Am Gallon Man!"

Alina Irish
3rd-Grade Teacher
Westwood Primary School
Phoenix, Arizona, USA

"I have used the technique of creating songs for teaching content quite a few times in my classes. In fact, I have kind of become known as 'the song lady' in my grade level!

"Here are two examples I have used (and continue to use) for math. The first one I wrote about four years ago or so, when the movie *Iron Man* was big with all of the kids. I took the basic tune of 'Iron Man,' by Black Sabbath, and I put words to it to help them remember gallons, quarts, cups, and pints. I called it 'Gallon Man.' We create a gallon man as we sing it, and they see how each part of the song relates to the size of the volume measurements. I have used this song each year since, and it has been very helpful to students. Here are the lyrics:

Gallon Man (to the tune of "Iron Man")
I am Gallon Man
Look at me close and you'll understand
I am Gallon Man
I measure volume and give a hand
A gallon is my chest
It is the biggest and the best
Quarts start all my limbs

A gallon equals four of them
Pints come next, they aren't too small
There are eight of them in all
Cups are the smallest ones
Sixteen of them equals one gallon
That is all of me
Use me often and you'll see
A gallon man can be such fun
And you'll learn to measure some

"I also came up with one last year to help remember estimation rules. I took the popular song 'Billionaire' by Travie McCoy and Bruno Mars and changed it to 'I Wanna Estimate.' The students really enjoyed learning it, and it did seem to help them in remembering the estimation rules. Here are the lyrics for this one:

I Wanna Estimate So Superfast (to the tune of "Billionaire")
I want to estimate
So superfast
Round numbers in my head and add
Them up
I want to estimate
So superfast
Round numbers in my head and take
Away
Oh, every time I es-ti-mate
I find a number that is close—that's
Great
They end in zeros, then I add them up—
Or take away
That is why I say
That I can estimate
Oh oh oh oh
That I can estimate
Oh oh oh oh
I can estimate

Advice to Teachers: "Creating lyrics that help students learn content really works—it's almost like magic! Once I gave myself permission to get creative with my ideas, to just trust that it would work, it's become a wonderful—and power-ful—part of my classroom. Perhaps the most important thing this strategy has added is that while students really do remember the information, they have fun with it—they laugh while they learn. To me, that's the real magic hidden inside this idea."

Characteristics of Music for Learning

Are some types of music better carriers of information? Actually, no. Almost *any* song with embedded content will work well for learning, as long as students are given ample opportunity to hear and learn the song. Unlike the previous categories of music we've covered, we don't really have to worry much about issues such as tempo, instrumentation, mode, or volume. That said, if we are going to be particular, here are a few characteristics to look for when searching for music with which to teach content:

- ♪ **"Poetic" Text**: The more the lyrics read like poetry (and the less they read like prose), the better. Look for strong, regular *rhymes,* especially end rhyme (but internal rhyme and other sound effects like alliteration help, too); a clear, regular *rhythm* to the words (created by a repeated pattern of stressed and unstressed syllables); and lots of *repetition* (repeated phrases, lines, or whole stanzas). The more of these elements you find in the lyrics, the more memorable they will be, as they will provide many hooks for memory.
- ♪ **A Slower Rate of Presentation**: This primarily has to do with three factors: (1) the amount of content embedded in the song's lyrics, (2) the song's tempo, and (3) the amount of "breathing room" provided between verses and choruses by instrumental passages. In general, you want a song that has a decent amount of content embedded in the lyrics (enough to make it worthwhile spending time on it), but not so much that material delivery becomes too compressed. A slower tempo and more instrumental passages also help to give learners processing time.
- ♪ **A Familiar Tune**: If you have to choose between a well-known or novel tune, where the songs are otherwise equal (quality and quantity of embedded content, poetic structure, and presentation rate), go with the song with the familiar tune.

How to Use It

You have two main options for using music to help your students learn content:

1. Use existing songs with relevant lyrics

2. Turn your students into singer-songwriters

Using Existing Songs With Relevant Lyrics

Many songs have been specifically written with the intent of embedding content for learning in the lyrics. Many others, while not intended for this purpose, nevertheless include information in their lyrics that might be used for teaching purposes. *How much* information is embedded in the lyrics of a particular song dictates how we use the song as a teaching tool—and how useful it is for helping our students to memorize content. To help you distinguish between different content levels—and therefore understand how to use each one—here's a means of categorizing them.

- ♪ *Level One*—little or no actual content, but a useful frame or hook for your lesson
- ♪ *Level Two*—a limited amount of content, useful as supplemental materials
- ♪ *Level Three*—large amounts of content worth memorizing, useful as a core teaching tool

Let's look at each of these in action.

Level one songs are useful hooks or frames. For example, Simon and Garfunkel's short song "Bookends" contains only a single stanza that focuses on the power of photographs to preserve memories. An art teacher starting a unit on photography might play this short song to her students to introduce the mnemonic power and usefulness of photographs in our lives and sell the relevance of studying the topic in class. There is no content to learn in the song; it's merely topical and provides an engaging way to make a point.

Or a high school history teacher might play Elton John's "Goodbye Yellow Brick Road" in an economics unit discussing capitalism/materialism. In the song, the speaker is a "kept man" who alludes to the famed yellow brick road in L. Frank Baum's *The Wizard of Oz*, using the road as a symbol of the pursuit of high-society life and wealth at any cost—which he ultimately rejects.

Level two songs contain a little bit more useful content. For example, in Bruce Springsteen's "The Ghost of Tom Joad," the speaker talks about the struggle of the dispossessed and invokes Joad, the main character from John Steinbeck's novel *The Grapes of Wrath*, set during the Great Depression. In one stanza of the song, the lyrics combine and paraphrase several statements made in the novel by Joad and another main character, the Preacher, concerning the fight of the oppressed against all the forces—economic and political—that conspire to hold them in their place. A high school English teacher discussing the novel, or an American history teacher talking about the Great Depression, could use Springsteen's song as a conversation starter. It's a great way to engage teenagers with the plight of the dispossessed farmers who migrated out of the dust bowl of Oklahoma to California in hopes of finding work.

Level three songs have a good quantity of useful content in their lyrics, whether the primary intent of writing the song was for educational purposes or not. One well-known example of a level three song comes from the classic educational cartoon series *Schoolhouse Rock.* The first two stanzas of "Conjunction Junction" introduce the *function* of conjunctions (to "hook up," like train cars, words, phrases, and clauses) and introduce the three main coordinating conjunctions used in English (*and, but,* and *or*). The next stanza of the song goes on to give some examples of coordinating conjunctions in use. In the following stanzas, the song presents several of the common correlative conjunctions (*either . . . or, neither . . . nor*), as well as some examples (via one very long sentence) of another kind of conjunction— subordinating conjunctions (*when, where,* and *although* in this case). As you can see, well-written lyrics can pack a great deal of information into a very short space, and do so in memorable fashion. Once students have the lyrics in their heads, these lyrics become a touchstone to which they can return whenever they need to review some examples.

Space doesn't allow us to give more examples of level three songs in detail (that would be a whole book in itself), but we hope that you can see the great potential such songs have for helping your students to learn important information.

All three levels of the hierarchy have their usefulness for classroom teachers. Sometimes you want a song with a good deal of key information embedded in it (a level three song) to be used as a cornerstone piece in a unit of instruction, and when such a song is available, it can be a wonderful teaching vehicle. On the other hand, level two songs, while not providing as much content as level three songs, nevertheless allow you to sprinkle into your instruction nice musical interludes that provide some content while keeping engagement high. And level one songs give you the chance to bring (highly memorable) fun and emotion into your teaching, while introducing or reinforcing a point about a topic.

Grade-Level and Content-Area "Starter" Lists

Here are a number of lists of songs as a starting place. These lists are divided first by content areas (math, world literature, American history, etc.), then by usefulness (levels one, two, and three), and then by grade range (elementary, middle school, or high school). Please take these grade-range labels with a grain of salt. The only way you will know if you can use a song listed here in your curriculum will be to listen to it and check out the lyrics.

Art

Level One

"Colors," John McCutcheon—elementary

"Bookends," Simon and Garfunkel—middle school

"Paint It Black," The Rolling Stones—middle school

"True Colors," Cyndi Lauper—middle school

"Paint Me a Birmingham," Tracy Lawrence—high school

"What Light," Wilco—high school

Level Two

"Creativity," Music With Mar—elementary

"I Draw the Line," Greg Percy—elementary

"Walk Like an Egyptian," The Bangles—elementary

"Flowers Are Red," Harry Chapin—middle school

"Kodachrome," Paul Simon—middle school

"Painting by Chagall," The Weepies—high school

"Painting by Numbers," James McMurtry—high school

"Vincent," Don McLean—high school

Level Three

"Basic Shapes," School Art Theatre Productions—elementary

"Roy G. Biv," They Might Be Giants—elementary

"The Red and Yellow Blues," Greg Percy—elementary

"Big Sensation (Escher)," Greg Percy—middle school

"Georgia," Greg Percy—middle school

"Henri Matisse," Sharon Luanne Rivera—high school

"Leonardo da Vinci," Sharon Luanne Rivera—high school

"Michelangelo: His Biography," Sharon Luanne Rivera—high school

"Rembrandt van Rijn," Sharon Luanne Rivera—high school

"The Astounding Romantic Adventures of Goya/In the Middle of the Eighteenth Century," Cast of *Goya . . . A Life in Song*—high school

"Vincent van Gogh: His Biography," Sharon Luanne Rivera—high school

Language Arts: General

Level One

"'C' Is for Cookie," Cookie Monster—elementary

"La La La La Lemon," Barenaked Ladies—elementary

"READ (Reading)," Glenn Colton—elementary

"Stop Talking About Comic Books or I'll Kill You," Ookla the Mok—middle school

"Book of Love," The Monotones—high school

"Paperback Writer," The Beatles—high school

"Persuasion," Santana—high school

Level Two

"Adjective (Rock)," Songs of Higher Learning—elementary

"Alligators All Around," Carole King—elementary

"Super E," Mark D. Pencil and Friends—elementary

"The Writer's Song," Tim Bedley—elementary

"The Preposition Dance," Obie Leff—middle school

Level Three

"Adjective Song," Have Fun Teaching—elementary

"A Noun Is a Person, Place or Thing," Schoolhouse Rock—elementary

"Author's Purpose Song," Have Fun Teaching—elementary

"Capitals," Joe Crone—elementary

"Let Your Body Be a Punctuation Mark," Jack Hartmann—elementary

"The Tale of Mr. Morton," Schoolhouse Rock—elementary

"The Vowel Family," They Might Be Giants—elementary

"Verb: That's What's Happening," Schoolhouse Rock—elementary

"Conjunction Junction," Schoolhouse Rock—middle school

"Hey Mama, When Do You Use a Comma?" Kathleen Wiley—middle school

"Idioms," Jim Thompson—middle school

"Metaphors," Kathleen Wiley—middle school

"Rufus Xavier Sarsaparilla," Schoolhouse Rock—middle school

Language Arts: Children's Literature

Level One

"Green Eggs and Ham," The Learning Station—elementary

"Linus and Lucy," The Vince Guaraldi Trio—elementary

Level Two

"Beauty and the Beast," Celine Dion and Peabo Bryson—elementary

"Cruella De Vil," Dr. John—elementary

"Goodnight Moon," Mark Krantz—elementary

"Hey There, Goldilocks," Intelli-Tunes—elementary

"The Giving Tree," The Learning Station—elementary

"Wild Things," The Learning Station—elementary

"Riki Tiki Tavi," Donovan—middle school

Level Three

"Big Troubles for Little Red," Andrew Queen—elementary

"Cinderella," Andrew Queen—elementary

"Green Eggs and Ham," Mark Krantz—elementary

"House at Pooh Corner," Loggins and Messina—elementary

"Humpty Dumpty," Jack Hartmann—elementary

"I Had a Little Overcoat," The Learning Station—elementary

"I Know an Old Lady," The Learning Station—elementary

"Pierre," Carole King—elementary

"Puff (The Magic Dragon)," Peter, Paul and Mary—elementary

"The Lorax," Mark Krantz—elementary

"Where the Wild Things Are," Mark Krantz—elementary

Language Arts: American Literature

Level One

"Superman," R. E. M.—middle school

"Tender Is the Night," Jackson Browne—high school

Level Two

"Iron Man," Ozzy Osbourne—middle school

"Over the Rainbow," Judy Garland—middle school

"Resignation Superman," Big Head Todd & the Monsters—middle school

"Superman (It's Not Easy)," Five for Fighting—middle school

"Afternoons and Coffeespoons," The Crash Test Dummies—high school

"Catcher in the Rye," Datarock—high school

"For Whom the Bell Tolls," Metallica—high school

"Scarlet Letters," Mudvayne—high school

"Sylvia Plath," Ryan Adams—high school

"The Ghost of Tom Joad," Bruce Springsteen—high school

"The Raven," Alan Parsons Project—high school

"Tom Sawyer," Rush—high school

"Who Wrote Holden Caulfield," Green Day—high school

Level Three

"Solitude," The Dead Poets—middle school

"Atticus Taught Me," Cary Cooper—high school

"Emily Dee," The Dead Poets—high school

"Hey Jack Kerouac," 10,000 Maniacs—high school

"Richard Cory," Simon and Garfunkel—high school

"Sonnet," Luciana Souza—high school

"The Ballad of Annabel Lee," from *The Fall of the House of Usher,* Cast—high school

"The Tell-Tale Heart," The Alan Parsons Project—high school

"Tom Joad (Part 1 and Part 2)," Woody Guthrie—high school

Language Arts: British/Irish Literature

Level One

"Prince Caspian," Phish—middle school

"Brush Up Your Shakespeare," from *Kiss Me Kate,* Cast—high school

"I'll Never Read Trollope Again," Dave's True Story—high school

"Love Story," Taylor Swift—high school

"Xanadu," Olivia Newton John—high school

Level Two

"Second Star to the Right," James Taylor—middle school

"Guinnevere," Crosby, Stills, & Nash—high school

"I Am a Rock," Simon and Garfunkel—high school

"Prospero's Speech," Loreena McKennitt—high school

"Romeo and Juliet," Dire Straits—high school

"The Battle of Evermore," Led Zeppelin—high school

"Virginia Woolf," Indigo Girls—high school

"White Rabbit," Jefferson Airplane—high school

"Wuthering Heights," Kate Bush—high school

Level Three

"A Red, Red Rose," The Dead Poets—high school

"Daffodils—William Wordsworth," The Dead Poets—high school

"Ephemera," Carla Lother—high school

"Funeral Blues," The Dead Poets—high school

"John Barleycorn," Traffic—high school

"Rime of the Ancient Mariner," Iron Maiden—high school

"The Highwayman," Loreena McKennitt—high school

"The Lady of Shalott," Loreena McKennitt—high school

"The Tyger—William Blake," The Dead Poets—high school

"Xanadu," Rush—high school

Language Arts: World Literature

Level One

"Holding Out for a Hero," Jennifer Saunders—high school

"Out of Eden," Robert Cray—high school

"Summer I Read Collette," Roseanne Cash—high school

"When Kafka Was the Rage," Dave's True Story—high school

Level Two

"Dante's Prayer," Loreena McKennitt—high school

"Don't Stand So Close to Me," Sting—high school

"I Am a Man of Constant Sorrow," from *Oh Brother, Where Art Thou?* The Soggy Bottom Boys—high school

"Icarus (Borne on Wings of Steel)," Kansas—high school

"Impossible Dream," from *Man of La Mancha*, Various Artists—high school

"Man of La Mancha," from *Man of La Mancha*, Various Artists—high school

Level Three

"Don Quixote," Gordon Lightfoot—high school

"Flight of Icarus," Iron Maiden—high school

"The Minute I Heard—Rumi," The Dead Poets—high school

Math: Arithmetic

Level One

"I Can Add," They Might Be Giants—elementary

"MATHemACTION," Googol Power—elementary

"Love Potion Number Nine," The Searchers—middle school

"Multiplication," Bobby Darin—high school

"One," Three Dog Night—high school

Level Two

"Count It Higher," from *Sesame Street*, Chrissy and the Alphabeats—elementary

"Measurement Song," Rockin' the Standards—elementary

"Numbers in a Bag," Imagination Movers—elementary

"Six in a Bed," Countdown Kids—elementary

"Infinity," They Might Be Giants—middle school

Level Three

"Divisibility," Jim Thompson—elementary

"Fraction Rock," Joe Crone—elementary

"I Got Six," Schoolhouse Rock—elementary

"Lemonade Stand (Liquid Measurement)," Teacher and the Rockbots—elementary

"Long Division," Karl Roemer—elementary

"Math Pattern Chant," Googol Power—elementary

"Multiplying Magic for 6's, 7's, 8's, and 9's," Barbara Speicher—elementary

"Ready or Not, Here I Come," Schoolhouse Rock—elementary

"Rounding and Estimating," Karl Roemer—elementary

"Subtraction Blues," *Sesame Street* Cast—elementary

"The Place Value Rap," Rockin' the Standards—elementary

"The Switch," Jack Hartmann—elementary

"Three Is a Magic Number," Schoolhouse Rock—elementary

"Mean, Median & Mode," Mason Rather—middle school

"My Hero, Zero," Schoolhouse Rock—middle school

Math: Geometry

Level One

"(You're So Square) Baby, I Don't Care," Buddy Holly—elementary

"Geometry," Jim Thompson—middle school

"Straight Lines," Dawn Landes—high school

"Will It Go Round in Circles," Billy Preston—high school

Level Two

"Figure Eight," They Might Be Giants—elementary

"Polygon Song," Peter Weatherall—elementary

"Angles, Angles," Mindy Bauer—middle school

"Geometry," The Hipwaders—middle school

"Loving Pi," Pi Diddy—high school

"Parallel Lines," Joss Stone—high school [*Get the clean version*]

Level Three

"Nonagon," They Might Be Giants—elementary

"Polygon," Mindy Bauer—elementary

"Determining the Sum of the Angles in a Polygon," The Trigs—middle school

"Lines," Kathleen Wiley—middle school

"Parallel or Perpendicular," Rockin' the Standards—middle school

"Perimeter Area," Rockin' the Standards—middle school

"Perimeter, Circumference, Area, Volume," Kathleen Wiley—middle school

"The Angles Song," Rockin' the Standards—middle school

"Triangle," Rockin' the Standards—middle school

"Volume," Jim Thompson—middle school

"Determining the Surface Area of Prisms & Cylinders," The Trigs—high school

"Geometry Park," Joe Crone—high school

"Is the Name," The Trigs—high school

"My Apothem," The Trigs—high school

"Proofs Is Easy," The Trigs—high school

Math: Algebra and Advanced Math

Level One

"Don't Do the Math," Jim and Steve—middle school

"Math," Supernova—middle school

"Problems," The Everly Brothers—high school

"Rikki Don't Lose That Number," Steely Dan—high school

"The Math," Hilary Duff—high school

"You Do the Math," Tower of Power—high school

Level Two

"Equations," Bryan Johnson—middle school

"Point Plotting," Mr. Duey—high school

Level Three

"The Bar Graph Dance," Science Maniacs—middle school

"The Fundamental Algebra Song," Musical Recall—middle school

"A Constant Ratio," The Trigs—high school

"Linear Equations in Slope-Intercept & Point-Slope Forms," The Trigs—high school

"Proportion and Congruence: Missin' Parts," The Trigs—high school

"The Measurements I Know," The Trigs—high school

Music

Level One

"Don't Forget to Sing," Gemini—elementary

"Seven Days of the Week (I Never Go to Work)," They Might Be Giants—elementary

"Drift Away," Dobie Gray—high school

"Feeling Music Brings," Susan Tedeschi—high school

"Magick," Ryan Adams and the Cardinals—high school

"Walk of Life," Dire Straits—high school

Level Two

"Very Best Band," Margie La Bella—elementary

"Memphis Soul Stew," Solomon Burke—middle school

"The Sound of Music," from *The Sound of Music,* Cast—middle school

"Looking for an Echo," The Persuasions—high school

"Money for Nothing," Dire Straits—high school

"Mr. Tambourine Man," Bob Dylan—high school

"Music," Joss Stone—high school

"Rock 'n' Roll Band," Boston—high school

"Sir Duke," Stevie Wonder—high school

"Sultans of Swing," Dire Straits—high school

"The Minstrel in the Gallery," Jethro Tull—high school

Level Three

"Crescendo," Wendy Rollin—elementary

"C to C," Wendy Rollin—elementary

"Melody & Harmony," Wendy Rollin—elementary

"Rhythm—March & Waltz," Wendy Rollin—elementary

"The Orchestra Is Here to Play," Gemini—elementary

"Canon in D," Sing Your Way to the Classics—middle school

"Minuet in G," Sing Your Way to the Classics—middle school

"Giuseppe Verdi," Sing Your Way to the Classics—high school

Physical Education

Level One

"Getting Strong," The Wiggles—elementary

"Happy Tappin' With Elmo," Sesame Street—elementary

"Head to Toe Dance," The Learning Station—elementary

"Mover Music (Jump Up!)," Imagination Movers—elementary

"Pop N' Hop," Funky Mama—elementary

"The Freeze," Greg and Steve—elementary

"The Hokey Pokey," Ray Anthony—elementary

"The Shimmie Shake," The Wiggles—elementary

"Dance to the Music," Sly and the Family Stone—middle school

"I Like to Move It," from *Madagascar,* The Party Cats—middle school

"Jump," Van Halen—middle school

"Gonna Fly Now," from *Rocky,* Bill Conti—high school

"Gonna Make You Sweat (Everybody Dance Now)," C & C Music Factory—high school

Level Two

"Calling All Movers," Imagination Movers—elementary

"I Like to Run I Like to Jump," David Mead—elementary

"I Love Football," Funky Mama—elementary

"Get'cha Head in the Game," from *High School Musical,* Troy—middle school

"Kung Fu Fighting," Carl Douglas—middle school

"Walking," Mary Mary—middle school

"The Hockey Song," The Hockey Champs—high school

Level Three

"Champion," Queen Latifah—middle school

"Ballad of Eddie Klepp," Chuck Brodsky—high school

"Did You See Jackie Robinson Hit That Ball?" Buddy Johnson—high school

"Jackie Robinson's Legacy," Phil Coley—high school

Science: General

Level One

"Science Is . . . ," Tickle Tune Typhoon—elementary

"Science Is Real," They Might Be Giants—elementary

"Superstition," Stevie Wonder—high school

Level Two

"Physical Property Sense," Musically Aligned—elementary

"Put It to the Test," They Might Be Giants—elementary

"Scientific Method," Teacher and the Rockbots—elementary

"Scientific Method Blues," Kathleen Carroll—elementary

"Scientific Process," Jim Thompson—elementary

"The Scientific Method (to the Madness)," Miz B—elementary

"Evidence and Inference," Science Maniacs—middle school

"Science ROCKS!" Rock Chick and Science Geek—middle school

Level Three

"Nature of Science," Musically Aligned—elementary

"Nature of Science," Professor Boggs—middle school

"Science Discoveries," Science Maniacs—high school

"Scientific Inquiry Rap," Allendale's Got Talent—middle school

Science: Biology (Including Anthropology, Botany, Ecology, Genetics, Human Physiology, and Zoology)

Level One

"Circle of Life," Elton John—elementary

"Dinosaur Song," Johnny Cash—elementary

"What on Earth?" Earth Mama—middle school

"Golgi Apparatus," Phish—high school

"My Brother the Ape," They Might Be Giants—high school

Level Two

"Baby Beluga," Raffi—elementary

"Give Plants a Chance," Banana Slug String Band—elementary

"I Am a Paleontologist," They Might Be Giants—elementary

"Over in the Endangered Meadow," Sally Rogers—elementary

"3 R's," Jack Johnson—elementary

"Cell Castle," Professor Boggs—high school

"Darwin's Children," Edwin McCain—high school

"In The Year 2525 (Exordium & Terminus)," Zager and Evans—high school

"Mercy Mercy Me (The Ecology)," Marvin Gaye—high school

"The Mitosis Square Dance," Robin Walling—high school

Level Three

"Do the Circulation," Schoolhouse Rock—elementary

"Food Chain," Teacher and the Rockbots—elementary

"Good Garbage," Tom Chapin—elementary

"Photosynthesis," They Might Be Giants—elementary

"The Double Life of Amphibians," Two of a Kind—elementary

"Where Will I Go (Digestive System)?" Teacher and the Rockbots—elementary

"FBI (Fungus, Bacteria, Invertebrates)," Banana Slug String Band—middle school

"Telegraph Line," Schoolhouse Rock—middle school

"Vascular Plants," Lyrical Learning—middle school

"Bacteria," Lyrical Learning—high school

Science: Physical Science (Including Astronomy, Chemistry, Earth Science, Geography, and Geology)

Level One

"*Big Bang Theory* Theme," Barenaked Ladies—high school

"Galileo," The Indigo Girls—high school

"See the Constellation," They Might Be Giants—high school

Level Two

"How Many Planets?" They Might Be Giants—elementary

"Landforms," Teacher and the Rockbots—elementary

"Matter Is Everywhere!" J. P. Taylor—elementary

"Meet the Elements," They Might Be Giants—elementary

"Roy G. Biv," They Might Be Giants—elementary

"Sedimentary Metamorphic Igneous," Kathleen Wiley—elementary

"The Tongue Twister Weather Song," Bob Swanson—elementary

"The Wheel of the Water," Tom Chapin—elementary

"What's the Matter?" Jack Hartmann—elementary

"Living on a Layer Cake," Chris Rawlings—middle school

"Moon Song," Have Fun Teaching—middle school

"Saturated Zone," Chris Rawlings—middle school

"What Is a Shooting Star?" They Might Be Giants—middle school

"The Bonding Song," Ellen McHenry—high school

Level Three

"Get Your Molecules Movin'," J. P. Taylor—elementary

"How to Read a Map," Teacher and the Rockbots—elementary

"Solids, Liquids, & Gas," Mason Rather—elementary

"The Rock Cycle," J. P. Taylor—elementary

"Kepler Said," Professor Boggs—high school

"The Elements," Robin Ray—high school

"Why Does the Sun Really Shine?" They Might Be Giants—high school

"Why Does the Sun Shine (The Sun Is a Mass of Incandescent Gas)?" They Might Be Giants—high school

Science: Physics and Engineering

Level One

"Marvelous Toy," Chad Mitchell Trio—elementary

"Beam Me Up, Scotty," Aliotta, Haynes and Jeremiah—high school

"Computer Assisted Design," They Might Be Giants—high school

"Gravity," John Mayer Trio—high school

"Particle Man," They Might Be Giants—high school

Level Two

"Electric Car," They Might Be Giants—elementary

"Sound," Intelli-Tunes—elementary

"Speed and Velocity," They Might Be Giants—elementary

"The Energy Blues," Schoolhouse Rock—elementary

"Conduction, Convection, Radiation," Professor Boggs—middle school

"Electricity," Teacher and the Rockbots—middle school

"Levers, Pulleys and Simple Machines," Twin Sisters Productions—middle school

"Objects and Light," Intelli-Tunes—middle school

"The Electric Connection Rap," Kathleen Carroll—middle school

"The Lever Rap," Ellen McHenry—middle school

"Newton's Laws of Motion," Jeff Mondak—high school

"The Neutron Blues," Mr. Nicky—high school

Level Three

"A Victim of Gravity," Schoolhouse Rock—elementary

"Mother Necessity," Schoolhouse Rock—elementary

"Thomas Alva Edison," Kathleen Wiley—elementary

"Electricity Electricity," Schoolhouse Rock—middle school

"Magnets," Intelli-Tunes—middle school

"Simple Machines," Teacher and the Rockbots—middle school

"Position, Velocity, Acceleration," Professor Boggs—high school

"The Ballad of Sir Isaac Newton," Dr. Chordate—high school

Social Studies: General

Level One

"History Repeating," Propellerheads and Shirley Bassey—high school

"It's All Been Done Before," Barenaked Ladies—high school

"Supply & Demand," Amos Lee—high school

Level Two

"Government," Jim Thompson—elementary

"States and Capitals," The Dream Team and the Hip Hop Professor—elementary

"If I Had a Hammer," Peter, Paul and Mary—middle school

"Unemployment Line," Arlo Guthrie—high school

"War," Edwin Starr—high school

"Where Have All the Flowers Gone?" Pete Seeger—high school

"Won't Get Fooled Again," The Who—high school

Level Three

"Branches of Government," Mr. Duey—elementary

"Branches of Government," Teacher and the Rockbots—elementary

"Cities, States, Countries & Continents," Teacher and the Rockbots—elementary

"Globe," Teacher and the Rockbots—elementary

"Social Studies Stomp," Dr. K—elementary

"I'm Just a Bill," Schoolhouse Rock—middle school

"Supply & Demand (Economics)," Teacher and the Rockbots—middle school

Social Studies: American History

Level One

"Back in the Saddle Again," Gene Autry—elementary

"The Yankee Doodle Boy (Yankee Doodle Dandy)," James Cagney—elementary

"Nobody Knows You When You're Down and Out," Eric Clapton—high school

Level Two

"1492," Sally Rogers—elementary

"Battle Hymn of the Republic," Judy Collins—middle school

"Ellis Island," Marc Cohn—middle school

"The City of New Orleans," Arlo Guthrie—middle school

"The Night They Drove Old Dixie Down," The Band—middle school

"This Land Is Your Land," Woody Guthrie—middle school

"When Johnny Comes Marching Home," Ronnie Gilbert—middle school

"Abraham, Martin and John," Dion—high school

"For What It's Worth," Buffalo Springfield—high school

"Mr. President (Have Pity on the Working Man)," Randy Newman—high school

"Sailing to Philadelphia," Mark Knopfler—high school

"The Ballad of the Green Berets," SSgt. Barry Sadler—high school

"When a Soldier Makes It Home," Arlo Guthrie—high school

Level Three

"Give Me Your Tired, Your Poor," The Mormon Tabernacle Choir—elementary

"Sacajawea," Jonathan Sprout—elementary

"The Battle of New Orleans," Johnny Horton—elementary

"The Shot Heard 'Round the World," Schoolhouse Rock—elementary

"Three-Ring Government," Schoolhouse Rock—elementary

"Harriet Tubman's Ballad (Part 1 and Part 2)," Woody Guthrie—middle school

"The Preamble," Schoolhouse Rock—middle school

"Allentown," Billy Joel—high school

"Boom! (Went the 50s)," History Tunes—high school

"Bury My Heart at Wounded Knee," Indigo Girls—high school

"I-Feel-Like-I'm-Fixin'-to-Die Rag," Country Joe and the Fish—high school

"Sufferin' Till Suffrage," Schoolhouse Rock—high school

"We Shall Overcome," Mahalia Jackson—high school

Social Studies: World History

Level One

"King Tut," Steve Martin—elementary

"Snoopy vs. the Red Baron," The Royal Guardsmen—elementary

1812 Overture, New York Philharmonic Orchestra and Leonard Bernstein—middle school

"Conquistador," Procol Harum—high school

"Marrakesh Express," Crosby, Stills, & Nash—high school

"This Was Pompeii," Dar Williams—high school

Level Two

"Canadian Railroad Trilogy," Gordon Lightfoot—high school

"Don't Cry for Me Argentina," Madonna—high school

"Freedom Now," Tracy Chapman—high school

"Imelda," Mark Knopfler—high school

"We Didn't Start the Fire," Billy Joel—high school

Level Three

"Done With Bonaparte," Mark Knopfler—middle school

"Fields of Athenry," Paddy Reilly—middle school

"Mother Russia," Iron Maiden—middle school

"Prime Ministers Are People Too," Shawna Audet and The Overlanders—middle school

"Butcher's Tale (Western Front 1914)," The Zombies—high school

"Krystallnacht Is Coming," Bob Franke—high school

"The Band Played Waltzing Matilda," Tommy Makem and Liam Clancy—high school

This is just a sample of what's available. You can find additional songs for teaching in Appendix F. Once you start looking for such songs, you will be amazed at how many good selections you will find. Elementary teachers will probably be aware of the many popular children's artists—for example, The Learning Station, Greg and Steve, Jack Hartmann, and Dr. Jean Feldman—who write songs with embedded learning content for young children. Middle school and high school teachers should know that there are also a number of artists who write content-rich songs specifically for older students, though unfortunately most of these artists are not as well known (primarily because teachers of older students tend not to use music for this purpose as much). However, a quick Google search will turn up many great choices (see Appendix H for a list of some of these resources).

INSIDE A CLASSROOM

Matching Song Lyrics With Content

Maureen Stolte
Special Education Reading Teacher, Grades 6–8
Brandon Middle School
Virginia Beach, Virginia, USA

"After my students have read a fiction or nonfiction selection, I often give them a critical thinking task to connect a specific song to the reading selection. I select a song that has a theme or main idea similar to the selection read. Then I play the song for the class and ask the students to listen carefully to the song, read the lyrics, and answer the prompt that requires the students to make connections between the song and the reading selections.

- "Here are a few examples of prompts I have used:
- How do the theme, conflict, and main idea of the short story entitled 'Thank You M'am' written by Langston Hughes connect with the song 'Someone to Watch Over Me' performed by Frank Sinatra?
- How does the song 'Stand by Me' performed by Ben E. King connect with the main idea, theme, and plot of the short story 'Rikki-Tikki-Tavi' written by Rudyard Kipling?
- After reading informational text about the events of September 11, 2001, and the article entitled 'Lifesaver Hero: Firefighters,' read the lyrics to the song 'Hero' and listen to Mariah Carey perform the song. Your task is to write a response to the following question: How do the viewpoint and the purpose of the informational text entitled 'Lifesaver Hero: Firefighters' connect with the song 'Hero' performed by Mariah Carey?

"Before I used music in my classroom, I would give my students a worksheet with comprehension questions to answer after reading a fiction or nonfiction selection. When grading their work, I discovered that most students were able to draw conclusions based on explicit information in the text, but struggled when asked inference questions or questions that required the use of implied cues in the text.

"After introducing critical-thinking performance tasks relating music to literature, my students have strengthened their understanding of the elements of literature, found relationships between different forms of expression, improved comprehension skills, and used high level thinking skills to explain the connections between a song and a reading selection. This meaningful and rigorous task requires students to communicate their thoughts effectively as well as think critically and creatively. As a result, students are better able to compare fiction and nonfiction stories with poetry, respond to inference questions with greater depth and complexity, and answer compare and contrast prompts with ample details. Relating a specific song to literature also enables students to demonstrate a deeper understanding of main idea and theme, more easily analyze relationships, and transfer concepts learned to other situations. Best of all, my students truly enjoy strengthening their academic skills with this critical-thinking task that ties music to literature."

Advice to Teachers: "My advice is to use music to enhance the curriculum and reinforce skills. When students hear music that connects to a concept they learned or literature that they have read, they can make connections to academic concepts, demonstrate a deep understanding, and strengthen analytical skills. Music is a medium that can allow students to reflect upon the human experience as it is portrayed in literature and felt throughout history."

Suggested Songs:

For the reading selection "Thank You Ma'am," written by Langston Hughes:
Song Title: "Someone to Watch Over Me," Ira and George Gershwin
Artist: Frank Sinatra

For the reading selection "Rikki-Tikki-Tavi," written by Rudyard Kipling:
Song Title: "Stand by Me," Ben E. King, Jerry Leiber, and Mike Stoller
Artist: Ben E. King

For the reading selection "Lifesaver Hero: Firefighters," found online at http://www.myhero.com/myhero/hero.asp?hero=firefighters:
Song Title: "Hero," Mariah Carey and Walter Afanasieff
Artist: Mariah Carey

The above activity is dedicated to a friend of Maureen's family, New York City Police Officer Walter Weaver of the Emergency Services Unit, who died while rescuing others on September 11, 2001, in the collapse of the World Trade Center.

Guidelines for Using Existing Songs for Teaching Content

♪ First, and most important, *you still have to teach!* Even if you find a level three song with tons of great embedded content, no song will ever cover everything you want students to know about a topic, so don't expect the song to do this crucial teaching work for you. A good song can, however, be a powerful aid for anchoring key information in students' memories, so by all means, use it, but only as *one part* of your instruction.

♪ Where there's a benefit in students memorizing a song (some level two songs and most level three songs), make sure you build the appropriate time into your lesson plan. As with just about anything we learn, most of us don't learn a song in one exposure. You'll find that distributed practice (multiple exposures stretched out over time) works much better for learning than massed practice (going over the same thing multiple times in one sitting). Introduce the song early in the unit, perhaps at the very beginning even before students know what any of the content means, and then repeat it when you teach the embedded content in class. Finally, solidify the learning by playing the song several more times between the learning of the content and your final evaluation of the learning, especially during review time. You can also use "sponge times" throughout the unit when no academic work is being done (cleanup time, transitions between activities, etc.) to play the song in the background. Why are multiple exposures better? Research suggests that, if students hear a song with embedded content only once, there is no advantage over hearing the same information spoken. However, exposing students to the song version multiple times shows a distinct advantage over listening to the same information being spoken multiple times.[6]

Use the following process:

1. Play the song before introducing the topic by laying a general foundation for the more specific discussion to come.

2. Distribute the relevant lyrics to students and either read the lyrics to them out loud or have them read them silently (you can find the lyrics to just about any song on the Internet).

3. Ask your students to briefly discuss (with their neighbors or tables) the meaning of the lyrics and identify the main idea(s).

4. Guide a more detailed group discussion of the lyrics, helping students understand tricky passages, metaphors, and symbols.

5. Play the song again, while students are reading along with the lyrics.

6. Bring closure to the activity by having students reflect on the song and process on their own (through writing, drawing, etc.).

7. If you want your students to memorize the song, play it again and lead the group in singing the lyrics (you will have to repeat this several times during the unit to achieve memorization).

Please note: You may not consider yourself to be a singer, but the simple fact is that your students will learn the song much better by singing it than by just listening to it, so you have to put yourself out there and lead them in the singing until they start getting it, and then you can let your voice become just one of the many voices singing the song. If you're timid about singing in front of and with your students, just remember *embarrassment is temporary, but learning is forever!*

One great way to incorporate music into a lesson is to ask *your students* to research and bring to class music related to the theme or topic under study, and then find ways to work that music into your instruction. For example, California English teacher and author Alan Sitomer, when teaching a text, asks his students to research and find a song whose lyrics connect to the text in some way. He then asks them to write down their thoughts about how the song's lyrics connect to the text and present their interpretations to the class. When teaching a long text (like a novel), he often parcels out the book and asks students to choose songs for each chapter, main event, or character, and then compiles these into a *soundtrack* for the book (a concept with which today's film-savvy students are quite familiar). Students can also be asked to name the album and create an appropriate album cover for it. Such activities raise student engagement (they love listening to music), and as a bonus you will be exposed to great music you didn't even know existed. Of course, you may need to screen student suggestions for appropriateness before playing them for the whole class.

Turn Your Students Into Singer-Songwriters

Perhaps the best method for using music to cement learning in place is asking *your students* to write lyrics that embed key content into a well-known tune ("The Beverly Hillbillies," "Gilligan's Island," "Row, Row, Row Your Boat," etc.). This may be tough for students below about fourth or fifth grade to do on their own, but it works amazingly well with middle school, high school, and even adult students. In every case, the process of writing and singing the lyrics creates powerful memories. We frequently hear from adult participants who are still singing the song they wrote in a workshop several years ago.

This is a really worthwhile teaching strategy. Not only will your students remember the content they embed in their lyrics; they will be engaged throughout the process and remember fondly the whole experience for years to come.

Here's the basic process to create these powerful and positive memories:

1. Teach the material for understanding first. This use of a song as a mnemonic aid is to be used *following* instruction (as a review and solidification of learning).

2. Put students together into pairs or teams. Writing lyrics is a challenging activity, and multiple heads work better than one. Plus, most kids are inherently social, and this allows them to get their social needs met while getting their learning needs met.

   If you are a primary grades teacher, you can still use this approach, but we recommend you make this an interactive writing activity, with you leading the whole group to create the lyrics.

3. Explain the reason for the activity and *model* (if this is the first time you've used this technique). This means that, if you want the students to do good work, you need to show them how it's done. Take some material that the class has already covered (say, in the previous unit) and write a song, either in front of your students in real time (if you are supremely confident in your on-the-spot composing abilities) or at home, embedding the key content into the lyrics. If you do this work at home and bring it into class, be prepared to explain your composing process—simply showing students a finished product is not enough for them to understand how to do it themselves. Also be prepared to sing your song, as your students will demand to hear it (you may enlist some students to help, if you're shy). Give students a copy of your lyrics to look at while you perform and as an example to refer to later.

4. Identify the content to be worked with. If the number of key points to be embedded is not too large, and if they are the same for everyone, all groups can work with the same content. Just make sure each group uses *different* tunes, and students will come up with a variety of ways to represent the material. When the groups share, while all of the compositions will be somewhat different, the performances will be repeating the same key material in a variety of ways, thus further solidifying the learning for the whole group.

INSIDE A CLASSROOM

Music and Math: A Perfect Match

Marion Gural
2nd Grade Teacher
South Euless Elementary
Euless, Texas, USA

"I have a passion for music and have long known the power of music. I'm always on the lookout for new ways to incorporate music in my classroom. Music is a natural extension of the classroom experience for me: as an energizer or to create a calming effect, as an engager, as a transition signal, as a memory aid, or just to make students 'feel good.' There is something magical about musical notation (math anyone?), rhythm (the beat goes on), and lyrics (word power). Kids seem to have an innate love of all things musical.

"The Math Goal Team at South Euless wanted something exciting that would engage all students, K–6. Using CUBES (a problem-solving strategy sometimes used in conjunction with TAPS, Thinking Approach to Problem Solving), our team put our heads together and decided to create a math rap. Two of the members of our team (our music teacher, Jeff Brooks, and our Suzuki Strings teacher, Patty Purcell) proved invaluable in this effort. CUBES is a mnemonic device meaning C—circle the numbers; U—underline the question; B—bracket information; E—eliminate extra information; S—solve and show your thinking. In previous years, we had made posters for all classrooms and asked teachers to post them and to teach this strategy. This probably helped some students some of the time. However, turning it into a rap (see lyrics below) made it an irresistible and effective strategy that most students could quickly recall and apply. The Math Goal Team performed it for the faculty, and then a small group of students presented it to the entire school during morning announcements. Mr. Brooks made a CD for all math teachers, making it easy to teach and learn in any classroom. In my classroom, this rap became a favorite way to transition to math as well as an engager that raised interest in solving math problems. As time went on, my students added simple movements to match the words, making the strategy even easier to remember. I knew when the CUBES were being applied simply by observing my students making circles in the air or pointing to their temples (showing their thinking) and by listening to students softly murmuring the lyrics in their WhisperPhone headsets."

Lyrics for **"The CUBES Rap"**

C-U-B-E-S! C-U-B-E-S! (Boys) [Boys and girls are rapping these two lines simultaneously]

Use Cubes! Use Cubes! (Girls) [Repeat four times]

Use the CUBES to solve your math!

Think it through, don't make a guess!

C-U-B-E-S! C-U-B-E-S! (Boys) [Boys and girls are rapping these two lines simultaneously]

Use Cubes! Use Cubes! (Girls) [Repeat four times]

C, circle all the numbers!

U, underline the question!

B, bracket only the important information!

C-U-B-E-S! C-U-B-E-S! (Boys) [Boys and girls are rapping these two lines simultaneously]

Use Cubes! Use Cubes! (Girls) [Repeat four times]

E, eliminate the words that clutter and confuse!

S, solve the problem with facts that you can use!

C-U-B-E-S-! C-U-B-E-S! (Boys) [Boys and girls are rapping these two lines simultaneously]

Use Cubes! Use Cubes! (Girls) [Repeat four times]

Where's the bracket? Did you bracket?

What is it that you need to know?

C-U-B-E-S! C-U-B-E-S! (Boys) [Boys and girls are rapping these two lines simultaneously]

Use Cubes! Use Cubes! (Girls) [Repeat four times]

CUBES!

Advice to Teachers: "I have found that if you can make it rhyme, give it rhythm, and/or put it to music, most (if not all) of your students will remember it!"

If, however, there is a lot of material to be worked with, you might set up a jigsaw-type situation, where each group is responsible for different key points. Either you can let students choose what material they want to work with, or you can assign it. When the songs are performed, they will add up to a representation of all of the key material.

Of course, if you are a primary-grades teacher and you will be leading the whole group in this activity, you will need to decide how much content you want to embed in your song lyrics. If there are only a few key points, you can easily put them into a single song. If you have more information than will comfortably fit into the lyrics of one song, you may choose to create several songs with your students to cover the whole territory. Just remember that this is only *one way* to learn the material, so you have to balance its usefulness with the amount of time the activity will take.

5. Give students time to write their songs. In our experience, high school students and adults usually need about twenty minutes to come up with a satisfactory effort. If you want to quality control the result, you might call this first effort a "first draft." You can then take them up, check them over, and offer feedback for improvements. Groups can then get together a second time to finalize their lyrics.

6. Give groups five or ten minutes to practice before their performances. Be prepared to let groups go out into the hallway or find somewhere to practice in private. This will encourage shy students to participate (keeping the embarrassment to a small group as long as possible) and build the suspense before the actual performance.

   By the way, some groups may have one or two strong singers who are used to performing. In these cases, these students can take the lead while other members of the group do something else (background vocals, sound effects, dance moves, etc.). Other groups won't have any strong performers in them, so these groups will probably choose to sing in chorus (there's safety in numbers). When we do this, our only requirement is that everyone in the group must contribute to the performance in some way—no free-loaders allowed.

7. Perform! Usually, this only takes about a minute per group. Get ready for the hilarity! You may choose to record the performances to be listened to or viewed again later (as a review, or for posterity).

8. Decide how to follow up. Of course, if all groups are covering the same content, each group can just keep a copy of their own song and memorize it to further solidify the content prior to a test or other end-of-unit evaluation. If you go the jigsaw route, however, you will need to make copies of all of the songs (with a notation reminding students which tune each song is sung to) and distribute copies to everyone. Students can add singing these songs to themselves several times to their other study practices and study aids to create a powerful mix of mnemonic strategies for the material. Of course, if you have recorded the performances, and if you have the technology available to do so, you can provide students with their own

copies of the performances to listen to or view as many times as they wish.

Why does this technique work so well? Because students are put into the position of meaning-makers. In contrast to just memorizing a preexisting song such as "Conjunction Junction," students in this case have to think about what they've learned, isolate and summarize key points (you can only get so much into a song lyric), and then reword the material so that it fits the syllabic pattern of the tune they have selected. This is high-level problem solving, and the working and reworking students must do to make the content fit into the song form helps to establish the material even more firmly in memory. Then, at testing time, all your students have to do is "play" that song in their heads to retrieve the content. Be prepared for some students, especially younger children, to hum or sing the song to themselves quietly under their breath.

What to Avoid

You Must Still Teach!

Songs with embedded content are great teaching tools, but don't go overboard. Even if you find a song that has lyrics that cover a good deal of a unit's key content, your students are still going to need to learn a lot of background detail and context from you, and they are still going to need to participate in carefully sequenced processing activities (reading, writing, group discussions, etc.) to solidify their learning. So, please keep your use of music in the proper perspective—as one tool, but *only* one, in your toolbox of effective teaching strategies.

Single Exposures Won't Do the Job

One reason we warn teachers not to go overboard is that it takes time to do it right. Using a level three song and making sure that every student in your class learns it is a commitment. You must build in the time necessary to introduce the song, frame its relevance to your students' learning objectives, practice the song multiple times during the unit, and ensure learning by assessing students' memory of the lyrics. Some teachers try to "cheat" the process by using a song, but only playing it once or twice. This won't get the job done. If you're going to use a song with embedded content in your teaching, you must be sure that the lyrics contain enough high-quality information to make the necessary investment of time worthwhile, and then you need to build that time into your unit. If you aren't willing or able to build in the time to do it right, you're better off not using the song at all.

If Transfer Is the Goal, Don't Stop at Recall

It's important to ask, "What, exactly, are my goals for this unit of instruction?" If the answer to this question is along the lines of "I simply want my students to store in long-term memory certain key facts and ideas," then music is a powerful tool for achieving that goal. If, however, the goal is the longer-term goal of *transfer* (being able to *use* the information in some way in the future), content-embedded music can only do *part* of the job. It can solidify key content in long-term memory so students will have it available for use in various situations, but whether or not students actually *use* the information depends on how well you teach them to apply their learning in a variety of situations.

Playing Music While Inputting Content—Accelerated Learning Techniques

In the 1970s, Georgi Lozanov, a Bulgarian psychotherapist, developed a method of foreign language instruction called Suggestopedia that focused on the physical surroundings and emotional climate of the classroom, including specific uses of art and music. Over the years, elements of this approach to foreign language instruction morphed into a more general educational approach called Superlearning or Accelerated Learning. Some of the strategies recommended in these programs have stood the test of time, while others have not been supported by research. Here we address two Accelerated Learning practices involving music:

1. "Active concert"—Using this approach, the teacher reads a text to students while engaging, dramatic classical music is played in the background. The teacher's voice "surfs" along on top of the music, rising and falling in volume and pitch to match the music. Students are instructed to focus on comprehending the text, not on the music. Theoretically, this music-enhanced presentation of the material will create emotional associations and more robustly encode the content in memory.

2. "Passive concert"—Sometimes called "concert review," this occurs toward the end of the learning cycle. The key material is once again read to a musical background (this time using more sedate, often Baroque, classical pieces), but the goal here is different. The teacher this time reads the text as one would normally read prose out loud, making no attempt to match the content to the music, and students are instructed to focus on the music and let the content being read slip into the background. The idea is that, in the state of relaxed awareness engendered by the music, the student will rehearse the content at an unconscious level.

Do these practices work? To be honest, it's hard to say. There appears to be a decent amount of research and anecdotal evidence to support the original use of these techniques in teaching foreign language vocabulary. However, there seems to be very little research to support the use of these techniques for inputting or reviewing material in other content areas.

Our concern is that, in both the active and passive concerts, a great deal of auditory information (the content being read, plus the music being played) is thrown at the learner all at once. We have to wonder if it is possible to effectively attend to all of this auditory information. In fact, some research suggests that it is possible to overload a single input channel (sense), meaning that the brain may only be able to process a portion of the information present in rich auditory environments such as those produced by the active and passive concert approaches.[7] If this is the case, instead of enhancing the encoding of the content, the music may actually limit the amount of attention that can be brought to bear on it—meaning that there is a high probability that students will actually process (and therefore learn) *less* of the content than they would without the added musical component.

Playing Music During Testing

A good deal of evidence supports the hypothesis that people are better able to retrieve memories when there are contextual cues around them that remind them of the initial learning—context-dependent memory. The idea is, if background music was playing during the initial encoding of the memory, playing that same music when we try to remember that information will act as a cue to facilitate recall.[8]

Research also supports the hypothesis that people access memories more easily when their emotional state during encoding is matched by their emotional state during retrieval—mood-dependent memory.[9] And since music has been shown to be a powerful mood inducer (see Chapter 2), it stands to reason that playing the same music used during encoding just prior to or during recall could help put one into the same emotional state as during the learning of the material, which would in turn help with recall during testing.

So, can you improve recall at testing time by carefully using music either to match the learning and testing contexts or by inducing and matching students' moods between the learning and testing contexts? Yes, you probably can. Whether you *should* do so is a question for you and your school. One of the counterarguments is the issue of *transfer*. If your goal for your students is that they be able to recall and apply the information in various situations over the long term, perhaps we need to ensure they have learned the information at a deep enough level to be able to recall it when the testing conditions do *not* match the learning conditions.

Getting Started

How do you find good music whose lyrics address a specific curricular topic you will be teaching? This chapter has already offered you some starter lists, and you'll find more in Appendix F, where we give you 101 additional songs for teaching. There are also some very good online resources that can help you in your search for great embedded-content music (see Appendix H). For now, here are two of the best: www.greenbookofsongs.com and www.songsabout.com.

The website www.greenbookofsongs.com began its life in 1982 as a printed book, *The Green Book of Songs by Subject*, by Jeff Green (get it?). Now in its fifth edition, this book was the first of its kind. Unlike other list publications that focused on the popularity of songs (such as the *Billboard* chart lists) or on those selected for awards (such as Grammy winners), *The Green Book of Songs by Subject* was the first effort to organize the totality of 20th century (and now 21st century) popular music by *topics*. The book quickly became the go-to resource for DJs, advertisers, and those putting together soundtracks for TV shows and movies. But you don't have to be a DJ or television producer to use the content of *The Green Book*. Anyone (including teachers, of course) can use this easy-to-navigate reference. All you have to do is look up a topic (the book is arranged by topics and subtopics in alphabetical order, with a cross-referenced index in the back), and there you will find a list of songs from the past 100-plus years about that topic!

However, for those of you who prefer searching for your music online (at 1,600 pages, the physical *Green Book* is pretty hefty), all the great content of *The Green Book* and much more can be found on the website. Members can search this vast database—more than 116,000 songs by 10,000 artists covering more than 2,200 topics—as much as they want for a truly affordable annual subscription fee. The site offers three ways to search for subjects, as well as hyperlinked "see also" categories and an extensive thesaurus, that make it easy to find whatever you're looking for. Users can also search by five major genres and for "hits" only. The site also gives you not only the name of the song and the artist, but also at least one discography and its record label.

The most important feature of both the site and the book is the way songs have been indexed. There are many music sites where you can search by keyword, and if that keyword happens to be in the title of the song, these sites will retrieve the song for you. But for www.greenbookofsongs.com, actual humans have listened to the lyrics of each song and categorized the song not just by keywords from the title, but by what each song is *actually about*. So, if a song has content in its lyrics about your topic but no mention of the topic in the song's title, your topic search will still find the song for you. This site even has a "Teacher's Page" section specifically about using music for teaching, with links to several great lesson plans, two of which were developed in conjunction with the Rock and Roll Hall of Fame.

The other site we will recommend here is *The Green Book*'s sister site, www.songsabout.com. This site is a repository of topical song lists already created for you by the people at www.greenbookofsongs.com. These ready-to-use playlists are, to quote the site, "about holidays, current events, and interesting topics of every kind!" Is it getting close to Christmas, Halloween, the Fourth of July, or any other major holiday? Do you want some great ideas for songs to match the holiday? Just go to www.songsabout.com, and you will find ready-made lists of songs of all musical genres. Are you a history teacher who wants to bring to class music related to current events and issues? This site has many lists of songs in broad categories such as current events, history, political issues, and social issues. In addition to these broad categories, there are hundreds of song lists categorized under more specific keyword tags—everything from arithmetic to vacation. We believe that, with these two sites, you can find a song for just about any topic you could imagine. Happy hunting!

Our Top 40 Songs for Teaching Academic Content

The Top 40 list for this chapter will be a bit different than those found in previous chapters. Since we have already provided a number of lists categorized by content areas, grade levels, and levels of usefulness in this chapter, and since we provide another 101 such songs in Appendix F, we will simply take this opportunity to list alphabetically forty of our favorites from these lists, regardless of content area or grade level. These songs offer the dual advantages of providing excellent content while also being high quality musical performances.

1. "Abraham, Martin and John," Dion (American history, Level 2, high school)

2. *Big Bang Theory Theme,*" Barenaked Ladies (physical science, Level 1, high school)

3. "Circle of Life," Elton John (biology, Level 1, elementary)

4. "Conjunction Junction," Schoolhouse Rock (language arts, Level 3, middle school)

5. "Drift Away," Dobie Gray (music, Level 1, high school)

6. "FBI (Fungus, Bacteria, Invertebrates)," Banana Slug String Band (biology, Level 3, middle school)

7. "Flowers Are Red," Harry Chapin (art, Level 2, middle school)

8. "Galileo," The Indigo Girls (physical science, Level 1, high school)

9. "Gonna Fly Now," from *Rocky,* Bill Conti (physical education, Level 1, high school)

10. "Gravity," John Mayer Trio (physics and engineering, Level 1, high school)

11. "House at Pooh Corner," Loggins and Messina (children's literature, Level 3, elementary)

12. "I Am a Man of Constant Sorrow," from *Oh Brother, Where Art Thou?* The Soggy Bottom Boys (world literature, Level 2, high school)

13. "I Am a Paleontologist," They Might Be Giants (biology, Level 2, elementary)

14. "I Like to Move It," from *Madagascar,* The Party

Cats (physical education, Level 1, middle school)

15. "I'm Just a Bill," Schoolhouse Rock (social studies, Level 3, middle school)

16. "Infinity," They Might Be Giants (arithmetic, Level 2, middle school)

17. "It's All Been Done Before," Barenaked Ladies (social studies, Level 1, high school)

18. "Kung Fu Fighting," Carl Douglas (physical education, Level 2, middle school)

19. "Meet the Elements," They Might Be Giants (physical science, Level 2, elementary)

20. "Mercy Mercy Me (The Ecology)," Marvin Gaye (biology, Level 2, high school)

21. "Painting by Chagall," The Weepies (art, Level 2, high school)

22. "Persuasion," Santana (language arts, Level 1, high school)

23. "Ready or Not, Here I Come," Schoolhouse Rock (arithmetic, Level 3, elementary)

24. "Rime of the Ancient Mariner," Iron Maiden (British/Irish literature, Level 3, high school)

25. "Romeo and Juliet," Dire Straits (British/Irish literature, Level 2, high school)

26. "Rufus Xavier Sarsaparilla," Schoolhouse Rock (language arts, Level 3, middle school)

27. "Stop Talking About Comic Books or I'll Kill You," Ookla the Mok (language arts, Level 1, middle school)

28. "Sultans of Swing," Dire Straits (music, Level 2, high school)

29. "Superman (It's Not Easy)," Five for Fighting (American literature, Level 2, middle school)

30. "Superstition," Stevie Wonder (science, Level 1, high school)

31. "The City of New Orleans," Arlo Guthrie (American history, Level 2, middle school)

32. "The Elements," Robin Ray (physical science, Level 3, high school)

33. "The Ghost of Tom Joad," Bruce Springsteen (American literature, Level 2, high school)

34. "Vincent," Don McLean (art, Level 2, high school)

35. "We Didn't Start the Fire," Billy Joel (world history, Level 2, high school)

36. "We Shall Overcome," Mahalia Jackson (American history, Level 3, high school)

37. "Why Does the Sun Shine (The Sun Is a Mass of Incandescent Gas)" They Might Be Giants (physical science, Level 3, high school)

38. "Will It Go Round in Circles," Billy Preston (geometry, Level 1, high school)

39. "Won't Get Fooled Again," The Who (social studies, Level 2, high school)

40. "Wuthering Heights," Kate Bush (British/Irish literature, Level 2, high school)

Notes

1. Wallace and Rubin (1991) studied Appalachian folk ballads to determine if structural characteristics such as verse length, refrains, poetics, rhymes, and metrical patterns explained the stability of retrieval of lyrics during performance. They conclude that the many constraints provided by the structural elements act to limit possible word choices and therefore lead to more stable transmissions. They state, "These devices work by organizing and constraining the words, as well as providing multiple links to aid recall" (181). Purnell-Webb and Speelman (2008) focused more specifically on rhythm and found that rhythm, with or without musical accompaniment, can facilitate recall of text, "suggesting that rhythm may provide a schematic frame to which text can be attached" (927). On the other hand, Wallace (1994) argues that melody is the more powerful mnemonic factor, as melody, being more variable than rhythm, is the more salient feature that "chunks words and phrases, identifies line lengths, identifies stress patterns, and adds emphasis" (1471).

2. Ginsborg and Sloboda (2007) asked subjects to learn a new song (both the melody and lyrics were new to the subjects) in several ways. Some subjects learned the words first, then the melody, and finally the whole song (words and melody together). Other subjects learned the melody first, then the words, and then both together. The researchers found that

learning the words and melody separately is not nearly as effective as learning the song intact (words and melody together) from the beginning. They conclude that "words and melody are . . . recalled in association with one another, so that retrieving one enables retrieval of the other . . . suggesting that the formal structure of a song provides a framework for recall" (421). Chazin and Neuschatz (1990) found that, when information (in this case science content about colors and minerals) was embedded in a song format, it was more easily recalled than when the same information was learned through lecture. This finding was true of both eight-year-old subjects and young adults (1067–1071).

3. Kilgour, Jakobson, and Cuddy (2000) conducted a study where subjects listened to material that was either spoken or sung. In addition, they presented the material either at a "normal" pace or in a slowed-down version. In all conditions, subjects with musical training performed better than those without training (700–710). Ginsborg and Sloboda (2007) found that musically trained subjects performed better on the learning of a new song than untrained subjects, but only when the lyrics and the melody were learned together. They concluded that "the melody provides a framework for retrieving the words that is more meaningful and therefore more memorable for those with musical expertise" (434–435). The results of these two studies, and others like them, suggest that musical training leads to enhanced recall of verbal material, which is perhaps one reason that students who take music classes have often been found to outperform other students across all academic subjects.

4. Yalch (1991) found that music enhanced memory for advertising slogans when they were incorporated into ads as jingles, as opposed to when they were spoken only (268–275).

5. Samson and Zatorre (1991) studied memory in patients who had undergone brain excisions for the relief of intractable epilepsy. They found that patients who had undergone excisions in the left temporal lobe demonstrated a deficit in text recognition, while patients who had undergone excisions of the right temporal lobe demonstrated deficits in melody recognition (793–804). This shows that memory of songs probably uses dual memory codes involving both temporal lobes. The verbal part of the code is consistently related to left

temporal lobe function, while the melodic code may depend to some extent on both temporal lobes.

6. Wallace (1994) had subjects listen to a text presented either in spoken form or in song form and then tested for recall. When subjects heard the text only once, recall was better for the spoken version. But when subjects heard three verses of the text sung to the same melody (repetition of the song structure), recall was better than for the same text when spoken (1471–1485).

7. Moreno and Mayer (2000) had students view and listen to an animated program with narration about either the formation of lightning or the operation of hydraulic braking systems. For some students, the researchers added background music, sound effects, or both to the narration. On tests of retention and transfer, those students listening to the program without music and/or sound effects outperformed those who had the extra auditory information added (117–125). It appears that the more "bells and whistles" added to the same input channel, the less effectively subjects are able to process the content.

8. In experiments conducted by Smith, Glenberg, and Bjork (1978), context-dependent memory was shown to work in two different ways. First of all, they showed that recall is facilitated when the initial learning conditions and testing conditions match. This was proven by having subjects learn two different lists of terms in different environments on back-to-back days. On the third day, subjects were tested on both lists in contexts that matched their Day 1 learning environment, their Day 2 learning environment, or a neutral environment. It was found that subjects consistently recalled information better when the testing condition matched the learning context. (While music was not used in this experiment as part of the external context, commonsense extrapolation from the findings suggests that, if music was indeed part of the initial learning environment, it would help facilitate recall if the same music was played during testing.) In another experiment, the researchers had two groups of subjects learn the same list twice, with a three-hour lag between learning sessions. The difference between the two groups was that one group studied the list twice in the same environment, while the other group studied the list in two different environments (different contextual information). The results were striking, with the group that studied the

words in different environments vastly outperforming the group that studied twice in the same environment (342–353). This finding points out that it is better for learning to process information multiple times in different environments, thus encoding a larger variety of contextual information along with the content to be learned and therefore embedding more retrieval cues through which the content can be recalled. It thus follows (to add music into the equation) that students who study the content multiple times in multiple locations with *different* background music playing each time will perform better at testing time than those students who studied with the same music playing each time. To get the full benefit of *both* of the effects described here, it follows that a teacher would be wise to rotate different playlists of background music as students study the material at different times and in different locations, and then play a set of background music during testing that mixes pieces from the various lists. To be clear, no one to our knowledge has conducted experiments on the exact situation just described. We are only making commonsense extrapolations from various research findings. Teachers are encouraged to do their own research into this subject (and let us know what you discover).

9. Teasdale and Fogarty (1979) used a mood-induction procedure to put subjects into either happy or depressed states, and then asked them to relate stimulus words to pleasant and unpleasant memories. They found that subjects took much longer to retrieve pleasant memories when they were in a depressed state, as opposed to when they were happy, suggesting a negative effect on retrieval of memories when the current mood state and the mood state in which the memory was encoded do not match (248–257). Many studies have shown that music can be used to manipulate mood (see Chapter 2). Several studies have also shown that this mood-inducing power of music can be used to facilitate recall by getting students into a certain mood state at the time of learning and then repeating the procedure prior to testing. For example, Thaut and de l'Etoile (1993) showed that subjects recalled the most information (in this case, a list of adjectives) when they listened to mood-induction music prior to the initial learning and then again prior to testing. This mood-induction effect was greater than that produced by using background music

during learning and testing, which was in turn more effective than learning and testing in silence (70–80). De l'Etoile (2002) later replicated and expanded upon these findings (145–160). Other research, including that conducted by Eich and Metcalfe (1989), has shown that the impact of mood on retrieval is more robust when the material to be recalled is the result of internal mental operations such as reasoning, imagination, and thought than if the material to be recalled is simply that of external, episodic events (443–455). These findings highlight the important role of mood for learning and retrieval in school contexts, where the material to be recalled during testing is almost always the memory of internal mental operations.

8

Your Magical, Musical Bag of Tricks

Fun and Effective Management Strategies Using Music

Where words fail, music speaks.

—Hans Christian Anderson

When music changes, so does the dance.

—African proverb

What It Is

This chapter covers classroom management strategies that have been tried and found effective by many classroom teachers. They include using music

1. As a signal to start an activity

2. As a "timer" to speed up transitions

3. With embedded directions as a management tool

4. As a match for classroom activity

In some ways, we believe these uses of music are just as important for creating a well-managed classroom as anything else covered in this book. Teachers who master the strategies in this chapter will find that everything they do in their classrooms will go much more smoothly, they will lose much less instructional time, and their students will consistently be in a better mood for learning.

Why It Works

Using Music to Activate Episodic Memory

Probably the most common management use of music in the classroom (especially at the elementary level) is as a *signal* to start a particular activity. Many teachers use a specific song to signal that it's time to line up to go to recess, or time to put away the art materials and get out the math manipulatives, or time to clean their desks in preparation to leave for the day. This simple management trick works like a charm, saving the teacher time otherwise wasted giving verbal directions. When the designated song comes on, students know immediately what needs to be done, and they hop to it right away.

Why does this simple management use of music work so well? It has to do with the specific memory system at work in these situations: episodic memory. Unlike semantic memory (our memory of words and numbers), episodic memory is our memory of the *events* of our lives (our where-were-you-when memory). And while it's true that we don't store away in long-term memory everything we experience (and what we *do* store is subject to change over time), episodic memory is nevertheless far superior to semantic memory in at least one key way: it's practically effortless. Want proof? Take this little test:

Visualize where you were for dinner last night. Now, answer these questions: Who were you with? What were you wearing? What did you eat? What did you have to drink? Did you have dessert? If so, what did you have?

Easy, right? We bet you were able to recall all of that information effortlessly. You didn't even have to study! How could we know that you would perform so well on this test? Because we know that, at least in the short term, we all hold the events of our lives quite easily in memory (as opposed to facts, which are much more difficult to commit to memory). Now, if we asked you what you ate and had to drink for dinner three weeks ago, you probably wouldn't do as well, because unless we deem some event to be important for some reason, it eventually slips away.

When you introduce a song to students and tell them that, each time the song plays, they will be expected to do *(fill in the blank)*, and when you then consistently use that same song for the same purpose, students form an *associative link* between the song and the actions they are to perform. Each time the song comes on, their effortless episodic memories kick in and automatically search for the last time they heard the song. And there it is—they remember the song and, along with it, what they did in response. Each time they hear the song and perform the same actions in response, they strengthen the associative links between the two—until they reach a point where the response becomes a *conditioned* response. They don't even think about it; they just start performing the action immediately upon hearing the song. Now that is a strong classroom management tool!

In addition to using music as a signal to start an action, many teachers also use music as a *timer* to alert students to how long they have until a task needs to be completed. The teacher selects a song (or, more likely, just a portion of a song) and uses that same song or portion each time the task is done. Once students hear the selection a few times, they get a sense for how much time they have and how quickly they need to move to finish in time. Again, this strategy is very effective, and again, episodic memory plays a role, as students remember whether they finished on time previously and adjust their pace accordingly. But we suspect that the effectiveness of this management strategy has even more to do with the enjoyment students clearly get from trying to "beat the clock." In fact, you will often see even the hard-core laggards hustle to finish on time.

Using Music to Activate Semantic Memory

The above process works well for simple procedures such as, "When song X plays, come to the carpet for story time." However, it may not be quite enough when you want students to quickly learn, remember, and consistently perform more complex procedures such as multistep directions. In this situation, you may need a song with lyrics that actually describe the procedure students must follow.

As we discussed in Chapter 7, there is a good deal of evidence that embedding content in song lyrics is superior for mnemonic purposes to learning the same material through traditional methods

INSIDE A CLASSROOM

Transitions—At the Beginning of Activities and at the End of the Day

Shari Rindels
1st Grade Teacher
Catalina Ventura School
Phoenix, Arizona, USA

"I use the song entitled 'Jack Be Nimble,' by Jack Hartmann, to signal that it is time to get ready for any whole group activity, especially spelling, when students need to get out their spelling journals or spelling games, or when they need to take the weekly spelling test. The song is about two minutes long and has the line, 'Get ready, get set' in it, which fits well with 'getting ready' for something. The kids know it is time for spelling when the song starts, and they get out their journals, open them to the correct page, sharpen their pencils, get a quick drink, and are in their seats, sitting quietly, ready to go by the end of the song. Instead of me having to say, 'One, two, three, eyes on me,' and verbally giving them directions, they have learned what steps are needed by simply listening to the song. It saves my voice, gives the students a break from my talking, allows me to get my materials ready, and best of all adds energy to the room! Another song I use to get ready for spelling activities is 'Glamorous,' by The Kidz Bop Kids—they spell out the letters g-l-a-m-o-r-o-u-s in the song.

"I also like the song 'One Two, Buckle My Shoe,' by Jack Hartmann, to get the students geared up for a math lesson. The students like to stand up and act out this counting song as they sing along. When the song ends, they are back in their seats and our math lesson begins. The song and the music do the work for me; it allows the students to stand and stretch, make some noise, and re-energize—the teacher too! And if I need to organize math materials, I have a couple of extra minutes to do just that, without any down time for the kids.

"I also use a couple of different songs for packing up to go home. For our regular five-minute pack-up time, I use the song 'Home,' by Chris Daughtry, as sung by The Kidz Bop Kids. But when we are late and/or in a rush, I use the song 'Who Let the Dogs Out,' by The Kidz Bop Kids. The upbeat tempo gets the kids moving faster, and it is a shorter song. Funny how, when the music is playing, the noise involved in packing up no longer seems too much! What I like best of all is that the students work hard to be ready and in line by the time the song ends without me having to tell them to hurry up."

Advice to Teachers: "As Nike says, 'Just do it!' You will see a phenomenal increase in student engagement, enjoyment, and increased focus. Plus, your school day will seem to fly by! Give it a try; you will never be without it again. And as you use music in the classroom, you'll find more and more songs out there that fit your routines, lessons, and activities. Music truly is the universal language—have fun with it!"

Suggested Songs: "Jack Be Nimble," Jack Hartmann; "Glamorous," The Kidz Bop Kids; "One Two, Buckle My Shoe," Jack Hartmann; "Home," The Kidz Bop Kids; "Who Let the Dogs Out," The Kidz Bop Kids.

such as reading or listening to the material delivered verbally.[1] This is especially true when students have the opportunity to hear the song multiple times.[2] So, if you want students to learn a multistep procedure more quickly, embed those steps into the lyrics of a song and teach the song to them.

As we pointed out in Chapter 7, there are a number of theories about exactly *why* learning content through song lyrics works so well. Some believe that rhythm is the most salient element,[3] others believe that melody is the most important factor,[4] and still others point to the controlled rate of presentation found in songs.[5] Research also suggests that learning content through a song (whether the embedded material is content area knowledge or procedural directions doesn't matter) is facilitated when the tune is familiar to students.[6] So, while there are many wonderful songs that have been created and recorded specifically to teach students certain procedures (see the song suggestions later in this chapter and in Appendix G), writing your own song to a well-known tune might be especially effective.

When you teach students a song with embedded directions and then use that song consistently each time the actions need to be performed, you combine the power of both the episodic and semantic memory systems. Students hear the song begin, and this reminds them of the previous times they've heard the song and the actions they performed (episodic memory). And, if the actions have not yet become conditioned (habitual), the song's lyrics are there to be reviewed until they become stored in long-term semantic memory. It is truly a powerful combination.

Creating Positive Learning States by Matching Songs to the Activity

We can also increase student engagement by matching songs to the activities going on in class. This use of music might be termed an *indirect* management strategy, with the main goal being to create an enjoyable learning environment. You might be wondering how this use of music differs from the use of feel-good music discussed in Chapter 2. The difference is that with feel-good music, the approach is more *general*, with the teacher choosing songs to play during transitions that he or she thinks will promote a better mood in the class as a whole. The use of music we are talking about in this chapter is *specific* to the activity taking place at the moment.

For example, imagine you are teaching a lesson on sound waves in a science class. After some direct instruction, you ask students to stand up and walk to form groups of three or four students to discuss some point you just made. While students are walking to find their partners, you play (to match the waves theme) "Catch a Wave,"

"Surfin' Safari," "Surfer Girl," or "Surfin' U.S.A." by the Beach Boys, or "Surf City" by Jan and Dean, or "Heat Wave" by Martha and the Vandellas, or even "Wipeout" by the Surfaris.

Or imagine your students have recorded their ideas about a topic on chart paper and posted them on the walls. Now you want them to walk around the room, reading and responding to the ideas of the other groups. You might pick up on the concept of *walking* and play, in the background while students do their gallery tour, songs such as "Walking on Sunshine" by Katrina and the Waves, "I Get Around" by the Beach Boys, "The Wanderer" by Dion, "Walk Like an Egyptian," by The Bangles, or "I'm Gonna Be (500 Miles)" by The Proclaimers, which features the chorus, "I would walk 500 miles, and I would walk 500 more, just to be the man who walks 1,000 miles to fall down at your door."

While this may seem a little dorky, many students will get a laugh out of it, and as a result, they will enjoy their time in your classroom just a little bit more. Even more important, the musical association may help them to remember the information on the posters. Be aware that some students won't even notice what song is playing, but they will still benefit from the mood-enhancing quality of the music.

You may be wondering at this point if matching music to classroom activities is worth the effort. It certainly *does* take some time to decide what songs would be a good match for certain activities, locate the songs, and build them into your play lists for class. But here's some research to consider before you write off this idea as "too hard." In Chapter 2, we discussed how music has been proven to be a powerful mood inducer in practically all humans.[7] In fact, studies done using PET scans have shown that pleasurable music causes blood flow changes in brain regions associated with reward, emotions, and arousal (Blood and Zatorre, 2001), and have also detected the release of dopamine (the brain's main feel-good neurotransmitter) in the striatum, the brain's reward center, during pleasurable music listening (Salimpoor, Benovoy, Larcher, Dagher, and Zatorre, 2011). "OK, that's nice," you might say, "but I already knew that music can make people feel good. Is there any other benefit beyond simply manipulating mood?"

Well, it turns out that there *is* another benefit—a very important one. In his book *Brain Rules: 12 Principles for Surviving and Thriving at Work, Home, and School,* molecular biologist John Medina (2008) talks about the importance of creating "emotionally charged" events during our teaching. When students respond emotionally to something in class, Medina says, the amygdala (one of the most important brain structures involved with emotion, and one that is "chock-full of . . .

dopamine") releases dopamine into the system. And, because dopamine has been proven to aid in information processing and memory formation, it's as if a sticky note is placed on the event, saying "Remember this!"(pp. 80–81). So, any time we can get students emotionally engaged in their learning (whether it's by getting them to laugh about a song you're playing, or in any other way), we are raising the chances that they will process and commit to memory the content under consideration at that time. The bottom line is this: the more students *enjoy* their learning, the more *effectively* they will learn—and music can play a powerful role in creating this enjoyable, effective learning environment.

INSIDE A CLASSROOM

Music as a Signal to Start Class

Bo Power
Katitjin Program Leader, Year 8 (equivalent to 8th Grade in the US)
Wesley School, Perth, Australia

"Before we began using music, getting class started wasn't a positive experience. I would call out to the students multiple times to get themselves ready for the start of the lesson. The routine would involve my loud and assertive voice as the cue, and begrudgingly the boys would respond, with varying levels of urgency. My valuable lesson time was fast evaporating, as was the boys' willingness to take a break from socializing to get ready to learn.

"Since introducing music as a cue to start class, the mood has altered significantly, and we have reduced the amount of time it takes. As the students are lingering around before class, I start the music. It acts as a cue to get their books and supplies to start the day. My incessant reminders to get ready are no longer needed, which means I'm off the 'public enemy number one' list. More importantly, the music lifts their mood so the lesson starts with a positive mindset. I'm relaxed, and the students are in good spirits."

Advice to Teachers: "Have a go. Play around with the concept, and let the results speak for themselves. With the right choice of songs, there will be a noticeable difference in student engagement, energy, and even learning outcomes. Have a play list that is well-researched and refined through trial and error. The students will respond to the music; all you have to do is notice whether the response is what you are looking for."

Suggested Songs: "Let's Get It Started," The Black Eyed Peas; "I Don't Like Mondays," The Boomtown Rats; "Get Up Offa That Thing," James Brown.

How to Use It

Here are a few ideas to add to your bag of management tricks.

Using Music as a Signal to Start an Activity

At the elementary level, this might include activities such as lining up to go outside or to lunch, gathering at a particular location in the room, or putting away the materials from one content area activity and getting out the materials for the next content area.

At the secondary level, a language arts teacher might use a certain song as the signal to begin silent reading time, a math teacher might use a particular song as the signal for students to move from individual practice to cooperative learning groups to compare their work, or a history teacher might use a particular song such as "It's All Been Done" by The Barenaked Ladies to signal that students should pair up to compare how something that happened in the past is like something going on in today's world.

To start using music as a signal in your classroom, just look through your lesson plans and find those procedures and instructional activities that you use every day, or at least several times a week. You will probably get good results by adding a signal song to any such repeated activity, whether it's a management procedure or a repeated instructional activity. And it doesn't matter if your signal song is instrumental or one with lyrics. Since you will only be using such songs during transitions, lyrics won't disrupt student learning.

Using Songs With Embedded Directions as a Management Tool

Embedding content about routines into tunes and teaching these tunes to the students is a technique often used by effective preschool, kindergarten, and primary-grades teachers around the world, but there's no reason why a teacher at any grade level couldn't use it. At the elementary level, a teacher might have a song for getting in line (when it's time to go to lunch or recess, for example), or for hand washing (at bathroom break time), or for putting away materials and coming to a specific location in the room for story time. These could be prerecorded songs specifically written for the purpose, or songs the teacher makes up herself. At the higher grade levels, a science teacher might find or create a song to sing or play prior to lab work that reviews the important safety steps all students need to remember. Or a math teacher might create a song that embeds in its lyrics the important steps for solving word problems (we gave you an example of this in the previous chapter). Or a language arts teacher might create a song that embeds the main steps for supporting an argument with rhetorical techniques. Any multistep process is a candidate for being turned into a management song.

Here are just a few examples of such songs. If you are an elementary teacher who struggles with getting students to follow the correct procedures at bathroom time, you could teach students Jack Hartmann's clever song, "Here's What You Do Do and What You Don't Do When You Go to Use the Bathroom." Embedded in the lyrics are instructions covering getting permission to go, walking to the bathroom and waiting patiently for your turn, knocking before you enter, washing your hands when you're done—even flushing and closing the lid! Similarly, "Wash Your Hands" by Miss Jenny reminds students to wash their hands after sneezing, coughing, or going to the restroom. And then there's "Helper Train" by Caroline and Danny, which directs students to help clean up while adding an element of fun, as students are directed to make various train noises while they clean. There are also many songs written for young children that embed in their lyrics directions for developing positive traits and becoming successful students (you might think of these as "long-term management songs"). For example, Ben Stiefel's song, "Never Be Afraid to Ask Questions," exhorts students to ask questions if they are wondering about something. Asking questions is obviously an important trait for success in the classroom and in life, and such songs can help to instill these kinds of traits in students.

Putting such content into song form makes it memorable and more easily retrievable, but there's one more major benefit of using songs in which directions are embedded: it saves your voice! Instead of repeating the same steps multiple times, you simply push *play* on your CD player or MP3 player or begin singing the song, and the song does the work for you. The students hear the directions in an enjoyable song format, and you don't have to play the "bad guy" always nagging at them to perform certain actions correctly.

A Simple Musical Management Trick for Beginning Class

Many teachers struggle with getting students settled in at the beginning of the school day or the beginning of a class period. One popular strategy for dealing with this problem is to establish a routine for the beginning of class—some activity that students know they will be expected to do as soon as the class bell rings. Often called a "Bell Ringer" or a "Do-Now" activity, these activities often involve some type of journal writing, writing in response to a quotation or other short reading selection, or reflective writing to review the previous day's lesson. However, you still need to get students to settle in to start the Do-Now activity.

Here's how to cut through the classroom chatter: as students transition into the classroom, have some engaging transitional music (feel-good or pump-up music) playing at medium volume. The engaging music will begin the process of getting students' minds off what they were thinking or talking about in the hallway prior to entering your class. Then, as you prepare to get class started, over the span of three or four seconds, raise the volume of the music from medium to medium-loud. Students will begin to turn toward the source of the music as you do this, since any change in the environment activates our stimulus-driven attention systems. As students turn toward you, abruptly cut the music off. Students who were talking loudly enough to be heard over the music find themselves speaking too loudly for the suddenly quiet room, and they tend to either stop talking entirely or at least lower their voices significantly. The abrupt ending of the music also causes any student who had not already turned toward you when you raised the volume to do so at this point. The result is that you have secured the attention of most of the students in the class, and most if not all of them have turned toward you and stopped talking—all without you having to say a word! Now, all you have to do is speak into the silence.

Be aware that you need to be prepared to jump in and begin your lesson immediately. Raising the volume of the music and then abruptly cutting it off will only get your students' attention for a few seconds. If you don't step into the resulting silence quickly, your students will assume their attention isn't required after all, and they will begin new conversations or take up their previous conversations where they left off. So, know what you're going to say *before* cutting the music!

Distributing Materials

In his book *Impact Teaching*, Rich Allen (2001) talks about the creative distribution of materials (pp. 72–76). The old-fashioned way to distribute materials is for the teacher to walk around the room, passing out one item at a time (or have a student do it), or to pass a stack of items out to the person in front to pass back (if in rows), or to pass a stack to each table (if in groups). There are a couple of major drawbacks to these methods. First, these traditional ways of getting materials out are slow. Nothing drags on like a teacher walking around the room giving one item to each student sequentially. Second, the traditional methods are just so *boring!* This is an area where most teachers are missing a golden opportunity to raise the level of student engagement.

Here are some ways to distribute materials more efficiently, while keeping your students fully engaged.

Color Songs

Ask a representative from each table to collect and distribute their materials. To make this fun, you might say, "Identify the person in your group wearing the most black today." Students look around and figure out who that person is. You then say, "Please send that person up here to pick up the materials for your group." As soon as you say this, pop on the song "Black Magic Woman" by Santana (or "Black Is Black" by Los Bravos, or "That Old Black Magic" by James Darren). Some students will laugh when they get the joke. There are tons of songs that mention a color in the lyrics, from "Blue Moon" by The Marcels, to "Red, Red Wine" by UB40, to "Itsy Bitsy Teenie Weenie Yellow Polka-Dot Bikini" by Sha Na Na. *The Green Book of Songs by Subject,* mentioned in Chapter 7, has literally hundreds of color songs listed. Just look up "Colors" and you will see entire subsections for every color in the rainbow.

Songs That Match Student Traits

Identify a trait of one or more students and have the student(s) with that trait distribute the materials—and then have a song ready to go that matches the trait, of course. For example, you might say, "Identify the person in your group who is wearing the most jewelry. Send that person up to get your materials." You then play Madonna's "Material Girl" while they do so (or "Diamond Girl" by Seals and Croft). Or what about identifying the person with the longest hair (play "Hair," from the Broadway musical) or the shortest person ("Short People" by Randy Newman) or the person wearing the newest shoes ("New Shoes" by Paolo Nutini)? No matter how you match the song to the distribution of the materials, having one person from each group pick the materials up and distribute them to their own groups is faster than traditional methods, and a lot more engaging, as well. And the music adds an element of fun to the entire process.

Here are just a few more ideas to get your creative juices flowing: Ask students to add up some number specific to them, like their phone numbers, and then have the one with the highest (or lowest) total pick up the materials to pass out. Meanwhile, play "Beechwood 4-5789" by The Marvelettes, or "867-5309/Jenny" by Tommy Tutone, or some other number song like "Rikki Don't Lose That Number" by Steely Dan. Or have students identify which student in their group is closest to having their next birthday, and play "Birthday" by The Beatles while these students pass out the materials. Or have students identify who they think is the fastest runner in their groups, and have those students pass out the materials while you play the theme song from the classic Roadrunner and Coyote cartoon series (or play the live version by The Barenaked Ladies). You are truly only limited by your imagination.

Songs That Match Student Names

Even if you really do want to have a single student pass out the materials sequentially, you can still use music to make it more of a light-hearted moment. One way to do this is to use songs with people's names in them. For example, let's say that you had a student named Amy in your class. You say, "Amy, would you please pass out the papers?" As she does so, you play "Amie" by Pure Prairie League. If you have a Jim in your room, have him pass things out to "You Don't Mess Around With Jim" by Jim Croce. Here are just a few others: Amanda ("Amanda" by Boston), Barbara ("Barbara Ann" by The Beach Boys), Bernadette ("Bernadette" by The Four Tops), Caroline ("Sweet Caroline" by Neil Diamond), Daniel ("Daniel" by Elton John), Duke (or Earl) ("Duke of Earl" by Gene Chandler), Georgia ("Georgia on My Mind" by Ray Charles), Gloria ("Gloria" by Laura Branigan), Henry ("I'm Henry the VIII I Am" by Herman's Hermits), Jack (or Diane) ("Jack and Diane" by John Mellencamp). . . . well, you get the idea. There really is a song to go with just about any name. We haven't even tried very hard to collect these name songs, and we have a playlist of such songs in iTunes with more than 300 songs in it. Again, the *Green Book of Songs by Subject* is a fabulous resource here. Just look up "Men's Names" or "Women's Names," and you will find alphabetical listings of hundreds of songs.

Paper Scramble

Every once in a while, as a change-up, try literally throwing the papers up in the air and have students scramble to pick them up and pass them to the appropriate people. If you have students seated in groups, you can presort the papers by group. Then pop on an appropriate song such as "Come Fly With Me" by Michael Buble or "Up, Up, and Away" by The 5th Dimension, and walk from group to group, throwing their papers up in the air over their tables. Students grab the papers as they flutter down and pass them to the appropriate people. This gets the papers passed out quickly, the students get to move around a bit, and everyone enjoys a quick break from the normal classroom routine. Similarly, anytime you want to pass out other (nonpaper) materials such as colored markers or pencils, you could toss a handful in the general direction of each group (be careful, please) and have students scramble for them. While you do this, you could play "It's Raining Men" by The Weather Girls or "Raindrops Keep Falling on My Head" by B. J. Thomas. It's great fun for everyone!

Beginning and Ending Songs

Another easy way to have fun by matching music to classroom activity is to use a song at the beginning of the day that says something about *morning* or *beginnings*. As students transition into the classroom, you could play songs such as "Back in the Saddle Again" by Gene Autry; "Beautiful Day" by U2; "A Beautiful Morning" by The Rascals; "Begin" by Ben Lee; "Brand New Day" by Sting; "Daydream Believer" by The Monkees; "Good Morning Good Morning" by The Beatles; "Good Morning, Starshine" by Oliver; "Lovely Day" by Donavon Frankenreiter; "Morning Has Broken" by Cat Stevens; "The Promise of a New Day" by Paula Abdul; "Start Me Up" by The Rolling Stones; "Starting All Over Again" by Hall and Oates; "Wake Up Little Susie" by The Everly Brothers; or "Woke Up This Morning" by Joe McBride.

Of course, there are also many songs written about *endings* or *leaving* (about the end of relationships, usually), so there are many ways to use songs as a "musical joke" as students leave at the end of a class or the end of the day. We have more than 100 of these, but here is just a sample: "Bye Bye Love" by The Everly Brothers; "Closing Time" by Semisonic; "Come Back Baby" by Eric Clapton; "Day-O" by Harry Belafonte; "Every Time We Say Goodbye" by Steve Tyrell; "Exodus" by Bob Marley; "Farewell So Long Goodbye" by Bill Haley; "Get Back" by The Beatles; "Good Riddance" by Green Day; "Happy Trails" by Roy Rogers; and "Hit the Road Jack" by Ray Charles. Just make sure that you are OK with the lyrics of any song you play ("Closing Time" is about leaving the bar at closing time).

Musical Reviews

Try matching a song to a review activity. For example, one type of cooperative learning review involves tossing a ball or other object from student to student while reviewing the material. Small groups of students get into circles. One person in each group has a ball, and that person shares one thing he or she has learned during the lesson or unit. He or she then tosses the ball to someone else in the group, who catches it and then adds something he or she has learned. The ball is tossed around the group long enough for each person to share two or three items. You can spice up this activity by playing a song like Jerry Lee Lewis's "Great Balls of Fire" while students toss the balls around (or "Red Rubber Ball" by The Cyrkle, or "Rubber Ball" by The Coasters). The music in the background almost always elicits a laugh or a groan from those paying attention to it. Many other people never even notice what song is playing, but just enjoy hearing an upbeat song in the background during the activity.

Or conduct a "musical chairs review," where students stand around a group of chairs arranged in a circle or facing out from a table. There is one less chair than students in each group. When the music begins, students walk in the same direction around the chairs. When you stop the music, everyone tries to get to the nearest seat. The student left standing in each group is then asked to share something he or she learned during the lesson or unit. Those students then step outside of the activity, while the remaining students remove a chair from each group before repeating the activity. We like to use a song for this activity that matches the movement such as "Will It Go Round in Circles" by Billy Preston or "Rawhide" by Frankie Laine, which includes the line, "rollin', rollin', rollin', keep them doggies rollin'." You get the material reviewed, and everyone has a good time.

Movement for Movement's Sake—Energizing, Oxygenating, and Zapping the Wiggles

Sometimes the best thing a teacher can do is simply to get students up out of their seats and moving around. Some people criticize such movement breaks because they feel that students should constantly be engaged in "academically rigorous" tasks. But the reality is that no one can maintain constant attention and effort on academic tasks for too long at a stretch without needing a break. This is especially true of younger students, those students with ADHD, or those who are just more kinesthetically oriented.

Getting your students out of their seats and moving achieves several goals at once: it gives students a break from the demands of sustained on-task attentional focus; it helps them get their kinesthetic needs met, which can help them "get their wiggles out"; and it gives their brains a good dose of oxygen, especially if the movement is vigorous and sustained for more than a minute. For all of these reasons, students who are given periodic movement breaks are often in a better state to learn than their peers who are always expected to be on-task. Plus, classrooms that incorporate periodic movement tend to be more enjoyable learning environments as well!

Whatever movement activity you choose—from the simple (stand behind their chairs and do some toe raises, walk around their tables, do some stretching or Brain Gym movements, etc.) to the more elaborate (do more vigorous exercise movements such as jumping jacks, or play a quick, fast-paced round of blob tag, for example)— provide a soundtrack of energizing music. In a matter of a minute or two, you have given students a quick break, injected their brains with a shot of oxygen, and added an element of energy and fun into the learning environment. If you want to take this a step further, you can use a song with lyrics that match the movement or actually direct students in their movements via the lyrics—for example, "Follow the Leader," by The Socka Boys; "The Freeze," by Greg and Steve; or classics such as "The Hokey Pokey," by Ray Anthony or "The Chicken Dance," by Ray Castoldi (OK, technically "The Chicken Dance" doesn't have lyrics, but you know the movements).

And this just scratches the surface. There are songs to match the weather, songs to match the season, holiday songs, songs that match the day of the week . . . and on and on and on. We hope this quick look into some of the special uses of music for management purposes and to match classroom activities has sparked some ideas for how you can use it in your own teaching.

What to Avoid

Habituation Versus Novelty

We talked briefly about habituation—the process by which the brain gets used to a stimulus and gradually reduces its response to that stimulus—in the chapter on background music. Habituation, in the case of background music, is our friend, as the brain habituates to the music, which then becomes merely white noise in the background, covering distracting sounds and allowing students to focus on their work.

When we're talking about using music as a signal to start an activity or using a song with embedded directions, however, habituation can work against us. When a teacher uses the same song repeatedly to signal students to start an activity, the song acts as a trigger for episodic memory (and semantic memory as well, when there are directions embedded in the lyrics), which eventually leads to conditioned memory and an automatic response. But it is also possible that, over time, students will have heard your signal song so many times that they will habituate to it (it will no longer be novel), and they might begin to tune it out. If you notice this beginning to happen, you may have to reteach the response you want. If that doesn't work, you may need to switch to a new song.

INSIDE A CLASSROOM

Transitions—Music as a Cue and Directions for Lining Up

Zoie Moody
Key Stage One Coordinator, Year 2 (equivalent to 2nd Grade in the US)
St. Dennis Primary School
Cornwall, England

"We sing the 'We Are Lining Up' song when a quiet, orderly line is needed in the class or around school. I made up the lyrics ('We are lining up; we are lining up; fold your arms, face the front, we are lining up!'), and whenever I want the children to line up (especially if they are a bit noisy), I just start singing the song, and they automatically join in, following the actions, which results in the desired lining-up behavior. I use this song with Early Years and Key Stage One children. We sing it three times: the first time in a normal voice, the second time in a whisper, and the third time we just mouth the words silently, resulting in a quiet line of children ready to listen and move quietly.

"Before I used music in my classroom, lining up would be a bit of a hit or miss affair, with me normally having to shout to make myself heard, or I would have to spend time focusing on those not lining up correctly. As a result, lining up would take a long time and had the potential to be a quite hectic and negative experience. Since introducing music, lining up has become a quick, fun activity with most children complying the first time. The atmosphere is positive and purposeful."

Advice to Teachers: "Keep it simple with young children. Use it often so it becomes routine, and make it fun so the children want to join in."

Unclear Expectations for Student Response to Music

We have mentioned several times how a signal song can work like magic to get students to begin a routine action—and it definitely can. But the magic doesn't happen without a little work on the front end.

Let's say, for example, that you are a primary teacher, and you want to use a song as a signal for students to put away any materials on their desks and gather quietly at the carpeted area for read-aloud time. You can't just simply say, "OK, from now on, every time I play this song, I want you to put away your things and come to the carpet." Instead, you need to complete five basic steps to ensure your new signal song will work well from the very beginning:

1. **Frame the relevance**—Explain to students *why* it's important for you to be able to get their attention and get them started on the new activity quickly when necessary. Even very young students like to have a reason for doing the things they are asked to do, and they are more likely to participate willingly if given one.

2. **Introduce the song to your students**—Play the song (or portion of the song, if you are just going to use part of the song, like the chorus) a couple of times so students will recognize it when you start using it as a signal.

3. **Model**—*Show* your students how to do the action(s) correctly. In this case, you might pretend to be a student with a number of objects out on your desk. Start the signal song, and then model quickly clearing your desk, standing and walking quietly to the read-aloud area, and sitting down facing the teacher's chair, ready to pay attention. One clear visual demonstration is worth a thousand words, so *don't skip this crucial step.*

4. **Practice**—Tell students that it is now their turn to try. Ask them all to sit in their seats and simulate the end of the activity prior to read-aloud time. Turn on the music and instruct the students to clear their desks and move to the read-aloud area as you just demonstrated. When all students reach the designated area, turn off the music.

5. **Give feedback and practice again, if necessary**—Students need to know how good is good enough, so give them this crucial feedback. You might say, "On a scale of 1 to 10 that was a 6. We need to get to at least an 8 before I will be satisfied. Everyone please return to your desks, and let's try again." Tell them *exactly* what they need to do differently in order to improve their performance. Once students know what a competent performance looks, sounds, and feels like, they are much more likely to complete the action(s) to your satisfaction going forward.

Once students have been taught the song and practiced the routine a few times, all you have to do is turn the song on (or start singing the song softly, if it's a song with lyrics). It usually just takes a few notes to get them moving (remember that show, *Name That Tune.*), all without having to tell students a thing. If you take the time at the beginning to teach students your expectations, it really *does* work like magic!

Not Establishing or Following Through on Consequences for Misbehavior

While the uses of music discussed in this chapter tend to be fun and engaging for everyone involved, this doesn't change the fact that you, the teacher, have other reasons for using these strategies beyond simply creating a fun classroom environment (though, of course, that is certainly *one* of your goals). If you are using a signal song, it's because you want a certain type of repeated activity to start quickly and be accomplished smoothly each time. If you are using a short song clip as a timer for a certain repeated transition, you are doing so because you need that transition to take place quickly so you don't lose valuable instructional time. And when you use a song (such as a color song or a trait song) to designate certain students to distribute materials to their classmates, you are doing so because you need the materials passed out efficiently without having to designate five or six individual students to do the job.

So, what happens if your students fail to perform any of these management tasks as expected? Yes, being up front with students about your expectations can go a long way toward heading off problems down the road. Modeling, practicing, and giving feedback are also all crucial components for ensuring that your students perform well. But no strategy is foolproof, and in our experience, you can expect some students to test you to see if you really mean what you say.

Take signal songs, for example. Some students (and you know who they are) will hear the song come on and drag their feet, watching you the whole time to see how you will react. Rest assured that, if these students are successful at slowing down the entire transition with no repercussions for their actions, they will move even more slowly next time. Pretty soon, the transition is taking as long as it did before you established the signal song. Or let's say that you establish a short musical selection as a timer for a certain repeated transition. It might work beautifully for a while, but then you notice that one or more students are intentionally moving slowly and waiting until the music is almost over, and then trying to move at hyperspeed to complete the action in the nick of time. This usually results in unsafe movement, and someone is likely to get hurt. Or let's say that you use a color song like "Green Acres" to designate that the student in each group wearing the most green needs to come up and get the materials to pass out to his group. But then you look around and you notice that one of the students passing out materials is wearing no green at all. Either the person in his group who *was* wearing the most green found a way (begging? threatening? bribing?) to get this student to do the task for him or her, or the student passing out the materials volunteered to do it. Either way, if one of your goals for using such songs is to randomize student help and get everyone involved consistently over time, students not following your directions work against that goal, and you need to put a stop to such behavior.

What should you do about such situations? A little proactive planning can go a long way toward keeping such exasperating behavior from happening in the first place—or at least from being repeated if it does happen. The best thing you can do is to anticipate such possibilities and establish consequences for noncompliance from the beginning. For example, if you anticipate that some of your students may try to make a game of the timer song, waiting until the last second to accomplish the task, and then running at full speed to get done just as the final note dies away, you should bring this up *at the very beginning.* In fact, you might even want to model the *wrong* way to do things (students will get a kick from seeing you "misbehave") before you model the *right* way to do them. If you do this, students can't behave incorrectly later and claim that they didn't know that you would consider the behavior to be unacceptable. You also need to establish a consequence for anticipated incorrect behaviors. And, of course, if you establish a consequence, you *must* follow through and administer the consequence each and every time the misbehavior occurs until the behavior is extinguished. Anticipate noncompliance, discuss and model both correct and incorrect behavior, establish consequences for incorrect behavior, and follow through by administering consequences when necessary, and you will have very few problems—and the ones you do have will be short-lived.

When Lyrics and Processing Clash

Some of you may have noticed an inconsistency between some things we've said in this chapter and some issues we discussed in

Chapters 5 and 6 about background music. In those chapters, we talked about how important it is to use instrumental music *only* for background behind individual or group tasks. We pointed out that words are inherently attention-getting, and that introducing them (via lyrics) into the learning environment when students are attempting to think can be distracting and lead to poorer work quality. And we stand by that statement.

On the other hand, in this chapter, when talking about using music that matches the activity, the songs we have used as examples all contain lyrics. Isn't this a contradiction? That's a great question, and the answer is, "Yes, in *some* cases, it is a contradiction, and in such cases, you have to think carefully about your goals and the task at hand in order to make good instructional decisions."

INSIDE A CLASSROOM

Transitions—Cleaning Up After Activities

Alistair Johnson
Year 6 Teacher (equivalent to 6th Grade in the US)
Dobwalls CP School
Dobwalls, Liskeard, Cornwall, England

"I use music after an art activity as a cue for students to quickly tidy up. I will play the music (the main theme to *Mission Impossible* or *Countdown*, from the British word/number quiz show), and the children are expected to complete the task before the music ends.

"Before I used the music, the children generally wanted to continue what they were currently doing or just chat with friends instead of focusing on tidying up. Since I have started using the music, the children work together to get the cleanup done as quickly as possible to beat the music."

Advice to Teachers: "I really would recommend the use of music in the classroom. I have found that children respond so positively to music, whether it be a quick 'clean up' piece of music or a slow background tune that helps them focus—it really does seem to help them (and me) get things done much more easily!"

Suggested Songs: "Main Title Theme, *Mission Impossible*," Danny Elfman; "*Countdown* Theme," Pipa and the Four From the Top.

Let's look at some examples. First of all, you have to think about the activity that will be taking place while you play the music. If you are simply asking students to stand and walk twenty steps in any direction, then pair up with someone near them to have a pair share, you can play a song such as "Gimme Three Steps" by Lynyrd Skynyrd to match the activity and add a little fun into the environment. This is simply a transition, so there is no student processing taking place while they walk to find partners. As soon as students are paired up, however, you would need to turn "Gimme Three Steps" off, give students directions for their pair shares, and then switch to a background song such as those described in Chapter 6. When students finish their discussions and are ready to return to their seats, you can use another song to match the activity, or just use a feel-good or pump-up song to keep the mood and energy high. Such flexible use of music accomplishes several objectives in a short three- to five-minute span—adding fun and energy into your transitions, while maximizing student processing during the actual share time.

But what about the example we used previously, where students did a gallery tour around the room, examining the work of other groups and adding their own comments? This is where it gets tricky. We talked previously about playing walking songs to match the activity and add some fun into the atmosphere. This would probably be acceptable if students were simply seeing what their classmates thought about an issue, but didn't have to think too hard about responding. However, if students are expected to do some real critical thinking about their classmates' work and put their thoughts into words, which is a challenging task, having extra words in the environment in the form of lyrics would probably not be a good idea. So, instead of playing walking songs throughout the activity, you might play a walking song at the very beginning, as students are gathering in their groups and walking to the first poster, and then switch to group background music during the rest of the activity. Or, if you are a real pro at it, you could switch back and forth, playing a song to match the activity each time students rotate to the next poster, and then switching back to background music as they do the actual work.

Here's one more example. Remember when we talked about playing ball songs while having students complete a ball-toss review? Is this a good idea? Well, again, it depends on what the students are sharing and how challenging the task is. If they are simply sharing their opinions about something, or sharing ideas they have already written down (that is, the thinking is easy or has already been done), then it's probably OK to have a song such as "Great Balls of Fire" playing while students share. It won't impair thinking too much, and the added element of fun might be just what the class needs. On the other hand, if the review activity involves higher-level processing, you might play a ball song during the transition into the activity (while students get into groups, pick up a ball to use, etc.), but then switch to instrumental background music during the actual review.

Bottom line, you need to think about the activity carefully, and if students are going to have to do some heavy "mental lifting," avoid music with lyrics during that processing time. However, you still may be able to use a song that matches the activity at hand as students transition into and out of the activity. With a little common sense and proactive planning, you will be using music as an effective management tool in no time.

Beware of Inappropriate or Hurtful Lyrics

One final warning. It's easy to get caught up in finding songs to match classroom activities, and if you're not careful, you can get careless and inadvertently hurt someone's feelings or send inappropriate messages. Let's say you decide to use some name songs in your classroom as musical jokes to add an element of fun into your classroom, so you start thinking about the names of the students in your class and what songs might include those names in their lyrics. Like we've said, there are literally hundreds of songs that include names, so you will probably be able to find songs for most of your students. But just because you find a song that includes a student's name, that doesn't mean that the rest of the lyrics will be appropriate to use. Say, for example, that you have a student named Jim, and he has a macho reputation. In this case, he (and everyone else in the class) might get a kick of you playing Jim Croce's "You Don't Mess Around With Jim" while Jim passes out materials or does some other management task. Or let's say you have three girls in your class named Jennifer (not an uncommon occurrence these days), and you want the three of them to do something for you while simultaneously making light of the fact that there are three of them in a single class. You could play "27 Jennifers" by Mike Doughty, and everyone will probably get a kick out of it. But playing a song like Night Ranger's "Sister Christian," or Eric Clapton's "Lay Down Sally," or The Beatles' "Sexy Sadie" just because you have girls in your class named Christian, Sally, or Sadie would probably be a very bad choice, for obvious reasons. Just make sure that you listen to *all* of the lyrics to any song you plan on using. If the lyrics may hurt someone's feelings or send an inappropriate message, you would be better off not using the song—even if you really like it.

Getting Started

You can get started with some of these strategies right away with very little work, while others may be a bit more labor-intensive. For example, it takes very little work to get started with implementing signal songs or timer songs. You can literally use any song you want, either instrumental or with lyrics, for these purposes. Many teachers use a feel-good song that their students like as a signal song. For timer songs, a fast-paced song is often good, or you can make a joke out of the situation by using something like the theme song to the classic game show *Jeopardy*.

For matching a song to an activity, you can probably think of a lot of songs that will work for certain situations right off the top of your head. But as we've already mentioned, there's really no better tool for coming up with music to match activities than *The Green Book of Songs by Subject* or the website www.greenbookofsongs.com. Simply search for your topic and you will find tons of great songs you can use to inject that extra element of fun and engagement into your classroom.

Of all of the management uses of music mentioned in this chapter, the biggest challenge, as you might expect, is finding good songs with directions for certain tasks embedded in the lyrics. For this purpose, the best source we have found is the website www.songsforteaching .com. This site, in addition to many other great features, includes a page titled "Classroom Management Songs for Teachers," with lists of songs for different uses such as establishing procedures, starting the day or ending the day, lining up, and cleaning up. Unfortunately, as you might guess, most of these songs are more for the elementary level. It is very difficult to find management songs for the secondary level, so you secondary teachers may just need to get the creative juices flowing and write your own!

Our Top 40 Classroom Management Songs

Similar to our Top 40 in Chapter Seven, there's not much new material here. Most of the songs in the following list have been mentioned already in this chapter. We are simply taking this opportunity to give you a few of our overall favorite songs from the different subcategories we've covered. Also check out Appendix G, where we give you many more song ideas *not* mentioned in this chapter, as well as our website, www.rockandrollclassroom.com.

Timer Songs

1. "Jeopardy!" Merv Griffin

Songs With Embedded Directions

2. "Helper Train," Caroline and Danny
3. "Here's What You Do Do and What You Don't Do When You Go to Use the Bathroom," Jack Hartmann
4. "Never Be Afraid to Ask Questions," Ben Stiefel

Songs That Match Classroom Activities: Color Songs

5. "Black Magic Woman," Santana
6. "Blue Moon," The Marcels
7. "Green Acres," Eddie Albert
8. "Itsy Bitsy Teenie Weenie Yellow Polka-Dot Bikini," Sha Na Na
9. "Mrs. Brown You've Got a Lovely Daughter," Herman's Hermits
10. "Red, Red Wine," UB40

Songs That Match Classroom Activities: Student Traits

11. "Material Girl," Madonna
12. "New Shoes," Paolo Nutini

13. "Rikki Don't Lose That Number," Steely Dan
14. "Short People," Randy Newman

Songs That Match Classroom Activities: Student Names

15. "Amie," Pure Prairie League
16. "Barbara Ann," The Beach Boys
17. "Duke of Earl," Gene Chandler
18. "Georgia on My Mind," Ray Charles
19. "I'm Henry the VIII I Am," Herman's Hermits
20. "Johnny B. Good," Chuck Berry
21. "Sweet Caroline," Neil Diamond
22. "You Don't Mess Around With Jim," Jim Croce

Songs That Match Classroom Activities: Paper/Materials Scramble

23. "Come Fly With Me," Michael Buble
24. "It's Raining Men," The Weather Girls
25. "Raindrops Keep Falling on My Head," B. J. Thomas
26. "Up, Up, and Away," The 5th Dimension

Songs That Match Classroom Activities: Beginning Songs

27. "A Beautiful Morning," The Rascals

28. "Beautiful Day," U2

29. "Daydream Believer," The Monkees

30. "Start Me Up," The Rolling Stones

31. "Wake Up Little Susie," The Everly Brothers

Songs That Match Classroom Activities: Ending Songs

32. "Bye Bye Love," The Everly Brothers

33. "Happy Trails," Roy Rogers

34. "Hit the Road Jack," Ray Charles

Songs That Match Classroom Activities: Review Songs

35. "Great Balls of Fire," Jerry Lee Lewis

36. "Rawhide," Frankie Laine

Songs That Match Classroom Activities: Movement Songs

37. "Follow the Leader," The Socka Boys

38. "The Chicken Dance," Ray Castoldi

39. "The Hokey Pokey," Ray Anthony

40. "Walking on Sunshine," Katrina and the Waves

Notes

1. Chazin and Neuschatz (1990) found that information embedded in a song format was more easily recalled than when the same information was learned through lecture. This finding was true of both eight-year-old subjects and young adults (1067–1071).

2. Wallace (1994) found that, when subjects listened to a text presented either in spoken form or in song form and then were tested for recall, they performed better in the spoken condition if the text was heard only once. But when subjects heard three repetitions of the text sung to the same melody, recall was better than in the spoken condition (1471–1485).

3. Purnell-Webb and Speelman (2008) focused more specifically on rhythm and found that rhythm, with or without musical

accompaniment, can facilitate recall of text, "suggesting that rhythm may provide a schematic frame to which text can be attached" (927).

4. On the other hand, Wallace (1994) argues that melody is the more powerful mnemonic factor, as melody, being more variable than rhythm, is the more salient feature that "chunks words and phrases, identifies line lengths, identifies stress patterns, and adds emphasis" (1471).

5. Kilgour, Jakobson, and Cuddy (2000) found presentation rate to be an important factor in the mnemonic power of songs with embedded content. When they slowed down the presentation rate of material presented verbally to match the presentation rate of the same material presented through a song, they found that subjects learned the material when spoken as well as they did when it was presented in song format (700–710). This finding suggests that the typically slower presentation rate of material as presented in song format is a key reason for its mnemonic value.

6. Pereira, Teixeira, Figueiredo, Xavier, and Castro (2011) scanned subjects using fMRI to determine the brain's response to familiar and unfamiliar music. They found that a number of limbic and paralimbic brain regions, as well as the brain's reward circuitry, were significantly more active when listening to familiar music. This suggests that listening to familiar music is an emotionally engaging activity, and heightened activation of these structures may well play a role in the increased mnemonic effectiveness of songs with content embedded in familiar tunes.

7. Shatin (1970) found that, while people are individual in their reactions to the same songs, "there is certainly a common or modal type of mood response which is predictable for various pieces of music" (81). That is, the same type of music produces, in general, the same type of response from most people.

9

Putting It
All Together

Policies and Procedures, Hardware and Software, Planning and Implementation

Music is like making love: either all or nothing.

—Isaac Stern

What It Is

To this point, you've read about each use of music in the classroom in a separate chapter. Now that you have seen each use separately, it's time to step back and look at the big picture. The question before us here is, "What does the daily, flexible, integrated use of music in the classroom look like?" To answer this question, we need to address a number of issues you may have been wondering about. For example, "Do I need to think about policy issues and procedures? What about equipment? How do I use music for a variety of purposes all within a single lesson?" And that's exactly what this final chapter is about. Our goal here is to answer these and other "big picture" questions so that when you're finished reading, you will feel ready to give this whole music thing a shot.

How to Use It—Policies and Procedures

In the final analysis, only *you* can figure out what works best for your specific students. As with most classroom methodologies, the use of music can only be fine-tuned by the teacher-researcher willing to try different approaches and reflect on the efficacy of those approaches. However, here are a few principles that will support you in integrating music into your classroom.

Get in the Habit of Collecting and Categorizing Music

This is not a *classroom* procedure, but rather a *personal* procedure—that is, a habit—all teachers should cultivate. The teachers who are best at incorporating music into their classrooms have developed a certain mindset. First, they are always on the lookout for music to use in their classrooms. They even listen to the radio differently than others. Whereas most people listen to a radio station simply for enjoyment, these master music-users are also thinking along the lines of, "That would be a great feel-good song for my classroom," or "I could use that song to introduce my unit on astronomy." You will often see these teachers frantically searching for a scrap of paper and a pen so they can write down a song's title and the name of the artist so they can purchase the song later.

But collecting the music is only the first step. The necessary second step is to categorize your music. Programs such as iTunes make this easy. Simply create a playlist for all of your feel-good songs, another playlist for your calming songs, another for your background music, and so on. When it's time to add music to your lesson plans, all you have to do is think, "OK, at this point, I'm going to ask my students to find a partner from another group, and I want them to do it quickly, so I need a pump-up song here." You then go to your pump-up playlist, pick a song, and drag it into your lesson plan playlist. Easy! But if you don't precategorize your music into playlists, it makes the whole process much harder. If you have thousands of songs in your music library, you don't want to be sifting through the whole library every time you need a song. This would quickly become time-consuming and overwhelming, and you will probably give up on the whole thing.

INSIDE A CLASSROOM

Music to My Ears

Anne Kerby
Resource Teacher
Desert Trails Elementary School
Phoenix, Arizona, USA

"I have had the joy of teaching students with autism, emotional disabilities, learning disabilities, and cognitive disabilities for fifteen years. It can be tricky finding a variety of techniques that are effective for these unique learners. At times, the life skill of learning can be arduous. Educators must find an avenue that opens the mind and prepares students to receive new and challenging information. Music has been one technique that has been extremely successful in motivating, focusing, and at times soothing my students so they are ready to learn.

"Some of my students with autism are ultrasensitive to sound. Music must be pleasant to their ears and individualized. Two of my students with autism use iPods with headphones when they are required to complete tasks. When they are working, they can listen to their specific, self-selected, teacher-approved play lists. I use this as a motivator to get perceived, mundane tasks completed. General education teachers are typically pleased with the completed tasks such as projects, worksheets, or tests. At times, parents question if this strategy is appropriate; however, I assure them the students have a higher level of productivity when listening to music, free from other stimuli in the classroom or school. The goal is to have them practice the academic skill. When they refuse to work, or if they go into 'shut-down' mode, learning stops. I use whatever it takes to keep the momentum of learning moving forward, and music is a great motivator.

"One of my students struggles significantly because her distraction involves voices in her head. The voices never tell her how beautiful or smart she is. Instead, they tend to be a stream of insults that make her lash out in a violent manner. As a result, she had very little opportunity to learn or grow in the educational environment. She is very sensitive to sound and has a great deal of difficulty filtering, especially when the voices are taunting her. My first task was to find a genre of music she enjoyed. Her verbal skills are advanced, so she told me when she objected to the music. After exhausting my library, I accidentally stumbled upon a genre she responded to in a positive manner. Who would have guessed Roy Rogers would be music to her ears? Her favorite song was 'Hold That Critter Down.' She laughed and tapped her foot. When she listens to her individual playlist, the voices are quiet, and she works happily writing stories about horses, cows, and yes, other critters she loves.

"I also work with students with emotional disabilities who experience extreme difficulty with impulse control, lack social skills, and at times show violent tendencies. When one of my students has such an episode, he or she is typically escorted to my room, where he or she is given the opportunity to calm down and regroup before going back into the mainstream. One day, I was teaching a lesson on nouns, and *Schoolhouse Rock* was on my Smart Board. The kids were all singing along while the student who was just brought to my room was in the cooling off period. He got a huge smile on his face and asked if we were going to watch a few more episodes of the *Schoolhouse Rock* series. As a group, we decided to review adverbs, conjunctions, and adjectives. He was so happy and productive when he returned to his classroom that his teacher called to get my secret. Who knew conjunctions could sooth in such a positive manner?

"These are three quick examples of how music can be individualized to support the needs of students with a variety of special needs. The key is to find the genre of music that inspires and soothes. It may not be what you have in mind, hence the individualization. My goal is to do whatever it takes to increase student engagement and productivity. When distractions get in the way, I attempt to remove the barriers to moving forward so learning can happen. Music is just one way to accomplish the goal. Happy Trails!"

Policies Around Choice of Music

Perhaps the most important policy issue today's teacher must consider concerning music in the classroom is this: Who decides what students listen to, and when? Clearly, you as the teacher will control the musical selections played as students transition into and out of the classroom, and during movement activities. But what about the music students listen to while working independently—who chooses the background music while they work?

As explained in Chapter 5, the most effective music for students to listen to while focusing on a task is music of medium tempo (60 to 80 bpm) that is instrumental, structurally repetitive, simple in instrumentation, unfamiliar (no instrumental versions of well-known pop songs), in the major mode, and played at low volume (just loud enough to cover distracting sounds). The issue is, if we let our students listen to anything they want on their iPods (or through headphones connected to music on their laptops) while they work, will they choose to listen to the right kind of music? The answer is almost certainly, "No way!" They will choose to listen to the music they *like best*—which for most students will be what this book calls feel-good or pump-up music. And this is exactly the *wrong* kind of music for them to be listening to while they work, because it calls attention to itself and away from the task at hand!

So, what are your options as the adult responsible for ensuring that maximum learning takes place in your classroom? Most teachers choose to keep control in their own hands and play general background music for the whole class—the approach described in Chapter 5. This is probably the best approach for elementary and middle school teachers. However, high school teachers, whose students have access to iPods or other MP3 players (or access to music through their laptop computers), have another option. This option involves *educating* your students about the effects of different kinds of music on attention and then giving them some control over the music they listen to.

If you wish to pursue this option, here are a few suggestions: First, as stated above, educate your students. Explain how music with words distracts their minds when thinking in words; explain how fast-paced music and loud music cause arousal, which makes them more distracting; explain how familiar music calls attention to itself and splits their attentional focus, making them more error-prone in their work. Once you have explained these issues, play some examples of the kind of music that works best for background music while working. This will help your students to understand what kind of music they should be listening to while they work. Finally, *give them ongoing guidance and support.*

At this stage, some teachers may be comfortable leaving things up to their students, trusting that they will make good choices. Other teachers may want to more tightly control things—by offering students a playlist of approved songs or at least showing them where to find the kind of music they should be listening to. However tightly you decide to control the use of individual music listening in your classroom, the major advantage of going with this option is that, in addition to giving older students a sense of ownership and control in the classroom, you also help them to develop lifelong learning habits. You can be the one who teaches them that music can be used for a variety of purposes in their lives—inside and outside of school—helping them to develop a greater sense of self-efficacy.

Equipment Security

Sadly, some teachers are hesitant to use audio equipment and iPods in the classroom in case the equipment is damaged or stolen. If this is the case where you teach, you will clearly need to develop policies and procedures to safeguard your equipment.

First, if at all possible, make sure that your equipment is portable, so you can take it home with you each day after school and bring it back the next day. For example, the Bose SoundDock, which we both use in our workshops, not only has great sound quality, but is wonderfully portable. It's very lightweight, and packs away neatly into a small carrying case that your iPod or other MP3 player can fit into, as well.

So, if your player is portable, that takes care of the issue of your equipment being stolen after school hours, but what about *during* the school day? What about those times when you have to step out of your classroom to monitor the hallway, or to take students to recess, or to go to lunch? What will prevent someone from slipping into your room during these times and taking your equipment? Sure, if no one else needs the room, you could lock the door. But what if another class uses the room during part of the day? Or what if you have students in the room and you just need to step out for a couple of minutes? What procedures do you have in place for equipment security at these times?

Some teachers actually secure their players in place—literally bolt or chain equipment to the spot (not exactly portable, but then no one else is going to walk off with it, either). Others have created a type of wire "cage" around the player, with a doorway on it that can be locked with a padlock when necessary. Going to such extremes may seem over the top to you, but it may be necessary in some situations.

Another way to handle equipment security is by putting in place procedures that bring your students into the equation. Some teachers create a classroom "job" for music security (a "music monitor"). Students can be assigned to the duty on a rotating basis. Whenever the teacher must be out of the room, the designated student is responsible for making sure the equipment remains safe. This procedure adds the nice benefit of sending the message that the chance to have music in the classroom is a privilege, and that along with that privilege comes the responsibility of taking care of the equipment that makes it possible.

How to Use It—Hardware and Software

This section could be a whole book in its own right. Here, we simply give you a few thoughts on your options for music equipment in the classroom.

The easiest and most convenient equipment for integrating music into your classroom is some sort of MP3 player (it doesn't have to be an iPod) and a portable music player (you can get them for under $100 at Best Buy or some other mega-electronics store). That said, if you feel more comfortable burning CDs and using a boom box CD player in class, that can work perfectly well too.

If you're buying an MP3 player, here are three very useful features:

1. Portability—Being able to easily carry your music with you is a huge benefit. Look for something light, with a carrying case.

2. A remote control—Ideally, you want to be able to quickly start and stop a song or to fast-forward to the next song, from anywhere in your room. If you have to walk back to the player each time you need to start or stop the music, it will quickly become a chore.

3. Battery power—It's great to be able to take your music with you during a quick "field trip" outside for a lesson, or if you're teaching somewhere without an available electrical outlet.

Beyond these basic suggestions, feel free to use whatever equipment you are comfortable with—as long as it works for learning, that's all that matters.

As far as software goes, your iPod or MP3 player comes with its own software (iTunes in the case of the iPod), allowing you to purchase music through an online store, manage it (by creating categories and playlists on your computer), and transfer that music to your player. If you have a SMART Board, SMART Notebook will allow you to play music through the interactive whiteboard. While this can be a bit clunky, it does certainly solve the problem of having equipment stolen. It's a whole lot easier to grab an iPod and sneak off with it than it is to wheel a SMART Board out of the classroom without being caught!

How to Use It

Planning and Implementation

If you haven't used music extensively in your teaching before, you will need to get used to thinking about the musical component of your lessons and units as you plan for effective instruction. While incorporating music into lessons is both exciting and fun, it does add an extra layer of prep time. The more you can precategorize your music, either in your MP3 software program or on CDs, and the more familiar you get with the music in your library, the more quickly this planning will go. With practice, you will learn to add music to your lessons quickly and it will become less of a burden.

INSIDE A CLASSROOM

Music Throughout the Day

Tania Smith
4th Grade Teacher
R. E. Simpson Elementary
Phoenix, Arizona, USA

"I use music in a variety of ways throughout the day. One way I use music is during our 'Brain Breaks.' We usually do Dance Freeze or a game I made up called Survivor (much like Hot Potato). I sometimes use classical music during writing time. I also use songs in math to help the kids remember math facts. For example, the kids sing a song to the tune of 'Mary Had a Little Lamb' to remember how to calculate area. We also use another song to remember how to find perimeter. And, at the end of the day, I play the Rodgers and Hammerstein song 'So Long, Farewell' from the soundtrack of the movie *The Sound of Music* during our cleanup time.

"Before I began using music, the kids didn't enjoy the Brain Breaks we used all that much, but they love them now with music added. They often even sing along with the music. When this happens, I feel a sense of community within the classroom. When I play classical music during writing time, it really seems as though the students concentrate on the task at hand. They don't talk to each other during the time the music is on because the volume is very low, and they want to be able to hear it. When I asked my students why they like the music, a few students stated that it makes them 'happier' and that it is 'cool.' As far as cleanup time goes, I used to use my voice to signal that it was time to start cleaning. During cleaning time the room was silent, which is much less enjoyable than playing *The Sound of Music* song. Since adding the music, the kids actually look forward to cleaning the room, and it goes faster!"

Advice to Teachers: "Music is a tool that works! It saves my voice, makes learning more fun, and expedites transitions and tasks in my classroom."

Suggested Songs: "So Long, Farewell," by the Cast from *The Sound of Music*.

Here are a few skeleton lesson plans showing how music can be used for a variety of purposes within a single class period or portion of the school day. The intent here is just to show you how and where you can build music into a few example lessons, not to provide you with complete lesson plan ideas.

Example Lesson Plans

A Morning in Kindergarten

Before 8:45 a.m.   Opening Transition: Play music as students enter the classroom. You have several options here, depending on your students and your goals for the morning. Most teachers choose to use feel-good music for this morning transition time, but you could also use pump-up music or calming music or songs that match an activity you will be doing that morning.

8:45–9:00 a.m.   Morning Work: Independent reading, partner reading. During this "quiet time," students are choosing books to read by themselves or with a partner. The goal here is for students to develop the stamina to sit and read for an extended period of time, so focus is crucial. Use background music during this time to cover distracting noises, so students can concentrate on their reading and develop this stamina.

9:00–9:15 a.m.   Morning Meeting: During this time, the class comes together for community building activities (sharing what they did over the weekend at home, for example) and to set the agenda for the day. You could use a consistent signal song here, telling students to transition to the morning meeting. If not using a signal song, pump-up or feel-good music is also a good choice. No music would be played during the meeting itself, as it would interfere with teaching and discussion.

9:15–10:15 a.m.   Writing Workshop: This block of time offers several opportunities to use music. The typical workshop period consists of a transition into a minilesson (direct instruction and modeling); the lesson itself, which lasts typically five to ten minutes; a longer period of time during which students work on their writing independently (or sometimes with partners); and finally, the period usually ends with some type of communal share time. You can use music for each transition, using different kinds of music depending on your goals and the mood and energy level of the class—signal songs, timer songs, feel-good music, pump-up music, or calming music could all have value here. The long stretch of independent work time in the middle of this period is a perfect place to use background music. Of course, no music should be played during the minilesson itself or the share time (if it is done whole group). If students share their work with a partner in a pair-share format, or in small groups, background music can be used behind this group activity.

10:15–10:20 a.m.   Brain Break: Between Writing Workshop time and the following Reading Workshop time, students often need at least a stretch break or some type of more vigorous movement activity to reset their attentional clocks and provide some energy. This is a perfect place to use pump-up music or movement music with directions for how to move embedded in the lyrics (like "The Freeze").

10:20–11:00 a.m.   Reading Workshop: Once the Brain Break is over, students transition into Reading Workshop. Structurally, Reading Workshop looks like Writing Workshop. The only difference is that the minilesson at the beginning is designed to teach about some aspect of reading instead of writing, and the students work on their independent reading during the long stretch of time in the middle of the period. The options for incorporating music into this period of time mirror those discussed above in the Writing Workshop description.

11:00–11:30 a.m.   Work Stations: During station time, students move from one station to another to complete various tasks (working ABC puzzles, working on white boards, reading with a partner, etc.) while the teacher works with a small group in guided reading. This is a perfect opportunity to use several types of music. If students are going to work fairly independently and decide when they are ready to move, background music will work. If, however, you are going to tell students when to rotate to the next station, short stretches of pump-up or feel-good music could be used during the movement. You can then switch over to background music again while students do the work at the next station.

11:30–11:35 a.m.   Cleanup Time: This is a great opportunity to use a song with embedded cleanup lyrics such as those mentioned in the previous chapter. Or any fun, up-tempo music would work to put students into a good mood and speed them up as they get the work done. You could also use a timer song to count down the amount of time left.

11:35 a.m.–12:20 p.m. Lunch/Recess: The transition from Cleanup Time to lunch gives you another opportunity to use either a line-up management song or feel-good or pump-up music.

An Afternoon in Fourth Grade

In this example, the heavier content focus of the science/social studies time period provides an opportunity to work in music with embedded content in addition to all of the management uses described in the previous lesson outline.

12:35–1:20 p.m.   Lunch/Recess: As students transition back into the classroom from lunchtime, you have the option of raising the mood with feel-good music, raising energy levels with pump-up music, or calming students down with calming music. Additionally, you could use a content song that foreshadows the content of the lesson to come.

1:20–2:15 p.m.   Science/Social Studies: This lesson is about Harriet Tubman and the Underground Railroad using several activities: silent reading/reciprocal teaching, whole class discussion, song analysis, and reflective writing. In this case, students read a section from their textbooks about the Underground Railroad and Harriet Tubman's role in it. During this silent reading time, play some background music to facilitate focus. Using the reciprocal teaching approach, each student reads the selection with a different focus (to summarize, to ask questions, or to identify key quotes, for example), and then brings his or her thinking to the group discussion that follows. Use music behind these discussions to allow each group to hear and focus on only their own discussion. After these discussions, distribute the lyrics to Woody Guthrie's "Harriet Tubman's Ballad"; then play the song while students read along with the lyrics. Afterward, students fill out a T-Chart with the headers "Information that matches the reading" and "New information," with background music playing again. You can then lead the class in a discussion of what students now know about Harriet Tubman's role in the Underground Railroad, combining what they've learned from their reading and the song lyrics. Class ends with a short piece of reflective writing where students write about how the information garnered through songs is the same as or differs from information learned through reading.

2:15–2:30 p.m.   Recess: Fourth graders are probably too old (or think they are) to need a line-up song to get ready to go to recess. However, you can still use a pump-up song to get students to move quickly to prepare to leave the room, or a timer song to make sure preparation takes place quickly. On the way back in, use another timer song by the end of which students need to have settled back into their seats, prepared to work. Alternatively, use a calming song if your students are hyped up from recess and need to settle down.

2:30–3:20 p.m.   Writing Workshop: This block of time looks very similar to the Writing Workshop block discussed previously in the kindergarten outline. There are several opportunities for transition music within the period, plus a long stretch of independent writing time (around thirty minutes) during which background music should be used. Again, no music should be used during the instructional minilesson or during whole-class sharing activities.

3:20–3:30 p.m.   Get Ready to Dismiss: At the end of Workshop time, students need to prepare to be dismissed to the buses or to be picked up by parents. This final tidying-up time might require a number of activities (putting away materials, gathering homework, putting on coats, etc.), and it needs to be done in an orderly fashion and quickly. A signal or timer song could be used here to signal the beginning of cleanup time and how much time is left until the final bell. On the other hand, the end of the day is a good time to use an ending song. Fourth graders are old enough to get the joke when a teacher plays a song such as "Happy Trails" or "Who Let the Dogs Out" as they transition out of the classroom.

High School Literature: To Kill a Mockingbird

The following lesson, developed by Christian Goering and Lauren Virshup (2009), is drawn from a series of suggested lessons found on the website LitTunes (www.corndancer.com), incorporating music into the study of Harper Lee's 1960 novel, *To Kill a Mockingbird*. If you would like to see a number of more detailed lesson plans for teaching *Mockingbird*, check out the LitTunes site. In the original lesson plan, only the songs with embedded content were included. The following fifty-minute example fleshes out the rest of the class period to show you how a number of other uses of music could be integrated into this lesson.

9:50–10:00 a.m.   As students transition into the classroom, the teacher plays feel-good music to put students in a good mood for class. (Alternatively, he or she could play pump-up music to energize the class, or calming music if energy levels will be too high, or somber music to set the tone for the serious discussions soon to take place.)

10:00–10:01 a.m.   While the teacher takes attendance, students get out their materials for class. As the teacher finishes taking roll, he gradually raises the volume of the music and then suddenly cuts it off. Students turn to face the front of the room, and the teacher begins the lesson.

10:01–10:06 a.m.   The teacher-led whole-class discussion begins. The focus of this day's lesson is on moral character, as displayed by Atticus and other characters in the book. In this short discussion, the teacher prepares students for the next activity by reviewing several previously discussed examples of moral character from the book.

10:06–10:08 a.m.   The teacher assigns four or five groups randomly in some fashion (counting off, etc.). As the students move into their groups, the teacher plays either pump-up music or a song that matches the activity ("Travelin' Band" by CCR, for example). If students already have established teams, this movement step can be skipped.

10:08–10:09 a.m.   The teacher uses a color (student wearing the most purple, for example, while playing "Purple People Eater" by Sheb Wooley) or some trait (having the neatest dressed male in each group come up to get the materials while playing "Sharp Dressed Man" by ZZ Top) to designate one student from each group to pick up the song lyrics and pass them out to their groups. Each group gets lyrics to a different song that has some relationship to the theme of moral character. The seven songs suggested as possibilities for this lesson are "There But for Fortune," by Phil Ochs; "I Choose," by India.Arie; "Hands," by Jewel; "What Say You," by Travis Tritt; "He Was My Brother," by Simon and Garfunkel; "Lie on Lie," by Chalk Farm; and "Atticus Taught Me," by Cary Cooper.

10:09–10:25 a.m.   Students are directed to read the song lyrics for their song silently and then take a couple of minutes to discuss what they think the lyrics are saying. The teacher plays slower-paced background music at a low volume while students read, but then switches to a more up-tempo background selection during the group discussions. After groups have had the chance to discuss their lyrics for a few minutes, the teacher asks each group to listen to their song while following along with the lyrics. The logistics of this activity depend on available equipment. If students have the music on iPods, they can each listen to the song individually at the same time; if one student has the song downloaded on her computer, she can play the song for the group to listen to together (groups will need to move away from each other as much as possible, and volume must be controlled so each group can hear the song without being too distracted by the other songs playing in the other groups). After listening to the song and reading along, the group once again discusses what they take away from the song.

10:25–10:35 a.m.   Groups work together to write a one-paragraph summary of their song, plus a list of at least three scenes from the book that match the song's message well. During this group work, the teacher plays background music to put a wall of sound up between groups so they can focus on their own work. One student from each group is designated as the reporter.

10:35–10:40 a.m.   The reporter from each group gives a brief (one minute) report on the group's song.

10:40–10:50 a.m.   The teacher leads the class in a culminating discussion of the theme of moral character as demonstrated in the songs and in the novel.

As you can see from this lesson plan, music can be used flexibly for a variety of purposes (background behind reading, discussions, and writing, adding an element of energy to the distribution of materials, and for learning content) in a single fifty-minute class period. All in all, music is probably playing for about 60 to 70% of this class period.

What to Avoid

Giving Up Control of Music's Effects by Trying to Please Everyone

When we talk about the issue of *control* in the context of this book, we want to stress that we aren't talking about teachers being control freaks who need to make every decision in their classrooms. In fact, we are strong advocates for the practice of teachers allowing their students to make, or at least have a say in, any number of important decisions concerning instructional, curricular, and classroom community issues. But when it comes to music, what we're really talking about is *quality control*.

If you want to reap the benefits that music can bring to your classroom, you need to make sure that you are using music correctly, and this requires that you retain control of these crucial instructional decisions.

Some teachers give students too much say in what music is played and when. Often a teacher will start out with good, tight control over how music is used in her classroom, but over time she begins to slip. "What song do you want me to play when we come in from recess today?" she might ask, or, "Would you guys like to have fast-paced music on as we transition to the next subject, or would you like calming music?" And while giving students such choices does have the value of giving students some ownership over the classroom, it can be a dangerous practice. When given choices about what music to listen to in class, students generally choose the music they *like* best, which is often not the music most appropriate for the current educational goal. Allowing students to make uninformed choices about classroom music thus often works against the goals of the lesson, and learning suffers.

> Music is like girlfriends to me; I am continuously astonished by the choices other people make.
>
> —David Lee Roth

This is why we suggest that teachers make most, if not all, of the decisions concerning the use of music in their classrooms. The one possible exception is allowing—*with guidance*—older students to listen to self-selected background music on headphones while doing individual work. There's also nothing wrong with allowing students to nominate music to be used as feel-good music or pump-up music for transitions (which we discussed in earlier chapters). You get to make the ultimate decisions about what songs to use, and the more of their music you can find a way to work into the school day (even if you don't care for it), the more of a motivational benefit you will reap.

Radio and Internet Radio

Avoid using a radio station or Internet radio station as the source of background music in your classroom, even classical or smooth jazz stations. While such stations do play a good number of selections during the day that fit the guidelines we've discussed for good background music, radio stations have commercials. Nothing breaks the train of thought quite so much as having a commercial suddenly come on the radio. While that nice, soft classical music was playing, your students were really getting good work done, but now their heads have all popped up to hear what's being said, and it's likely to take three or four minutes for them to get back into the flow of the task.

And commercials are not the only problem. Genre doesn't always produce correct music. You have to look at each piece of music in its own right to see if it has the required characteristics to support your educational goals for the present activity. And since some DJ sitting in a studio somewhere is making the decisions, you have lost control. All of the songs he's playing may be in a genre you associate with proper background music, but that doesn't mean that each selection will be appropriate and effective for your purpose.

Even Internet radio stations programmed by you and played off of your own computer in the classroom are not immune to these problems. We have recommended Pandora as one way to *find* good music to use in your classroom. But this doesn't mean that you should *play* Pandora in your classroom. For one thing, Pandora's free version also has periodic commercials, so you would need to purchase the commercial-free upgrade. And that's not the only issue. Let's say you create an Internet radio station around one of your favorite background tunes. Pandora will then deliver through your computer what it considers to be similar songs. Chances are the station will deliver songs to your computer that don't quite match the characteristics you want at the time, and again, learning suffers. For these reasons, we discourage the use of both radio and Internet radio in the classroom.

> Take a music bath once or twice a week, and you'll find that it is to the soul what the water bath is to the body.
>
> —Oliver Wendell Holmes

Overusing Music

You've just read a couple of hundred pages of suggestions about how to go about using music in the classroom, so it might seem strange to you that we would warn against the *overuse* of music. But you know that old saying, "Too much of a good thing . . ."? Well, that applies in this situation, as well.

It's important to remember that your goal as a teacher is to *maximize learning*. And music can definitely be a powerful tool to increase learning by getting students in a good mood, regulating their energy levels, helping them focus, and even delivering content in a memorable fashion. But there are also times when you don't want music of *any* type playing—especially when you are delivering new content through lecture, demonstrating a new skill, or leading a whole-class discussion of some topic. Even if you use all of the types of music discussed in this book in an integrated fashion daily, you will probably not be playing music more than 40 to 50% of the time. There are definitely many reasons to use music in the classroom; just make sure you are only using it when it will increase learning.

Getting Started

Our most important piece of advice is this: *start slowly* and master the use of music in the classroom at a pace that doesn't overwhelm you.

Yes, we have given you all the information you need to use music for a variety of purposes in your classroom, and yes, in this chapter we have given you a few examples of what lessons can look like when a teacher is in control of using all of these types of music to achieve a number of different purposes within a single lesson, but trying to get to that point too quickly is probably the best way we know of to burn yourself out completely and never reach the goal.

This advice doesn't just apply to music, either. Whenever teachers get fired up about any new instructional approach or classroom management program, they tend to want to jump in and do it all right away. Inevitably, they run into problems because, instead of taking it slowly and mastering one aspect of the new methodology at a time, they try to do too much—and they end up not doing *any* of it well. Soon they become disillusioned and claim that the methodology *doesn't work*. The fact is, there are many good teaching methodologies out there, but they only work if you *work them correctly*.

So, to repeat, take it slowly. As the English novelist C. K. Chesterton said, "Anything worth doing is worth doing badly." You were probably expecting that last word to be "well," since that is the common version of this old saying. But Chesterton has it right. When tackling a new set of skills, *no one* starts off doing it well. There's always a learning curve. And the same will be true for you. What Chesterton is saying is that, if you want to become proficient at something, you have to be patient with yourself and be willing to continue to work through the challenges until you master the skill. This is why we suggest you pick one or, at most, two of the uses of music discussed in this book to start with and work on incorporating them into your teaching until they become so comfortable for you that you hardly have to think about them anymore. Then pick another use of music to incorporate and go through the process again. Yes, it will take some time—maybe a couple of years—until you have mastered all of the uses of music described in this book. But when you do, look out! You will have truly added an extremely powerful set of tools to your teaching tool belt, and your students will be the beneficiaries of your newly developed skill.

So, with that last bit of advice, there's only one thing left to say: "To those about to teach, we salute you. Rock on!"

Appendix A

101 More Feel-Good Songs

We hope that our Top 40 list from Chapter 2 gave you some good ideas for feel-good songs to use in your classroom. But just to make sure that you have enough ideas to get you off to a good start, here are 101 more selections. Of course, these are songs that *we* like, and we realize that your tastes may be very different. We also realize that most of these songs are popular songs, and therefore written for young adults and adults. For the elementary and middle school teachers reading this, some of these songs may not be suitable. We encourage you to check out the lyrics to any song before you use it in the classroom and make sure you are comfortable with it. Some of these songs may include subject matter and language to which you may not want to expose your students.

1. "Accidentally in Love," Counting Crows
2. "All Is Love," from *Where the Wild Things Are,* Karen O and the Kids
3. "All Night Long," Lionel Richie
4. "All Star," Smash Mouth
5. "Amazed," Lonestar
6. "Barbara Ann," The Beach Boys
7. "Boogie On Reggae Woman," Stevie Wonder
8. "Boogie Woogie Bugle Boy," The Andrews Sisters
9. "Breezin'," George Benson
10. "Catch My Disease," Ben Lee

11. "Come On Eileen," Dexys Midnight Runners

12. "Cruisin'," Smokey Robinson

13. "Dancing Queen," ABBA

14. "Dancing With Myself," Billy Idol

15. "Don't Stop Believin'," Journey

16. "Down Under," Men at Work

17. "Dynamite," Taio Cruz

18. "Everybody Have Fun Tonight," Wang Chung

19. "Everyday," Buddy Holly

20. "Feels So Good," Chuck Mangione

21. "Footloose," Kenny Loggins

22. "Gonna Fly Now," from *Rocky*, Bill Conti

23. "Good Lovin'," The Rascals

24. "Graduation (Friends Forever)," Vitamin C

25. "Hallelujah, I Love Her So," Ray Charles

26. "Happy Together," The Turtles

27. "Higher and Higher," Jimmy Barnes

28. "Hope," Shaggy

29. "I'll Be There for You," from *Friends*, The Rembrandts

30. "I'll Take You There," The Staple Singers

31. "I'm Gonna Be (500 Miles)," The Proclaimers

32. "I'm Henry the VIII I Am," Herman's Hermits

33. "I'm Yours," Jason Mraz

34. "I Can See Clearly Now," Johnny Nash

35. "I Love a Rainy Night," Eddie Rabbitt

36. "I Love Rock and Roll," Joan Jett and the Blackhearts

37. "I Think I Love You," The Partridge Family

38. "Joy to the World," Three Dog Night

39. "Jumpin' Jack Flash," The Rolling Stones

40. "Jump, Jive an' Wail," Brian Setzer Orchestra

41. "Kung Fu Fighting," Carl Douglas

42. "Let's Twist Again," Chubby Checker

43. "Lil' Red Riding Hood," Sam the Sham and the Pharaohs

44. "(Lime in the) Coconut," The Sugar Beats

45. "Lovely Day," Donavon Frankenreiter

46. "Love Train," The O'Jays

47. "Macarena (Bayside Boys Remix)," Los Del Rio

48. "Mah Na Mah Na," Piero Umiliani

49. "Make Me Smile," Chicago

50. "MmmBop," Hanson

51. "Morning Train (Nine to Five)," Sheena Easton

52. "Mr. Blue Sky," Electric Light Orchestra (ELO)

53. "My Girl," The Temptations

54. "Ob-La-Di, Ob-La-Da (Desmond and Molly)," The Beatles

55. "Our House," Crosby, Stills, Nash &Young

56. "Party Rock Anthem," LMFAO

57. "Pata Pata," Miriam Makeba

58. "Pinch Me," Barenaked Ladies

59. "Pretty Woman," Roy Orbison

60. "Red Red Wine," UB40

61. "Return to Innocence," Enigma

62. "River of Dreams," Billy Joel

63. "Rock Around the Clock," Bill Haley and the Comets

64. "Rock Your Baby (Club Version)," George McCrae

65. "Shout," The Isley Brothers

66. "Small Town," John Mellencamp

67. "Smile," Uncle Kracker

68. "Soak Up the Sun," Sheryl Crow

69. "Somebody to Love," Queen

70. "Spooky," The Classics IV

71. "Steal My Kisses," Ben Harper

72. "Stuck Like Glue," Sugarland

73. "Sweet Child o' Mine," Guns N' Roses

74. "Tequila," The Champs

75. "That's the Way I Like It," K. C. and the Sunshine Band

76. "The Champ," Nelly

77. "The 59th Street Bridge Song (Feelin' Groovy)," Simon and Garfunkel

78. "The Impression That I Get," The Mighty Mighty Bosstones

79. "The Lazy Song," Bruno Mars

80. "The Letter (Live)," Joe Cocker

81. "The Lion Sleeps Tonight," The Tokens

82. "The Longest Time," Billy Joel

83. "The Power of Love," Huey Lewis and the News

84. "The Sound of Sunshine," Michael Franti and Spearhead

85. "The Way I Am," Ingrid Michaelson

86. "Tomorrow," from *Annie*, Cast

87. "Tubthumping," Chumbawumba

88. "Twist and Shout," The Beatles

89. "Walk Like an Egyptian," The Bangles

90. "Walk of Life," Dire Straits

91. "We're Going to Be Friends," The White Stripes

92. "(What a) Wonderful World," Herman's Hermits

93. "What I Like About You," The Romantics

94. "Where Everybody Knows Your Name," Gary Portnoy

95. "Whip It," Devo

96. "Wild Thing," The Troggs

97. "Will It Go Round in Circles," Billy Preston

98. "Yoshimi Battles the Pink Robots (Part 1)," The Flaming Lips

99. "You Belong With Me," Taylor Swift

100. "You Can't Stop the Beat," from *Hair Spray*, Cast

101. "You've Got a Friend in Me," Lyle Lovett

Appendix B

101 More Calming Songs

Here you will find more calming selections. We have tried to provide a varied list here, with a good mix of instrumentals and vocals. We hope you find some new "chill out" favorites here to use in your classroom.

1. "Alice in Wonderland," Earl Klugh
2. "All Yours," Marc Johnson
3. "Amore Come Dolore (Needs Remix)," Ennio Morricone
4. "Andantino Grazioso," from Symphony No. 24 in B Flat Major, Wolfgang Amadeus Mozart
5. "An Ending (Ascent)," Brian Eno
6. "Angels of Hope," David Lanz
7. "A Summer Child," Fourplay
8. "Avalon Shores," John Tesh
9. "Bailero," from Chants d'Auverge, Dame Kiri Te Kanawa, vocal
10. "Baptism," Paul Cardall
11. "Beloved," David Lanz
12. "Be Thou My Vision," David Nevue
13. "Blossom/Meadow," George Winston
14. "Blue Moon (Live)," Art Blakey
15. "Both Sides Now," Dianne Reeves

16. "Breakdown," Jack Johnson

17. "Can't Take That Away From Me," Jeremy Davenport

18. "China Roses," Enya

19. "Clair de Lune," from *Suite Bergamasque*, Claude Debussy

20. Concerto in C Major for Flute, Harp, and Orchestra, Wolfgang Amadeus Mozart

21. "Dance of the Searching Souls," Kevin Kern

22. "Dawn Dancing," Karl Jenkins

23. "Dream a Little Dream of Me," The Mamas and the Papas

24. "Dreamland Express," John Denver

25. "Drifting," Enya

26. "Far From Turtle," Bob James

27. "Fly Me to the Moon," Anita O'Day

28. "Gee Baby, Ain't I Good to You," Diana Krall

29. "Gira Con Me," Josh Groban

30. "Halcyon Days," John Tesh

31. "Heartland," Jim Brickman

32. "Heritage," Hiroshima

33. "If," Bread

34. "I Feel Blue," Alif Tree

35. "I Got It Bad and That Ain't Good," Nina Simone

36. "Imagination," Stan Getz

37. "I'm Getting Sentimental Over You," Thelonious Monk

38. "I Remember Clifford," Milt Jackson

39. "Ill Wind," Ben Webster

40. "Innocence," Kenny G

41. "Is This America?" Pat Metheny

42. "John Dunbar Theme,"from *Dances With Wolves*, Hollywood Bowl Orchestra

43. "Liquid Soul," Chris Standring

44. "Love Me Tender," Elvis Presley

45. "Magic," Colbie Caillat

46. "Mana'o Pili," Brothers Cazimero

47. "Meditation on Two Chords," Avishai Cohen

48. "Mi Cosa," Wes Montgomery

49. "Moon Dreams," Miles Davis

50. "Mr. Lucky," Vince Guaraldi

51. "Muskrat Love," America

52. "Natural High," Tosca

53. "Never My Love," The Association

54. "No Wonder They Sing," Philip Aaberg

55. "On Earth as It Is in Heaven," Mission

56. "One Dream at a Time," David Benoit

57. "One Safe Place (Live)," Marc Cohn

58. "On Golden Pond," Dave Grusin

59. "On Your Shore," Enya

60. "Over the Rainbow," Eva Cassidy

61. "Over the Rainbow," Jane Monheit

62. "Peace Piece," Liz Story

63. Piano Sonata No. 14 in C Sharp Minor (*Moonlight Sonata*), Ludwig van Beethoven

64. "Precious and Few," Climax

65. "Resting," Greg & Steve

66. Rhapsody on a Theme of Paganini, 18th Variation, Sergei Rachmaninoff

67. "Sanctuary Medley," Greg Maroney

68. "Shepherd Moons," Enya

69. "Shower the People," James Taylor

70. "Since I Fell for You (Live)," Ramsey Lewis

71. "Sleep Baby Mine," George Winston

72. "Solitude," Herbie Hancock

73. "Some Children See Him," George Winston

74. "Something in the Way She Moves," James Taylor

75. "Songbird," Eva Cassidy

76. "Song for Somalia," Fourplay

77. "Sophisticated Lady," Dave Grusin

78. "Sound of Invisible Waters," Deuter

79. "Spring," Peter Kater

80. "Stranger on the Shore,"from *The Majestic,* The Spencer Wyatt Big Band

81. "Summertime," Booker T. and the MGs

82. "S'Wonderful," Diana Krall

83. "The Bighorn Medicine Wheel," Laura Sullivan

84. "The Comb of the Winds," Enya

85. "The Fairy Queen," Clannad

86. "The Long Day Is Over," Norah Jones

87. "The Luckiest," Ben Folds

88. "The Oh of Pleasure," Ray Lynch

89. "These Foolish Things," Lester Young

90. "Thinking of You," Milt Jackson

91. "Time Goes on," Pat Metheny

92. "Time on My Hands," Ben Webster

93. "To Take . . . to Hold," Yanni

94. "The Velocity of Love," Suzanne Ciani

95. "The Wedding Song," Kenny G

96. "Walk Katie Home," Seth Glier

97. "Whatever It Is," Ben Lee

98. "When I Fall in Love," Nat King Cole

99. "White Daisy Passing," Rocky Votolato

100. "World to Me," Four Shadow

101. "You Are So Beautiful," Joe Cocker

Appendix C

101 More Pump-Up Songs

In addition to our Top 40 list from Chapter 4, here are 101 more songs to stimulate your students. We hope you find some fun stuff here. The majority of these songs are instrumental, but our standard disclaimer about checking out lyrics before using songs in the classroom still stands (for those songs to which it applies). Have fun checking these out!

1. "Acoustic Jubilee," Dominic Gaudious
2. "Another Friday Night," Jeff Golub
3. "Applebutter," Bela Fleck
4. "Black Coffee," Fishbelly Black
5. "Boogie Wonderland," Earth, Wind, & Fire
6. "Cafe Carnival," Craig Chaquico
7. "Can't Be Still," Booker T. and the MGs
8. "Caribe," Michel Camilo
9. "Cha Cha Slide," Countdown Mix Masters
10. "Classical Gas," Mason Williams
11. "Cold Duck Time," Pancho Sanchez
12. "Crazy Horse Mongoose," Galactic
13. "Crazy Rhythm," Django Reinhardt
14. "Cuckoo's Nest," Nickel Creek

15. "Dance, Dance, Dance," The Beach Boys

16. "Dance Mania," Tito Puente

17. "Dance to the Music," Sly and the Family Stone

18. "Dawg's Due," Bela Fleck

19. "Dinner at the Sugarbush," Brent Lewis

20. "Don't Stop 'Til You Get Enough," Michael Jackson

21. "Doom Tac a Doom," Brent Lewis

22. _Eine Kleine Nachtmusik, Allegro_, Wolfgang Amadeus Mozart

23. "Electricity," Moby

24. "Flight of the Bumblebee," Nikolai Rimsky-Korsakov

25. "Funky Cha-Cha," Arturo Sandoval

26. "Get Down With It," The Woggles

27. "Giddyap Hoedown," Big Smith

28. "Glad All Over," Hush

29. "Gloria," Laura Branigan

30. "Gonna Make You Sweat," C & C Music Factory

31. "Grand Central," Jeff Golub

32. "Guancona," Tito Puente

33. "Heaven," Moby

34. "Hideaway," James Govan and the Boogie Blues Band

35. "Hoe Down," from _Rodeo_, Aaron Copland

36. "I Get Around," The Beach Boys

37. "Ijeliu," James Asher

38. "I'll Always Hold You Close," Down to the Bone

39. "I'm So Excited," The Pointer Sisters

40. "Indian Diary," Neos

41. "Instrumental," Galaxie 500

42. "Jellybread," Booker T. and the MGs

43. "Juke (Single)," Little Walter

44. "Jump," Van Halen

45. "Jump in Line (Shake, Shake Senora)," Harry Belafonte

46. "Kambu Angels," Samite

47. "Kenya," The Rippingtons

48. "Kim," Charlie Parker

49. "Land of 1,000 Dances," Wilson Pickett

50. "Last Night," The Mar-Keys

51. "Latin Note," St. Germain

52. "Le Freak," Chic

53. "Legs," ZZ Top

54. "Long Train Runnin'," The Doobie Brothers

55. "Mambo #5," Perez Prado 2000

56. "March of the Toreadors," from *Carmen*, Georges Bizet

57. "Night Train," Jimmy Smith and Wes Montgomery

58. "No Matter What Shape (Your Stomach's In)," The T-Bones

59. "Nut Popper #1 (Remastered '97 Version)," The Paul Butterfield Blues Band

60. "Nut Rocker," B. Bumble and the Stingers

61. "Out of Limits," The Marketts

62. "Peter Gunn Theme," Henry Mancini

63. "Ran Kan Kan," Tito Puente

64. "Ready, Steady, Go," Oakenfold

65. "Red Alert," Basement Jaxx

66. "Ghost Riders in the Sky (A Cowboy Legend)," Peggy Lee

67. "Roam," The B-52s

68. "Rockit," Herbie Hancock

69. "Rock Lobster," The B-52s

70. "Rock Prelude," David Garrett

71. "Rods and Cones," Blue Man Group

72. "Rhythm of the Night," DeBarge

73. "Se Escaparon," Bombon

74. "Shake Your Bootie," KC and the Sunshine Band

75. "Snap," David Benoit

76. "So Flute," St. Germain

77. "Soul Limbo (Single Version)," Booker T. and the MGs

78. "Stompin' at the Savoy," Harry Connick, Jr.

79. "Summer," David Garrett

80. "Super Strut," Deodato

81. "Sweet Georgia Brown," Les Paul

82. "Swing That Thing," Harmonious Wail

83. "Swingtown," Steve Miller Band

84. "That's It," Fishbelly Black

85. "The Ballad of Jed Clampett," Lester Flatt and Earl Scruggs

86. "The Fair of Ballydarreen," Anam Ri

87. "The Green Minute," Galactic

88. "The Hunt," from *Brideshead Revisited*, Geoffrey Burgon and the Philharmonia Orchestra

89. "The Locomotion," Little Eva

90. "The Work Song," Herb Alpert

91. "Tickle Toe," Lyle Lovett and His Large Band

92. "Tighten Up," The Bamboos

93. "Time to Start," Blue Man Group

94. "Travelin' Band," Creedence Clearwater Revival

95. "Traveling Without Moving," Jamiroquai

96. "We Got the Beat," The Go-Gos

97. "Whipped Cream," Herb Alpert and the Tijuana Brass

98. "Wipe Out," The Ventures

99. "Working for the Weekend," Loverboy

100. "Yakety Yak," The Coasters

101. "You Should Be Dancing," The Bee Gees

Appendix D

101 More Background Songs
(Individual Work)

Here are 101 more background selections to use while your students do individual seatwork. Again, we strive for variety in these lists—within the parameters we have set for each type of music—so you will see some classical, some jazz, and some electronic music, but easy listening and smooth jazz selections dominate, as they are such a good fit for this purpose. As we did in the Top 40 list in Chapter 5, we have subdivided this list into "Reading" and "Writing" subcategories.

Reading

1. "Autumn," Peter Kater
2. "Bossa," Harry Pickens
3. "Breathe," Greg Maroney
4. "Butter," Boney James
5. "Corcovado," Vince Guaraldi
6. "Dark Night of the Soul," Philip Wesley
7. "Dawn," Tim Neumark
8. "Day Dream," Johnny Hodges
9. "Did You Mean It?" Peter Buffett
10. "East of the Sun," George Shearing
11. Etude op. 10 No. 3 (*Tristesse*), Frederic Chopin

12. "Every Snowflake," from *Elizabethtown*, Nancy Wilson

13. "Far From Turtle," Bob James

14. "Flamingo," Don Byas

15. "Forever, Forever (Solo Piano)," Keiko Matsui

16. "For the Love of You (Live)," Russell Malone

17. "Gay Sons of Lesbian Mothers," Kaki King

18. "Gentle Breezy," Harry Pickens

19. "Goodbye," Keith Jarrett and Charlie Haden

20. "Good Dog, Happy Man," Bill Frisell

21. "Harmony Grove," Greg Maroney

22. "Heartbeat at High Knob," Zola Van

23. "Here's That Rainy Day," Joe Pass

24. "House of Cards," Vitamin String Quartet

25. "I Didn't Know What Time It Was," George Shearing

26. "I Love to See the Temple," Paul Cardall

27. "In a Sentimental Mood," John Coltrane and Duke Ellington

28. "Interplay," Royce Campbell

29. "Joseph Smith's First Prayer," Paul Cardall

30. "Le Jardin," Kevin Kern

31. Liebestraum No. 3 in A Flat Major, op. 62, Franz Liszt

32. "Living Without You," George Winston

33. "Lullaby of the Leaves," Art Tatum

34. "Memories," Ryan Stewart

35. "New River Dawn," Bill Leslie

36. "No More Tears," David Nevue

37. "One Day I'll Fly Away," Keith Jarrett and Charlie Haden

38. "One Dream at a Time," David Benoit

39. "Pastorale," Ray Lynch

40. "Peace and Joy," Gary Lamb

41. "Return to the Heart," David Lanz

42. "River," Peter Kater

43. "Sahara," Alto Reed

44. Serenade No. 13 for Strings in G Major, K. 525: I. Allegro (*Eine Kleine Nachtmusik*), Wolfgang Amadeus Mozart

45. "Sometimes I'm Happy," The Lester Young Quartet

46. "Spring Breeze," Greg Maroney

47. "Sueños de España (Dreams of Spain)," Charo

48. "The Bighorn Medicine Wheel," Laura Sullivan

49. "The Blink of an Eye," Jeff Golub

50. "The Comb of the Winds," Enya

51. "The Swan," from *Carnival of the Animals* (Chamber Version), Gaby Casadesus, Philippe Entremont, and Yo-Yo Ma

52. "Trail Magic at Rocky Comfort," Zola Van

53. "Watching the Night Fall," Gary Lamb

54. "Water Shows the Hidden Heart," Enya

55. "Wedding on the Mountain," Robin Spielberg

56. "What Lies Ahead," Scott Wilkie

57. "When I'm Alone," Peter White

58. "Where Can I Go Without You," Keith Jarrett and Charlie Haden

59. "Whisper Not," Milt Jackson

60. "Wonderland," David Nevue

Writing

61. "Billy's Blues," Philippe Saisse

62. "Blue Light Blues," Django Reinhardt

63. "Broken Mirrors," Urban Knights

64. "Cabrillo," Marc Antoine

65. "Colors/Dance," George Winston

66. "Dancing in the Quiet Rain," Robin Spielberg

67. "Drifting," Enya

68. "Elmina," Kofi

69. "February Sea," George Winston

70. "Flight of Fantasy," Yanni

71. "Glow," Peter White

72. "Heartland," Jim Brickman

73. "I Wish I Knew," Ken Navarro

74. "Kei's Song," David Benoit

75. "Life Story," Peter White

76. "Lilies," Harry Pickens

77. "Lo Fi Groovy," All India Radio

78. "Madison," Ola Gjeilo

79. "Maybe Tonight," Earl Klugh

80. "Middle of the Night," Rick Braun

81. "Montana Half-Light," Philip Aaberg

82. "No Moon at All," Keith Jarrett and Charlie Haden

83. "Oi Gata," Joe McBride and the Texas Rhythm Club

84. "Rain at Ghost Dance Canyon Trail: Dixon Springs," Zola Van

85. "Ray Dawn Balloon," Trey Anastasio

86. "Remembering You," Robin Spielberg

87. "Rhythm in the Pews," Ray Lynch

88. "Rooster," Toubab Krewe

89. "Same Road, Same Reason," Acoustic Alchemy

90. "See, My Love . . . ," Andreas Vollenweider

91. "Slow Jam," Euge Groove

92. "Softly," Harry Pickens

93. "Solitude (Reprise)," from *Kansas City*, Kansas City Band

94. "Soul Serenade," Jeff Golub

95. "Spring," from *The Four Seasons*, Antonio Vivaldi

96. "Steps: Battery Rock to Rock Creek," Zola Van

97. "Sugar," Count Basie and His Orchestra

98. "The Vigil," David Nevue

99. "Tune 88," Jeff Lorber

100. "Two Teeth Missing," D. D. Denham

101. "Valerio," Marc Antoine

Appendix E

101 More Background Songs (Group Work)

Here are 101 more songs to play behind group work. There's some great stuff here; we hope you find something you like. As we discussed in Chapter 6, we have subdivided the list into songs to be used while students do more challenging work ("Newer Material, Harder Tasks") or less challenging work ("Older Material, Easier Tasks").

Newer Material, Harder Tasks

1. "Above the Clouds, You Can't See Anything," D. D. Denham

2. "Ain't No Sunshine," Dwayne Kerr

3. "Blue Train," Black & Brown

4. "Celia," Bud Powell

5. "Desafinado," Stan Getz and Charlie Byrd

6. "Don't Lose Your Cool," Tab Benoit

7. "Dudeman," Viktor Krauss

8. "Gentle Rain," Joe McBride and the Texas Rhythm Club

9. "Hamp's Hump," Galactic

10. "Hispanic Dance (With a Blues Touch)," Claude Bolling and Alexandre Lagoya

11. "Jamaica Heartbeat," Acoustic Alchemy

12. "Living," Moby

13. "Look Who's Here," Russell Malone

14. "Madrid," Marc Antoine

15. "Mercamon," Galactic

16. "Metropolis," Boney James

17. "Monday Night, Tuesday Morning," Kofi

18. "Ooh La La," Jeff Lorber

19. "Paradise Cove," Paul Hardcastle

20. "Ready or Not," 3rd Force

21. "Red Dust," Zero 7

22. "Risin' (Instrumental)," Josh One

23. "Robin and Marian," Nickel Creek

24. "Signe (Live)," Eric Clapton

25. "Slam Dunk," Euge Groove

26. "Somebody Loves Me," Bud Powell

27. "Song 4 My Girl," Outta Nowhere

28. "Spring and October," Weathertunes

29. "Straight, No Chaser," Thelonious Monk

30. "Strong Man," Wynton Kelly

31. "The Inlaw Josie Wales," Trey Anastasio

32. "The Message," Urban Knights

33. "Tokido," Samite

34. "Turn It Out," Peter White

35. "What You Think About . . . ," St. Germain

36. "Why Don't You Dance," Jacob Varmus

37. "Willow Weep for Me," Wynton Kelly

Older Material, Easier Tasks

38. "Ain't Nobody," Jeff Lorber

39. "Anejo de Cabo," Craig Chaquico

40. "Asphalt Funk," Tea Leaf Green

41. "At the Backroom," Brian Culbertson

42. "Baby Steps," Peter White

43. "Beautiful Blues," L. Santanaga

44. "Boomtown," Fishbelly Black

45. "Bumpin' on Sunset," Wes Montgomery

46. "Caribbean Breeze," The Rippingtons

47. "Chatter," Mike Stern

48. "Club Nowhere," Blue Man Group

49. "Conversations," Lao Tizer

50. "Doo Rag," Galactic

51. "Down Low," Jeff Lorber

52. "Electra Glide," Down to the Bone

53. "Get Down on It," Wayman Tisdale

54. "Go Go," Galactic

55. "Gonna Be Alright," Mindi Abair

56. "Green Impala," Joyce Cooling

57. "Grover," Fishbelly Black

58. "Harlem Air Shaft," Duke Ellington

59. "Kisses in the Rain," Rick Braun

60. "Lavish," Soul Ballet

61. "Let Me Love You," Tha' Hot Club

62. "Lost in the Groove," Dan Kusz

63. "Lulu's Back," Jeff Golub

64. "Madagascar," Garaj Mahal

65. "Me, Myself, and Rio," Doc Powell

66. "Moomba," Richard Elliot

67. "Morning Magic," Larry Carlton

68. "Off Into It," Wayman Tisdale

69. "Palm Strings," Marc Antoine

70. "Parkside Shuffle," Down to the Bone

71. "Pebble Beach," David Benoit

72. "Pedro Blanco," Peter White

73. "Pick Up the Pieces," Avenue Blue and Jeff Golub

74. "Potato Hole," Booker T.

75. "Put It Where You Want It," Larry Carlton

76. "Rainbow Man," Earl Klugh

77. "Rendezvous," Eric Marienthal

78. "Reptile," Eric Clapton

79. "Return of the Eagle," Craig Chaquico

80. "Rewind," Euge Groove

81. "RSVP," Boney James and Rick Braun

82. "Save the Last Dance," Mindi Abair

83. "See What I'm Sayin'?" Boney James

84. "Shadow and Light," Craig Chaquico

85. "Shoot the Loop," Acoustic Alchemy

86. "Sittin' Back," Brian Culbertson

87. "Summer," Dan Kusz

88. "Sweet Home Chicago," Urban Knights

89. "S'Wonderful," Dave Brubeck

90. "Taking It Uptown," Fishbelly Black

91. "Tango in Barbados," David Benoit

92. "The Cello Song," Steven Sharp Nelson

93. "The Happy Organ," Dave "Baby" Cortez

94. "Thursday," Takenobu

95. "Toast & Jam," Joyce Cooling

96. "Tuscan Chica," Soul Ballet

97. "Westside," Theo Bishop

98. "What Exit," Spyro Gyra

99. "White Fang," Bill Frisell

100. "Written Hour," Wayne Jones

101. "X Marks the Spot," Joe Sample

Appendix F

101 More Songs for Teaching Content

In addition to the starter lists in Chapter 7, here are 101 more songs for teaching content. There are so many good choices out there, we could have easily listed several hundred more, but we are going to stick with the 101-songs theme we have established in these appendices. For more ideas, you can always check out our website, www.rockandrollclassroom .com, where we will add many more songs in the future.

4 More Art Songs

Level One

1. "Painting Flowers," All Time Low—middle school

Level Two

2. "What a Wonderful World," Louis Armstrong—elementary

3. "Painter Song," Norah Jones—middle school

4. "Sunday," from *Sunday in the Park*, Cast—high school

9 More Language Arts Songs

Level One

5. "Reading Is Magic," Mr. Billy—elementary

6. "Don't Pick a Fight With a Poet," Madeleine Peyroux—high school

Level Two

7. "ZYX," They Might Be Giants—elementary

Level Three

8. "Story Elements Song," Have Fun Teaching—elementary

9. "Unpack Your Adjectives," Schoolhouse Rock—elementary

10. "Verb Rap Song," Have Fun Teaching—elementary

11. "Busy Prepositions," Schoolhouse Rock—middle school

12. "Interjections," Schoolhouse Rock—middle school

13. "Lolly, Lolly, Lolly, Get Your Adverbs Here," Schoolhouse Rock—middle school

13 More Literature Songs

Level One

14. "Superman," Los Lonely Boys—American literature, middle school

Level Two

15. "Hey Nancy Drew," Price—children's literature, middle school

16. "Kryptonite," 3 Doors Down—American literature, middle school

17. "Remember the Tin Man," Tracy Chapman—American literature, high school

18. "Saint Augustine in Hell," Sting—world literature, high school

Level Three

19. "Five Little Monkeys," The Learning Station—children's literature, elementary

20. "Goldilocks and the 3 Bears," The Learning Station—children's literature, elementary

21. "Trees—Joyce Kilmer," The Dead Poets—American literature, middle school

22. "Cymbeline," Loreena McKennitt—British/Irish literature, high school

23. "Insomnia," Luciana Souza—American literature, high school

24. "Life Is Fine," The Dead Poets—American literature, high school

25. "Sea Fever—John Masefield," The Dead Poets—British/Irish literature, high school

26. "100s of Ways—Rumi," The Dead Poets—world literature, high school

21 More Math Songs

Level One

27. "Apartment Four," They Might Be Giants—arithmetic, elementary

28. "Eight Hundred and Thirteen Mile Car Trip," They Might Be Giants—arithmetic, elementary

29. "Got to Know Math," Miz B—arithmetic, elementary

30. "Math Monster," Silly Joe—arithmetic, elementary

31. "Math Song," Laura Freeman—arithmetic, elementary

32. "Number Two," They Might Be Giants—arithmetic, elementary

33. "The Number Rock," Greg and Steve—arithmetic, elementary

34. "Never Ending Math Equation," Modest Mouse—algebra and advanced math, high school

Level Two

35. "Ten Mississippi," They Might Be Giants—arithmetic, elementary

36. "The Math Game," Eric Herman and the Invisible Band—arithmetic, elementary

37. "Triops Has Three Eyes," They Might Be Giants—arithmetic, elementary

38. "Zeroes," They Might Be Giants—arithmetic, elementary

39. "Order of Operations, 'O, O, O,'" Mr. Duey—arithmetic, middle school

40. "Parallel Lines," Todd Rundgren—geometry, high school

41. "Pi," Kate Bush—geometry, high school

Level Three

42. "Elementary, My Dear," Schoolhouse Rock—arithmetic, elementary

43. "Even Numbers," They Might Be Giants—arithmetic, elementary

44. "Lucky Seven Sampson," Schoolhouse Rock—arithmetic, elementary

45. "The Good Eleven," Schoolhouse Rock—arithmetic, elementary

46. "My Apothem," The Trigs—geometry, high school

47. "Proofs Is Easy," The Trigs—geometry, high school

7 More Music Songs

Level One

48. "Where's the Music," Medeski, Martin and Wood—elementary

49. "Listen to the Music," The Doobie Brothers—middle school

50. "Turn the Beat Around," Vicki Sue Robinson—middle school

51. "Dear Mr. Fantasy," Traffic—high school

52. "More Than a Feeling," Boston—high school

Level Two

53. "It's the Same Old Song," The Four Tops—high school

54. "Radio Song," R. E. M.—high school

5 More Physical Education Songs

Level One

55. "Can You (Point Your Fingers and Do the Twist)?" The Wiggles—elementary

56. "Freeze Dance," Funky Mama—elementary

57. "Head, Shoulders, Knees and Toes," The Wiggles—elementary

58. "The Boogie Walk," Greg and Steve—elementary

59. "It Keeps You Runnin'," The Doobie Brothers—middle school

19 More Science Songs

Level One

60. "Robot Parade," They Might Be Giants—physics and engineering, elementary

61. "Chemistry," Semisonic—physical science, high school

62. "Gravity Fails," The Bottle Rockets—physics and engineering, high school

63. "Museums," Wall of Voodoo—biology, high school

Level Two

64. "Ecology," Banana Slug String Band—biology, elementary

65. "Mammals," They Might Be Giants—biology, middle school

66. "Mendel's Theme," Dr. Chordate—biology, high school

67. "The Chemical Compounds Song," Ellen McHenry—physical science, high school

Level Three

68. "Habitat," Walkin' Jim Stoltz—biology, elementary

69. "Latitude/Longitude," Mr. Duey—physical science, elementary

70. "RECYCLE," Tom Chapin—biology, elementary

71. "Solid Liquid Gas," They Might Be Giants—physical science, elementary

72. "The Bloodmobile," They Might Be Giants—biology, elementary

73. "The Rock Song," Ellen McHenry—physical science, elementary

74. "Water Cycle Boogie," Banana Slug String Band—physical science, elementary

75. "Animals Belong in Class," Teacher and the Rockbots—biology, middle school

76. "Them Not So Dry Bones," Schoolhouse Rock—biology, middle school

77. "Hey Avogadro," Professor Boggs—physical science, high school

78. "Parts of a Cell," Hip Science—biology, high school

23 More American History Songs

Level One

79. "Wabash Cannonball," Roy Acuff—elementary

80. "Don't Fence Me In," Leon Russell and Willie Nelson—middle school

81. "Only in America," Jay and the Americans—high school

Level Two

82. "True Story of Amelia Earhart," Plainsong—elementary

83. "Indian Reservation (The Lament of the Cherokee Reservation Indian)," Paul Revere and the Raiders—middle school

84. "Fortunate Son," Creedence Clearwater Revival—high school

85. "John Brown's Body," Pete Seeger—high school

86. "Living in the Promiseland," Willie Nelson—high school

87. "Ohio," Crosby, Stills, Nash & Young—high school

88. "Rain on the Scarecrow," John Mellencamp—high school

89. "Rosie the Riveter," The Four Vagabonds—high school

90. "The Downeaster 'Alexa,'" Billy Joel—high school

91. "What's Going On?" Marvin Gaye—high school

Level Three

92. "Ballad of Davy Crockett," Fess Parker—elementary

93. "Fireworks," Schoolhouse Rock—elementary

94. "Pretty Boy Floyd," Bob Dylan—middle school

95. "Trail of Tears," John Denver—middle school

96. "Remember the Alamo," The Kingston Trio—high school

97. "Society's Child," Janis Ian—high school

98. "The Ballad of Ira Hayes," Johnny Cash—high school

99. "Tom Joad (Part 1 and Part 2)," Woody Guthrie—high school

100. "White America," Eminem—high school [Get the clean version]

101. "You Don't Own Me," Lesley Gore—high school

Appendix G

101 More Songs for Classroom Management

Here are 101 more management songs, broken down by some of the different subcategories we discussed in Chapter 8. We could have easily listed 101 more such songs, but these lists are only intended to get you started, so we held back. Have fun building your lists!

3 More Timer Songs

1. "Countdown Theme," Pipa and the Four From the Top
2. "Get Smart," Bob Crane and his Drums and Orchestra
3. "Mission Impossible Theme," from *Mission Impossible*, Danny Elfman

6 More Songs With Embedded Directions

4. "It's Cleanup Time," Jack Hartmann
5. "I've Got Self-Control," Ben Stiefel
6. "Lunchtime Is Time to Eat," Jack Hartmann
7. "The Wigglies," Peace Pals
8. "Wash Your Hands," Miss Jenny
9. "When Words Don't Work," Peace Pals

Songs That Match Classroom Activities: 12 More Color Songs

10. "Bein' Green," Kermit the Frog

11. "Black Is Black," Los Bravos

12. "Blue Suede Shoes," Carl Perkins

13. "Blue Velvet," Bobby Vinton

14. "Devil With a Blue Dress On," Mitch Ryder

15. "Lil' Red Riding Hood," Sam the Sham and the Pharaohs

16. "Long Cool Woman (in a Black Dress)," The Hollies

17. "Mellow Yellow," Donovan

18. "Purple People Eater," Sheb Wooley

19. "That Old Black Magic," James Darren

20. "(The Angels Wanna Wear My) Red Shoes," Elvis Costello

21. "Yellow Submarine," The Beatles

Songs That Match Classroom Activities: 13 More Student Traits Songs

22. "Beechwood 4-5789," The Marvelettes (highest or lowest number)

23. "Birthday," The Beatles (closest to birthday)

24. "Diamond Girl," Seals and Crofts (wearing most jewelry)

25. "Elevation," U2 (tallest)

26. "Hair" from the musical *Hair,* Tom Pierson and Cast (longest hair)

27. "Little Old Lady From Pasadena," Jan and Dean (oldest)

28. "Long Cool Woman (in a Black Dress)," The Hollies (tallest girl)

29. "Only Sixteen," Sam Cooke (high school students, closest to 16th birthday)

30. "Physical," Olivia Newton-John (in best shape, person who works out most)

31. "Pick-A-Little, Talk-A-Little," from *The Music Man*, Hermione Gingold and the Biddys (person who talks the most)

32. "Sharp Dressed Man," ZZ Top (best dressed boy)

33. "When I'm Sixty-Four," The Beatles (youngest or oldest in group)

34. "867-5309/Jenny" by Tommy Tutone (highest or lowest number)

Songs That Match Classroom Activities: 25 More Name Songs

35. "Amanda," Boston

36. "Bad, Bad Leroy Brown," Jim Croce

37. "Ben," Michael Jackson

38. "Bernadette," The Four Tops

39. "Daniel," Elton John

40. "Donna," Ritchie Valens

41. "Gloria," Laura Branigan

42. "Help Me, Rhonda," The Beach Boys

43. "Jack and Diane," John Mellencamp

44. "Little Willy," Sweet

45. "Love Grows Where My Rosemary Goes," Edison Lighthouse

46. "Lucy in the Sky With Diamonds," The Beatles

47. "Melissa," The Allman Brothers Band

48. "My Maria," Brooks and Dunn

49. "Ob-La-Di, Ob-La-Da (Desmond & Molly)," The Beatles

50. "Peggy Sue," Buddy Holly

51. "Proud Mary," Creedence Clearwater Revival

52. "Sherry," Frankie Valli and the Four Seasons

53. "Smile a Little Smile for Me (Rosemarie)," Flying Machine

54. "Sweet Baby James," James Taylor

55. "Take the Money and Run (Billy Jo and Bobbie Sue)," Steve Miller Band

56. "Tracy," The Cuff Links

57. "Walk Away Renee," The Four Tops

58. "You Can Call Me Al," Paul Simon

59. "27 Jennifers," Mike Doughty

Songs That Match Classroom Activities: 14 More Beginning Songs

60. "Back in the Saddle Again," Gene Autry

61. "Begin," Ben Lee

62. "Brand New Day," Sting

63. "Brand New Day: A Call and Response Song for Starting the Day," Jack Hartmann

64. "Good Morning," Greg and Steve

65. "Good Morning, Starshine," Oliver

66. "If You're Ready (Come Go With Me)," The Staple Singers

67. "Let's Get It Started (Spike Mix)," Black Eyed Peas

68. "Lovely Day," Donavon Frankenreiter

69. "Morning Has Broken," Cat Stevens

70. "Ready for School," Jack Hartmann

71. "The Promise of a New Day," Paula Abdul

72. "Walk Right In," Dr. Hook

73. "Woke Up This Morning," from *The Sopranos*, Joe McBride and the Texas Rhythm Club

Songs That Match Classroom Activities: 14 More Ending Songs

74. "Day-O," Harry Belafonte

75. "Every Time We Say Goodbye," Steve Tyrell

76. "Exodus," Bob Marley

77. "Farewell, So Long, Goodbye," Bill Haley

78. "Get Back," The Beatles

79. "Goodnight Sweetheart," The Flamingos

80. "Good Riddance," Green Day

81. "It's Time to Go," Hap Palmer

82. "Mickey Mouse March," Aaron Neville

83. "Na Na Hey Hey Kiss Him Goodbye," Steam

84. "Never Can Say Goodbye," Gloria Gaynor

85. "See You Later Alligator," Jack Hartmann

86. "The Letter," The Box Tops

87. "Who Let the Dogs Out," Baja Men

Songs That Match Classroom Activities: 14 More Movement Songs

88. "Gimme Three Steps," Lynyrd Skynyrd

89. "I'm Gonna Be (500 Miles)," The Proclaimers

90. "I've Been Everywhere," Johnny Cash

91. "Macarena," Los Del Rio

92. "On the Road Again," Willie Nelson

93. "Ramblin' Man," The Allman Brothers Band

94. "The Boogie Walk," Greg and Steve

95. "The Freeze," Greg and Steve

96. "These Boots Are Made for Walkin'," Nancy Sinatra

97. "The Wanderer," Dion

98. "Time to Start," Blue Man Group

99. "Travelin' Band," Creedence Clearwater Revival

100. "Walk Like an Egyptian," The Bangles

101. "Will It Go Round in Circles," Billy Preston

Appendix H

Resources

Throughout this book, we have mentioned several resources you can draw upon to find and build your lists of music. For the sake of convenience, we list these resources (plus a few more) once again here. Happy hunting!

Websites—Music Lists, Internet Radio, Lesson Plans

www.greenbookofsongs.com

This website began life in 1982 as a printed book, *The Green Book of Songs by Subject*, by Jeff Green. Unlike other "list" publications that focus on award-winning or popular songs, *The Green Book of Songs by Subject* was the first effort to organize the totality of 20th century (and now 21st century) popular music by *topics*. Just look up a topic and you will find a list of songs from the past 100-plus years about that topic! For those of you who prefer searching for your music online, however, all the great content of *The Green Book* and much more can be found on the website. Members can search the database—more than 116,000 songs by 10,000 artists covering more than 2,200 topics—as much as they want for a truly affordable annual subscription fee. The site offers three ways to search for subjects as well as hyperlinked "see also" categories and an extensive thesaurus. Users can also search by five major genres and for "hits" only. This site even has a "Teacher's Page" section specifically about using music for teaching, with links to several great lesson plans, two of which were developed in conjunction with the Rock and Roll Hall of Fame.

www.songsabout.com

This site is *The Green Book's* sister site. It acts as a repository of topical song lists already created for you by the site's owners. These ready-to-use playlists are, to quote the site, "about holidays, current events, and interesting topics of every kind!" You can search for song lists using broad categories, or you can find hundreds of lists categorized under more specific keyword tags. If you are thinking of creating a topical song list, it makes sense to check here first to see if you can find a list already compiled for you. This site can save you hours of work!

rockhall.com/education/resources

The Rock and Roll Hall of Fame in Cleveland, Ohio, offers teachers interested in the history of rock and roll music a wealth of resources to explore the subject, including lesson plans for using rock music to teach a wide variety of educational content, primarily language arts and history topics.

www.songsforteaching.com

This site is packed with hundreds of songs with embedded educational content and is searchable by subject area and artist. You can listen to short clips of most of the songs on the site, and lyrics are included as well (and sometimes even sheet music). What you won't find here are songs by "big name" popular recording artists (we assume that would be prohibitively costly for the owners of the site). On the other hand, many of the songs on this site embed much more content into their lyrics than the typical pop song, so this is a great site to use to expand your classroom collection of content songs.

www.rdio.com

Rdio is a paid service that, for a low monthly fee, allows you to access more than 15 million songs and listen to them without having to buy them. You can create playlists, discover what your friends and other people with similar tastes are listening to, and share using Twitter and Facebook. You can even access your music using your smartphone.

www.pandora.com

Pandora, a company started in 2000, provides an easy way to listen to music you love and discover new music with which you are likely to fall in love. Their Music Genome Project analyzes hundreds of details of every song in their vast music library. Then, when you enter a song or artist, Pandora creates a "station" of music with similar characteristics that is delivered directly to you through your computer. This service also offers teachers a fantastic way to expand their classroom music lists; just find a song that works well for an educational purpose (calming students down, pumping them up, helping them focus and stay on task, etc.) and create a station around that song. Pandora does the rest of the work—playing songs with similar characteristics. All you have to do is sit back and take note of other songs you would like to try in your classroom.

www.last.fm

This is another Internet radio site similar to Pandora. While its recommendation tool is not as powerful as Pandora's, Last.fm offers some advantages for those who enjoy social networking. On this site, not only can you create stations based on songs or artists you like, but you can also share personal information and photos and interact with listeners who share your tastes in music.

www.grooveshark.com

This is yet another enjoyable Internet radio site with powerful built-in social networking capabilities. You can build your own playlists and then share your favorites with other users and with nonusers via social networking sites such as Facebook or MySpace.

www.garylamb.com

Gary Lamb is a pianist who composes music specifically in the 60 to 80 bpm range ideal for background music. Many teachers use his music to create that state of "relaxed alertness" so valuable when doing academic work. We have used a lot of his music for background music over the years, and we've found most of it to work very well. On his site, he has a six-CD set of music called *Music for the Mind* that is definitely worth checking out.

www.rockandrollclassroom.com

Last, but certainly not least, there is the companion website for this book. The site is organized like the book—separate pages for feel-good music, calming music, pump-up music, and so on, and in addition to offering you links to the music suggested here, it is also designed to expand these playlists over time so that you always have fresh ideas for your classroom at your fingertips.

References

Abikoff, H., Courtney, M. E., Szeibel, P. J., & Koplewicz, H. S. (1996). The effects of auditory stimulation on the arithmetic performance of children with ADHD and nondisabled children. *Journal of Learning Disabilities, 29*(3), 238–246.

Ahmadiasl, N., Alaei, H., & Hanninen, O. (2003). Effect of exercise on learning, memory and levels of epinephrine in rats' hippocampus. *Journal of Sports Science and Medicine, 2*, 106–109.

Allen, R. H. (2001). *Impact teaching: Ideas and strategies for teachers to maximize student learning.* Boston, MA: Allyn & Bacon.

Alley, T. R., & Greene, M. E. (2008). The relative and perceived impact of irrelevant speech, vocal music, and non-vocal music on working memory. *Current Psychology, 27*(4), 277–289.

Alpert, J. I. (1982). The effect of disc jockey, peer, and music teacher approval on music selection and preference. *Journal of Research in Music Education, 30*, 173–186.

Anderson, S. A., & Fuller, G. B. (2010). Effect of music on reading comprehension of junior high school students. *School Psychology Quarterly, 25*(3), 178–187.

Areni, C. S., & Kim, D. (1993). The influence of background music on shopping behavior: Classical vs. top 40 music in a wine store. *Advances in Consumer Research, 20*(1), 336–340.

Arkes, H. R., Rettig, L. E., & Scougale, J. E. (1986). The effect of concurrent task complexity and music experience on preference for simple and complex music. *Psychomusicology, 6*(1–2), 51–60.

Armstrong, G. B., & Sopory, P. (1997). Effects of background television on phonological and visuo-spatial working memory. *Communication Research, 24*(5), 459–480.

Balkwill, L.-L., & Thompson, W. F. (1999). A cross-cultural investigation of the perception of emotion in music: Psychophysical and cultural cues. *Music Perception, 17*(1), 43–64.

Ball, P. (2010). One world under a groove. *New Scientist, 206*(2759), 30–33.

Banbury, S. P., & Berry, D. C. (1998). Disruption of office-related tasks by speech and office noise. *British Journal of Psychology, 89*(3), 499–517.

Bartlett, J. C., & Snelus, P. (1980). Lifespan memory for popular songs. *American Journal of Psychology, 93,* 551–560.

Beckett, A. (1990). The effects of music on exercise as determined by physiological recovery rates and distances. *Journal of Music Therapy, 27*(3), 126–136.

Belojevic, G., Slepcevic, V., & Jakovljevic, B. (2001). Mental performance in noise: The role of introversion. *Journal of Environmental Psychology, 21*(2), 209–213.

Bernardi, L., Porta, C., & Sleight, P. (2006). Cardiovascular, cerebrovascular, and respiratory changes induced by different types of music in musicians and non-musicians: The importance of silence. *Heart, 92*(4), 445–452.

Birnbaum, L., Boone, T., & Huschle, B. (2009). Cardiovascular responses to music tempo during steady-state exercise. *Journal of Exercise Physiology Online, 12*(1), 50–57.

Blood, A. J., & Zatorre, R. J. (2001). Intensely pleasurable responses to music correlate with activity in brain regions implicated in reward and emotion. *Proceedings of the National Academy of the United States of America, 98*(20), 11818–11823.

Blood, D. J., & Ferriss, S. J. (1993). Effects of background music on anxiety, satisfaction with communication, and productivity. *Psychological Reports, 72*(1), 171–177.

Boyle, R. (1996). Effects of irrelevant sounds on phonological coding in reading comprehension and short term memory. *The Quarterly Journal of Experimental Psychology, 49*(2), 398–416.

Brodsky, W. (2001). The effects of music tempo on simulated driving performance and vehicular control. *Transportation Research Part F: Traffic Psychology and Behaviour, 4*(4), 219–241.

Caine, R. N., & Caine, G. (1991). *Making connections: Teaching and the human brain.* Alexandria, VA: Association for Supervision and Curriculum Development.

Caldwell, C., & Hibbert, S. A. (1999). Play that one again: The effect of music tempo on consumer behavior in a restaurant. *European Advances in Consumer Research, 4,* 58–62.

Cassidy, G., & MacDonald, A. R. (2007). The effect of background music and background noise on the task performance of introverts and extraverts. *Psychology of Music, 35*(3), 517–537.

Chan, M. F., Chung, Y. F. L., Chung, S. W. A., & Lee, O. K. A. (2008). Investigating the physiological responses of patients listening to music in the intensive care unit. *Journal of Clinical Nursing, 18,* 1250–1257.

Chazin, S., & Neuschatz, J. S. (1990). Using a mnemonic to aid in the recall of unfamiliar information. *Perceptual and Motor Skills, 71,* 1067–1071.

Cheek, J. R., Bradley, L. J., Parr, G., & Lan, W. (2003). Using music therapy techniques to treat teacher burnout. *Journal of Mental Health Counseling, 25*(3), 204–218.

Chetta, H. D. (1981). The effect of music and desensitization on preoperative anxiety in children. *Journal of Music Therapy, 18*(2), 74–87.

Chou, P. T.-M. (2010). Attention drainage effect: How background music effects concentration in Taiwanese college students. *Journal of the Scholarship of Teaching and Learning, 10*(1), 36–46.

Clark, M. E., McCorkle, R. R., & Williams, S. B. (1981). Music therapy-assisted labor and delivery. *Journal of Music Therapy, 18*(2), 88–100.

Clayton, M., Sager, R., & Will, U. (2004). In time with the music: The concept of entrainment and its significance for ethnomusicology. *ESEM CounterPoint, 1.*

Copeland, B. L., & Franks, B. D. (1991). Effects of types and intensities of background music on treadmill endurance. *Journal of Sports Medicine and Physical Fitness, 31*(1), 100–103.

Corhan, C. M., & Gounard, B. R. (1976). Types of music, schedules of background stimulation, and visual vigilance performance. *Perceptual and Motor Skills, 42,* 662.

Daltrozzo, J., Tillmann, B., Platel, H., & Schon, D. (2009). Temporal aspects of the feeling of familiarity for music and the emergence of conceptual processing. *Journal of Cognitive Neuroscience, 22*(8), 1754–1769.

Davenport, W. G. (1974). Arousal theory and vigilance: Schedules for background stimulation. *Journal of General Psychology, 91,* 51–59.

Davis, W. B., & Thaut, M. H. (1989). The influence of preferred relaxing music on measures of state anxiety, relaxation, and physiological responses. *Journal of Music Therapy, 26*(4), 168–187.

Day, R.-F., Lin, C.-H., Huang, W.-H., & Chuang, S.-H. (2009). Effects of music tempo and task difficulty on multi-attribute decision-making: An eye-tracking approach. *Computers in Human Behavior, 25*(1), 130–143.

De l'Etoile, S. K. (2002). The effect of musical mood induction procedure on mood state-dependent word retrieval. *Journal of Music Therapy, 39*(2), 145–160.

Devlin, H. J., & Sawatzky, D. D. (1987). The effects of background music in a simulated initial counseling session with female subjects. *Canadian Journal of Counselling, 21*(2–3), 125–132.

Dillman-Carpentier, F., & Potter, R. F. (2007). Effects of music on physiological arousal: Explorations into tempo and genre. *Media Psychology, 10*(3), 339–363.

Dube, L., Chebat, J.-C., & Morin, S. (1995). The effects of background music on consumers' desire to affiliate in buyer-seller interactions. *Psychology & Marketing, 12*(4), 305–319.

Duerksen, G. L. (1972). Some effects of expectation on evaluation of recorded musical performances. *Journal of Research in Music Education, 20,* 268–272.

Dunbar, R. (1997). *Grooming, gossip and the evolution of language.* Cambridge, MA: Harvard University Press.

Edworthy, J., & Waring, H. (2006). The effects of music tempo and loudness level on treadmill exercise. *Ergonomics, 49*(15), 1597–1610.

Eich, E., & Metcalfe, J. (1989). Mood dependent memory for internal versus external events. *Journal of Exceptional Psychology, 15,* 443–455.

Eroglu, S. A., Machleit, K. A., & Chebat, J.-C. (2005). The interaction of retail density and music tempo: Effects on shopper responses. *Psychology and Marketing, 22*(7), 577–589.

Fontaine, C. W., & Schwalm, N. D. (1979). Effects of familiarity of music on vigilant performance. *Perceptual and Motor Skills, 49,* 71–74.

Fox, J. G., & Embrey, E. D. (1972). Music—an aid to productivity. *Applied Ergonomics, 3*(4), 202–205.

Fritz, T., Jentschke, S., Gosselin, N., Sammler, D., Peretz, I., Turner, R., Friederici, A. D., & Koelsch, S. (2009). Universal recognition of three basic emotions in music. *Current Biology, 19*(7), 573–576.

Froehlich, M. A. R. (1984). A comparison of the effect of music therapy and medical play therapy on the verbalization behavior of pediatric patients. *Journal of Music Therapy, 21*(1), 2–15.

Furman, C. E., & Duke, R. A. (1988). Effect of majority consensus on preferences for recorded orchestral and popular music. *Journal of Research in Music Education, 36*(4), 220–231.

Furnham, A., & Allass, K. (1999). The influence of musical distraction of varying complexity on the cognitive performance of extroverts and introverts. *European Journal of Personality, 13,* 27–38.

Furnham, A., & Strbac, L. (2002). Music is as distracting as noise: The differential distraction of background music and noise on the cognitive test performance of introverts and extroverts. *Ergonomics, 45*(3), 203–217.

Gardstrom, S. C. (1999). Music exposure and criminal behavior: Perceptions of juvenile offenders. *Journal of Music Therapy, 36*(3), 207–221.

Geringer, J. M., & Madsen, C. K. (1987). Pitch and tempo preferences in recorded popular music. In C. K. Madsen & C. A. Prickett (Eds.), *Applications of research in music behavior* (pp. 204–212). Tuscaloosa: University of Alabama Press.

Getz, R. P. (1966). The effects of repetition on listening response. *Journal of Research in Music Education, 14*(3), 178–192.

Ginsborg, J., & Sloboda, J. A. (2007). Singers' recall for the words and melody of a new, unaccompanied song. *Psychology of Music, 35*(3), 421–440.

Goering, C. Z., & Virshup, L. (2009). Addressing social justice, political justice, moral character, and coming of age in *To Kill a Mockingbird:* A LitTunes lesson plan. Available from http://www.corndancer.com/tunes/tunes_lp019/lp08_mvkbrd.html

Goldstein, A. (1980). Thrills in response to music and other stimuli. *Physiological Psychology, 8*(1), 126–129.

Gomez, P., & Danuser, B. (2004). Affective and physiological responses to environmental noises and music. *International Journal of Psychophysiology, 53*(2), 91–103.

Gorn, G. J. (1982). The effects of music in advertising on consumer choice behavior: A classical conditioning approach. *Journal of Marketing, 46*(1), 94–101.

Gowensmith, W. N., & Bloom, L. J. (1997). The effects of heavy metal music on arousal and anger. *Journal of Music Therapy, 34*(1), 33–45.

Graham, F. K., & Clifton, R. K. (1966). Heart-rate change as a component of the orienting response. *Psychological Bulletin, 65,* 305–320.

Green, J. (2002). *The Green book of songs by subject: The thematic guide to popular music* (5th Ed.). Nashville: Professional Desk References, Inc.

Grewe, O., Katzur, B., Kopiez, R., & Altenmuller, E. (2011). Chills in different sensory domains: Frisson elicited by acoustical, visual, tactile and gustatory stimuli. *Psychology of Music, 39*(2), 220–239.

Grewe, O., Nagel, F., Kopiez, R., & Altenmuller, E. (2007). Emotions over time: Synchronicity and development of subjective, physiological, and facial affective reactions to music. *Emotion, 7*(4), 774–788.

Gueguen, N., Jacob, C., Le Guellec, H., Morineau, T., & Lourel, M. (2008). Sound level of environmental music and drinking behavior: A field experiment with beer drinkers. *Alcoholism: Clinical and Experimental Research, 32*(10), 1–4.

Guhn, M., Hamm, A., & Zentner, M. (2007). Physiological and musico-acoustic correlates of the chill response. *Music Perception, 24*(5), 473–483.

Haas, F., Distenfeld, S., & Axen, K. (1986). Effects of perceived musical rhythm on respiratory pattern. *Journal of Applied Physiology, 6,* 1185–1191.

Hadsell, N. A. (1989). Multivariate analyses of musicians' and nonmusicians' ratings of pre-categorized stimulative and sedative music. *Journal of Music Therapy, 26*(3), 106–114.

Hall, J. C. (1952). The effect of background music on the reading comprehension of 278 eighth and ninth grade students. *Journal of Educational Research, 45,* 451–458.

Hallam, S., Price, J., & Katsarou, G. (2002). The effects of background music on primary school pupils' task performance. *Educational Studies, 28*(2), 111–122.

Hammer, S. E. (1996). The effects of guided imagery through music on state and trait anxiety. *Journal of Music Therapy, 33*(1), 47–70.

Hansen, C. H., & Hansen, R. D. (1991). Schematic information processing of heavy metal lyrics. *Communication Research, 18,* 373–411.

Hanser, S. B. (1985). Music therapy and stress reduction research. *Journal of Music Therapy, 22*(4), 193–206.

Hanser, S. B., Larson, S. C., & O'Connell, A. S. (1983). The effect of music on relaxation of expectant mothers during labor. *Journal of Music Therapy, 20*(2), 50–58.

Hanser, S. B., Martin, P., and Bradstreet, K. (1982, November). *The effect of music on relaxation of dental patients.* Paper presented to the National Association for Music Therapy Annual Conference, Baltimore, MD.

Hargreaves, D. J., & Castell, K. C. (1987). Development of liking for familiar and unfamiliar melodies. *Bulletin of the Council for Research in Music Education, 91,* 65–69.

Hargreaves, D. J., & Hargreaves, J. J. (2004). Uses of music in everyday life. *Music Perception, 22,* 41–77.

Heller, G. N. (1987). Ideas, initiatives, and implementations: Music therapy in America, 1789–1848. *Journal of Music Therapy, 24*(1), 35–46.

Hevner, K. (1935). The affective character of the major and minor modes in music. *American Journal of Psychology, 47,* 103–118.

Hevner, K. (1936a). Experimental studies of the elements of expression in music. *American Journal of Psychology, 48,* 246–268.

Hevner, K. (1936b). Expression in music: A discussion of experimental studies and theories. *Psychological Review, 42*(2), 186–204.

Hilliard, O. M., & Tolin, P. (1979). Effect of familiarity with background music on performance of simple and difficult reading comprehension tasks. *Perceptual and Motor Skills, 49,* 713–714.

Holbrook, M. B., & Anand, P. (1990). Effects of tempo and situational arousal on the listener's perceptual and affective responses to music. *Psychology of Music, 18*(2), 150–162.

Hui, M. K., Dube, L., & Chebat, J. C. (1997). The impact of music on consumers' reactions to waiting for services. *Journal of Retailing, 73,* 87–104.

Husain, G., Thompson, W. F., & Schellenberg, E. G. (2002). Effects of musical tempo and mode on arousal, mood, and spatial abilities. *Music Perception, 20*(2), 151–171.

Infante, D. A., & Berg, C. M. (1979, June). The impact of music modality on perception of communication situations in video sequences. *Communication Monographs, 46,* 135–148.

Iwanaga, M., Ikeda, M., & Iwaki, T. (1996). The effects of repetitive exposure to music on subjective and physiological responses. *Journal of Music Therapy, 33*(3), 219–230.

Iwanaga, M., & Moroki, Y. (1999). Subjective and physiological responses to music stimuli controlled over activity and preference. *Journal of Music Therapy, 36*(1), 26–38.

Jancke, L., & Sandmann, P. (2010). Music listening while you learn: No influence of background music on verbal learning. *Behavioral and Brain Functions, 6*(3), 1–14.

Jones, D. M., Miles, C., & Page, J. (1990). Disruption of proofreading by irrelevant speech: Effects of attention, arousal, or memory? *Applied Cognitive Psychology, 4*(2), 89–108.

Juslin, P. N., & Laukka, P. (2004). Expression, perception, and induction of musical emotions: A review and a questionnaire study of everyday listening. *Journal of New Music Research, 33,* 217–238.

Kallinen, K. (2002). Reading news from a pocket computer in a distracting environment: Effects of the tempo of background music. *Computers in Human Behavior, 18*(5), 537–551.

Karageorghis, C. I., Jones, L., & Low, D. C. (2006). Relationship between exercise heart rate and music tempo preference. *Research Quarterly for Exercise and Sport, 77*(2), 240–244, 246–250.

Kellaris, J. J., Cox, A. D., & Cox, D. (1993). The effect of background music on ad processing: A contingency explanation. *Journal of Marketing, 57*(4), 114–125.

Kellaris, J. J., & Kent, R. J. (1992). The influence of music on consumers' temporal perceptions: Does time fly when you're having fun? *Journal of Consumer Research, 1*(4), 365–376.

Khalfa, S., Dalla Bella, S., Roy, M., Peretz, I., & Lupien, S. J. (2003). Effects of relaxing music on salivary cortisol level after psychological stress. *Annals of the New York Academy of Science, 999,* 374–376.

Khalfa, S., Roy, M., Rainville, P., Dalla Bella, S., & Peretz, I. (2008). Role of tempo entrainment in psychophysiological differentiation of happy and sad music? *International Journal of Psychophysiology, 68*(1), 17–26.

Kiger, D. (1989). Effects of music information load on a reading comprehension task. *Perceptual and Motor Skills, 69*(2), 531–534.

Kilgour, A. R., Jakobson, L. S., & Cuddy, L. L. (2000). Music training and rate of presentation as mediators of text and song recall. *Memory and Cognition, 28*(5), 700–710.

Klingberg, T. (2009). *The overflowing brain: Information overload and the limits of working memory.* New York, NY: Oxford University Press.

Knight, W. E. J., & Rickard, N. S. (2001). Relaxing music prevents stress-induced increases in subjective anxiety, systolic blood pressure, and heart rate in healthy males and females. *Journal of Music Therapy, 38*(4), 254–272.

Krumhansl, C. L. (1997). An exploratory study of musical emotions and psychophysiology. *Canadian Journal of Experimental Psychology, 51,* 336–353.

Labbe, E., Schmidt, N., Babin, J., & Pharr, M. (2007). Coping with stress: The effectiveness of different types of music. *Applied Psychophysiological Biofeedback, 32*(3/4), 163–168.

LaCasse, M. M. (2010). *Background music: Can it make a difference in the classroom?* (Unpublished master's thesis). Sierra Nevada College, Incline Village, NV.

Lacourse, E., Claes, M., & Villeneuve, M. (2000). Heavy metal music and adolescent suicidal risk. *Journal of Youth and Adolescence, 30*(3), 321–332.

Lai, H. L., & Good, M. (2005). Music improves sleep quality in older adults. *Journal of Advanced Nursing, 49*(3), 234–244.

Lammers, H. B. (2003). An Oceanside field experiment on background music effects on the restaurant tab. *Perceptual and Motor Skills, 96*(3, Part 1), 1025–1026.

LeBlanc, A. (1982). An interactive theory of music preference. *Journal of Music Therapy, 19,* 28–45.

Le Roux, G. M. (2005). "Whistle while you work": A historical account of some associations among music, work, and health. *American Journal of Public Health, 95*(7), 1106–1109.

Logan, T. G., & Roberts, A. R. (1984). The effects of different types of relaxation music on tension level. *Journal of Music Therapy, 21*(4), 177–183.

Lovell, G., & Morgan, J. (1942). Physiological and motor responses to a regularly recurring sound: A study in monotony. *Journal of Experimental Psychology, 30,* 435–451.

Lundqvist, L.-O., Carlsson, F., Hilmersson, P., & Juslin, P. N. (2009). Emotional responses to music: Experience, expression, and physiology. *Psychology of Music, 37*(1), 61–90.

Madsen, C. K. (1997). Focus of attention and aesthetic response. *Journal of Research in Music Education, 45*(1), 80–89.

Madsen, C. K., Byrnes, S. R., Capperella-Sheldon, D. A., & Brittin, R. V. (1993). Aesthetic response to music: Musicians versus nonmusicians. *Journal of Music Therapy, 30*(3), 174–191.

Martin, R. C., Wogalter, M. S., & Forlano, J. G. (1988). Reading comprehension in the presence of unattended speech and music. *Journal of Memory and Language, 27*(4), 382–398.

Mayfield, C., & Moss, S. (1989). Effect of music tempo on task performance. *Psychological Reports, 65*(3, Part 2), 1283–1290.

McElrea, H., & Standing, F. (1992). Fast music causes fast drinking. *Perceptual and Motor Skills, 75,* 362.

Medina, J. (2008). *Brain rules: 12 principles for surviving and thriving at work, home, and school.* Seattle, WA: Pear Press.

Meyer, L. (1956). *Emotion and meaning in music.* Chicago, IL: Chicago University Press.

Middleton, W. C., Fay, P. J., Kerr, W. A., & Amft, F. (1944). The effect of music on feelings of restfulness-tiredness and pleasantness-unpleasantness. *Journal of Psychology, 17,* 299–318.

Milliman, R. E. (1982). Using background music to affect the behavior of supermarket shoppers. *Journal of Marketing, 46,* 86–91.

Milliman, R. E. (1986). The influence of background music on the behavior of restaurant patrons. *Journal of Consumer Research, 13,* 286–289.

Miluk-Kolasa, B., Matejek, M., & Stupnicki, R. (1996). The effects of music listening on changes in selected physiological parameters in adult presurgical patients. *Journal of Music Therapy, 33*(3), 208–218.

Miluk-Kolasa, B., Obminski, Z., Stupnicki, R., & Golec, L. (1994). Effects of music treatment on salivary cortisol in patients exposed to pre-surgical stress. *Experimental and Clinical Endocrinology, 102,* 118–120.

Moreno, R., & Mayer, R. E. (2000). A coherence effect in multimedia learning: The case for minimizing irrelevant sounds in the design of multimedia instructional messages. *Journal of Educational Psychology, 92*(1), 117–125.

Mulder, J., Ter Bogt, T., Raaijmakers, Q., & Vollebergh, W. (2007). Music taste groups and problem behavior. *Journal of Youth and Adolescence, 36,* 313–324.

Mull, H. K. (1957). The effect of repetition upon the enjoyment of modern music. *Journal of Psychology, 43,* 155–162.

Mulliken, C. N., & Henk, W. A. (1985). Using music as a background for reading: An exploratory study. *Journal of Reading, 28*(4), 353–358.

Nilsson, U., Unosson, M., & Rawal, N. (2005). Stress reduction and analgesia in patients exposed to calming music postoperatively: A randomized controlled trial. *European Journal of Anaesthesiology, 22*(2), 96–102.

North, A. C., & Hargreaves, D. J. (1998). The effect of music on atmosphere and purchase intentions in a cafeteria. *Journal of Applied Social Psychology, 28,* 2254–2273.

North, A. C., & Hargreaves, D. J. (1999a). Can music move people? The effects of musical complexity and silence on waiting time. *Environment and Behavior, 31,* 136–149.

North, A. C., & Hargreaves, D. J. (1999b). Music and driving game performance. *Scandinavian Journal of Psychology, 40*(4), 285–292.

North, A. C., Shilcock, A., & Hargreaves, D. J. (2003). The effect of musical style of restaurant customers' spending. *Environment and Behavior, 35*(5), 712–718.

O'Connell, A. S. (1984). *The effects of sedative music on test-anxiety in college students.* Unpublished master's thesis. Stockton, CA: University of the Pacific.

Oldham, G. R., Cummings, A., Mischel, L. J., Schmidtke, J. M., & Zhou, J. (1995). Listen while you work? Quasi-experimental relations between personal-stereo headset use and employee work responses. *Journal of Applied Psychology, 80*(5), 547–564.

Park, C. W., & Young, S. M. (1986). Consumer response to television commercials: The impact of involvement and background music on brand attitude formation. *Journal of Marketing Research, 23,* 11–24.

Peery, J. C., & Peery, I. W. (1986). Effects of exposure to classical music on the musical preference of preschool children. *Journal of Research in Music Education, 34,* 24–33.

Pelletier, C. L. (2004). The effect of music on decreasing arousal due to stress: A meta-analysis reference. *Journal of Music Therapy, 41*(3), 192–214.

Pereira, C. S., Teixeira, J., Figueiredo, P., Xavier, J., & Castro, S. L. (2011). Music and emotions in the brain: Familiarity matters. *PLoS ONE, 6*(11), e27241.

Perham, N., & Vizard, J. (2011). Can preference for background music mediate the irrelevant sound effect? *Applied Cognitive Psychology, 25*(4), 625–631.

Phillips, C. (2004). Does background music impact computer task performance? *Usability News, 6*(1). Available online at http://www.surl.org/usabilitynews/61/music.asp

Phillips-Silver, J., & Trainor, L. J. (2005). Feeling the beat: Movement influences infants' rhythm perception. *Science, 308*(5727), 1430.

Phillips-Silver, J., & Trainor, L. J. (2007). Hearing what the body feels: Auditory encoding of rhythmic movement. *Cognition, 105*(3), 533–546.

Pinker, S. (1997). *How the mind works.* New York, NY: Norton.

Potter, R. F., & Choi, J. (2006). The effects of auditory structural complexity on attitudes, attention, arousal and memory. *Media Psychology, 8*(4), 395–419.

Pring, L., & Walker, J. (1994). The effects of unvocalized music on short-term memory. *Current Psychology, 13*(2), 165.

Prueter, B. A., & Mezzano, J. (1973). Effects of background music upon initial counseling interaction. *Journal of Music Therapy, 10,* 205–212.

Purnell-Webb, P., & Speelman, C. P. (2008). Effects of music on memory for text. *Perceptual and Motor Skills, 106,* 927–957.

Radocy, R. E. (1976). Effects of authority figure biases on changing judgments of musical events. *Journal of Research in Music Education, 24,* 119–128.

Rickard, N. S. (2004). Intense emotional responses to music: A test of the physiological arousal hypothesis. *Psychology of Music, 32,* 371–388.

Rider, M. S. (1985). Entrainment mechanisms are involved in pain reduction, muscle relaxation, and music-mediated imagery. *Journal of Music Therapy, 22,* 183–192.

Rider, M. S., Floyd, J. W., & Kirkpatrick, J. (1985). The effect of music, imagery, and relaxation on adrenal corticosteroids and the re-entrainment of circadian rhythms. *Journal of Music Therapy, 22*(1), 46–58.

Rieck, W., & Dugger-Wadsworth, D. (2008). From Broadway to classroom: Using entertainment media to get your point across. *Clearing House, 81*(4), 165–168.

Robazza, C., Macaluso, C., & D'Urso, V. (1994). Emotional reactions to music by gender, age, and expertise. *Perceptual and Motor Skills, 79,* 939–944.

Robb, S. L., Nichols, R. J., Rutan, R. L., Bishop, B. L., & Parker, J. C. (1995). The effects of music assisted relaxation on preoperative anxiety. *Journal of Music Therapy, 32*(1), 2–21.

Rosenbaum, J., & Prinsky, L. (1987). Sex, violence and rock 'n' roll: Youths' perceptions of popular music. *Popular Music and Society, 11*(2), 79–89.

Rosenfield, A. H. (1985, December). Music, the beautiful disturber. *Psychology Today,* 48–56.

Sacks, O. (1973). *Awakenings.* New York, NY: Doubleday.

Safranek, M., Koshland, G., & Raymond, G. (1982). Effect of auditory rhythm on muscle activity. *Physical Therapy, 62,* 161–168.

Salimpoor, V. N., Benovoy, M., Larcher, K., Dagher, A., & Zatorre, R. J. (2011). Anatomically distinct dopamine release during anticipation and experience of peak emotion to music. *Nature Neuroscience, 14*(2), 257–264.

Samson, S., & Zatorre, R. J. (1991). Recognition memory for text and melody of songs after unilateral temporal lobe lesion: Evidence for dual encoding. *Journal of Experimental Psychology: Learning, Memory, and Cognition, 17*(4), 793–804.

Sanders, G. S., & Barron, R. S. (1975). The motivating effects of distraction on task performance. *Journal of Personality and Social Psychology, 32*(6), 956–963.

Scartelli, J. P. (1984). The effect of EMG biofeedback and sedative music, EMG biofeedback only, and sedative music only on frontalis muscle relaxation ability. *Journal of Music Therapy, 21*(2), 67–78.

Schafer, T., & Sedlmeier, P. (2009). From the functions of music to music preference. *Psychology of Music, 37,* 279–300.

Schellenberg, E. G., Nakata, T., Hunter, P. G., & Tamoto, S. (2007). Exposure to music and cognitive performance: Tests of children and adults. *Psychology of Music, 35*(1), 5–19.

Schulkind, M. D., Hennis, L. K., & Rubin, D. C. (1999). Music, emotion, and autobiographical memory: They are playing our song. *Memory & Cognition, 27,* 948–955.

Schwartz, K. D., & Fouts, G. T. (2003). Music preferences, personality style, and developmental issues of adolescents. *Journal of Youth and Adolescence, 32,* 205–213.

Shatin, L. (1970). Alteration of mood via music: A study of the vectoring effect. *Journal of Psychology, 75,* 81–86.

Silva, K. M., & Silva, F. J. (2009). What radio can do to increase a song's appeal: A study of Canadian music presented to American college students. *Psychology of Music, 37,* 181–194.

Simpson, S. D., & Karageorghis, C. I. (2006). The effects of synchronous music on 400m. sprint performance. *Journal of Sports Science, 24*(10), 1095–1102.

Sloboda, J. A. (1991). Music structure and emotional response: Some empirical findings. *Psychology of Music, 19,* 110–120.

Smith, C. A., & Morris, L. W. (1977). Differential effects of stimulative and sedative music on anxiety, concentration, and performance. *Psychological Reports, 41*(3, Part 2), 1047–1053.

Smith, J. C., & Joyce, C. A. (2004). Mozart versus new age music: Relaxation states, stress, and ABC relaxation theory. *Journal of Music Therapy, 41,* 215–224.

Smith, P. C., & Curnow, R. (1966). Arousal hypotheses and the effects of music on purchasing behavior. *Journal of Applied Psychology, 50*(3), 255–256.

Smith, S. M., Glenberg, A., & Bjork, R. A. (1978). Environmental context and human memory. *Memory and Cognition, 6,* 342–353.

Soderlund, G., Sikstrom, S., & Smart, A. (2007). Listen to the noise: Noise is beneficial for cognitive performance in ADHD. *Journal of Child Psychology and Psychiatry, 48*(8), 840–847.

Stanton, H. E. (1975). Music and test anxiety: Further evidence for an interaction. *British Journal of Educational Psychology, 45,* 80–82.

Stekelenburg, J. J., & Van Boxtel, A. (2002). Pericranial muscular, respiratory, and heart rate components of the orienting response. *Psychophysiology, 39*(6), 707–722.

Stevens, K. (1990). Patients' perceptions of music during surgery. *Journal of Advanced Nursing, 15,* 1045–1051.

Stratton, V. N., & Zalanowski, A. H. (1984). The relationship between music, degree of liking, and self-reported relaxation. *Journal of Music Therapy, 21*(4), 184–192.

Svoboda, E. (2009). Beat your stress hormone. *Prevention, 61*(2), 95–98.

Sweeney, J. C., & Wyber, F. (2002). The role of cognitions and emotion in the music-approach-avoidance behavior relationship. *Journal of Services Marketing, 16*(1), 51–69.

Taylor, D. B. (1973). Subject responses to precategorized stimulative and sedative music. *Journal of Music Therapy, 10,* 86–94.

Teasdale, J. D., & Fogarty, S. J. (1979). Differential effects of induced mood on retrieval of pleasant and unpleasant events from episodic memory. *Journal of Abnormal Psychology, 88*(3), 248–257.

Teo, T., Hargreaves, D. J., & Lee, J. (2008). Musical preference, identification, and familiarity. *Journal of Research in Music Education, 56*(1), 18–32.

Ter Bogt, T. F. M., Mulder, J., Raaijmakers, Q. A. W., & Gabhainn, S. N. (2011). Moved by music: A typology of music listeners. *Psychology of Music, 39*, 147–163.

Thaut, M. H., & de l'Etoile, S. K. (1993). The effects of music on mood state-dependent recall. *Journal of Music Therapy, 30*(2), 70–80.

Thaut, M. H., Schleiffers, S., & Davis, W. (1991). Analysis of EMG activity in biceps and triceps muscle in an upper extremity gross motor task under the influence of auditory rhythm. *Journal of Music Therapy, 28*(2), 64–88.

Thayer, R. E., Newman, J. R., & McClain, T. M. (1994). Self-regulation of mood: Strategies for changing a bad mood, raising energy, and reducing tension. *Journal of Personality and Social Psychology, 67*, 910–925.

Tom, G. (1990). Marketing with music: Exploratory study. *Journal of Consumer Marketing, 7*(2), 49–53.

Took, K. J., & Weiss, D. S. (1994). The relationship between heavy metal and rap music and adolescent turmoil: Real or artifact? *Adolescence, 29*, 613–621.

Trehub, S. E. (2003). The developmental origins of musicality. *Nature Neuroscience, 6*(7), 669–673.

Van der Zwaag, M. D., Westerink, J. H. D. M., & van den Broek, E. L. (2011). Emotional and psychophysiological responses to tempo, mode, and percussiveness. *Musicae Scientiae, 15*(2), 250–269.

Wakshlag, J. J., Reitz, R. J., & Zillman, D. (1982). Selective exposure and acquisition of information from educational television programs as a function of appeal and tempo of background music. *Journal of Educational Psychology, 74*(5), 666–677.

Wallace, W. T. (1994). Memory for music: Effect of melody on recall of text. *Journal of Experimental Psychology: Learning, Memory and Cognition, 20*(6), 1471–1485.

Wallace, W. T., & Rubin, D. C. (1991). Characteristics and constraints in ballads and their effect on memory. *Discourse Processes, 14*(2), 181–202.

Wannamaker, C., & Reznikoff, M. (1989). Effects of aggressive and nonaggressive rock songs on projective and structured tests. *Journal of Psychology, 123*, 561–570.

Waterhouse, J., Hudson, P., & Edwards, B. (2010). Effects of music tempo upon submaximal cycling performance. *Scandinavian Journal of Medicine & Science in Sports, 20*(4), 662–669.

Watkins, G. R. (1997). Music therapy: Proposed physiological mechanisms and clinical implications. *Clinical Nurse Specialist, 11*(2), 43–50.

Webster, G. D., & Weir, C. G. (2005). Emotional responses to music: Interactive effects of mode, texture, and tempo. *Motivation and Emotion, 29*(1), 19–39.

Wininger, S. R., & Pargman, D. (2003). Assessment of factors associated with exercise enjoyment. *Journal of Music Therapy, 40*(1), 57–73.

Wolfe, D. E., & Horn, C. (1993). Use of melodies as structural prompts for learning and retention of sequential verbal information by preschool students. *Journal of Music Therapy, 30*(2), 100–118.

Yalch, R. F. (1991). Memory in a jingle jungle: Music as a mnemonic device in communicating advertising slogans. *Journal of Applied Psychology, 76,* 268–275.

Yalch, R. F., & Spangenberg, E. (1990). Effects of store music on shopping behavior. *Journal of Consumer Marketing, 7*(2), 55–63.

Yerkes, R. M., & Dodson, J. D. (1908). Relation of strength of stimulus to rapidity of habit-formation. *Journal of Comparative Neurology and Psychology, 18,* 459–482.

Ylias, G., & Heaven, P. C. L. (2003). The influence of distraction on reading comprehension: A big five analysis. *Personality and Individual Differences, 34*(6), 1069–1079.

Index

Note: n refers to the number of the endnote